Understanding BAKING

THIRD EDITION

THE ART AND SCIENCE OF BAKING

JOSEPH AMENDOLA
NICOLE REES

JOHN WILEY & SONS, INC.

Interior design by Vertigo Design, NYC
Chapter opening art by Carolyn Vibbert

This book printed on acid-free paper. ∞

Published by John Wiley & Sons, Inc., Hoboken, New Jersey
Published simultaneously in Canada.

For general information on our other products and services or to obtain technical support please contact our Customer Care Department within the U.S. at
800-762-2974, outside the U.S. at 317-572-3993 or fax 317-572-4002.

Wiley also publishes its books in a variety of electronic formats. Some content
that appears in print may not be available in electronic books.

Library of Congress Cataloging-in-Publication Data:

Amendola, Joseph.
    Understanding baking : the art and science of baking / Joseph Amendola,
Nicole Rees.—3rd ed.
        p.   cm.
    Includes bibliographical references and index.
    ISBN-13 978-0-471-40546-7 (pbk. : alk. paper)
    ISBN-10 0-471-40546-9 (pbk. : alk. paper)
        1. Baking.   I. Rees, Nicole.   II. Title.

TX683.A45 2002
641.8'15—dc21   2002028887

Printed in the United States of America

10 9 8 7

CONTENTS

ACKNOWLEDGMENTS

I am indebted to the writers, pastry chefs, and food scientists whose work has educated and inspired me. Lisa Montenegro, my pastry instructor, taught me the techniques and science that would be my foundation. Tish Boyle and Tim Moriarty, editors of *Chocolatier* and *Pastry Art & Design*, have given me unwavering support and guidance throughout my career. I would also like to thank my editor, Pam Chirls, for her enthusiasm for this project.

Many people have endured my obsessive baking habit over the past decade. During my tenure at *Woman's World* and *First for Women* magazines, colleagues helpfully served as critics for my efforts. Michelle Davis had the presence of mind to end the reign of chocolate cake terror. Sean Smith, friend and one-time husband, supported seemingly pointless baking experiment after baking experiment and explained tedious chemistry principles with great patience.

This revision of this book, and the *Baker's Manual*, would not have been possible without the help of Lisa Bell. Lisa was my pastry mentor and now she is my business partner. She helped research, develop, fine-tune, and edit these books, generously donating recipes and expertise. The chapters on flour and breadmaking were her gift to this project, and reflect up-to-date and comprehensive research. This project rejuvenated our enthusiasm for pastry, shifting our interests from publishing to having our own bakery. Working with someone as talented as she is has been the highlight of my baking career.

Many food companies and professionals have been generous with information—King Arthur Flour, Guittard Chocolates, Knox Gelatin, Red Star Yeast, and General Mills are among them. Tim Healea of Pearl Bakery in Portland, Oregon, provided valuable information regarding pre-ferments and wild yeast starters. The American Baking Institute proved to be an indispensable resource. I have also drawn information from articles I wrote for *Pastry Art & Design* magazine.

—*Nicole Rees*

PREFACE

When first published, *Understanding Baking* was one of the few resources available to the common professional baker that seriously attempted to address the science behind the bakery recipe, be it chemistry, physics, or biology. This edition has been thoroughly revised, maintaining that original intent, but with several new goals in mind.

The first, obviously, was to update and expand the scientific material. Newer ingredients such as osmotolerant instant active dry yeast are clearly defined, while discussions of staple ingredients such as chocolate are expanded to reflect changes in manufacturing and usage.

Second, products and production methods have been updated to reflect current trends. When *Understanding Baking* first emerged, a primary concern of the baking industry and hence, the young baker, was the mastery of large-scale production. Automated equipment, mixes, and time-saving methods were regarded with enthusiasm as the way of the future, liberating the baker from round-the-clock toil. And, today, in a bit of mixed blessing, most of the baked goods consumed in America do indeed come from large, state-of-the-art industrial plants. However, certain very popular movements in modern pastry and breadmaking seem to be heading, not forward into some brave new world of baking, but backward toward craft, quality ingredients, and uncompromised flavor. The artisanal bread movement that currently has the entire nation enthralled is a key example of this trend. Even large supermarket chains are rushing to produce their own specialty breads to cash in on the cachet of "artisan." The old ways are back by popular demand—upscale coffeehouses, specialty bakeries, and restaurants boasting quality local ingredients have crept into almost every town.

Our final goal, in this era of television celebrity chefs and vast numbers of magazines devoted to food and fine living, is to make *Understanding Baking* accessible to a wider audience. Today's culinary students anticipate working in restaurants, bakeries, or even as self-employed caterers or personal chefs. This edition of *Understanding Baking* is meant to be a handbook for all those rookie bakers, as well as a reference for enthusiasts. Whether your lemon meringue pie begins to weep or you need to review the list of foods that prevent gelatin from setting up, *Understanding Baking* is an easy-to-use reference for the pastry kitchen. Talented and curious amateurs with a desire to understand the hows and whys can come away (after study and practice, of course!) with good technical skills and the wherewithal to modify recipes for specific ends. Understanding how ingredients interact in the processes of mixing and baking, and why certain proportions and ratios are successful in recipes, means you won't ever be limited to recipes found in books.

In the spirit of the original edition, the text has been kept short and, we hope, succinct. Like the previous edition, this book relies heavily on E. J. Pyler's two-volume tome, *Baking Science & Technology*. Though Pyler's work addresses the complex chemistry of large-scale industrial baking, it summarizes many studies of specific ingredients and processes, providing detailed explanations of the chemistry behind baking.

CHAPTER 1

WHEAT AND GRAIN FLOURS

Any discussion of baking must begin with its most elemental ingredient: wheat flour. Not only is wheat the heart and soul of bread but its special properties allow bakers to produce an astonishing array of products, from pastry to cakes and cookies. This will be the longest chapter in the book, as understanding this primary ingredient is vital to baking.

Wheat (and to a much lesser extent rye) flours do one thing extremely well that the flours of other grains cannot: create a gluten network. Gluten is the substance formed when two proteins present in flour, glutenin and gliadin, are mixed with water. Gluten is both plastic and elastic. It can stretch and expand without easily breaking. A gluten structure allows dough to hold steam or expanding air bubbles, so that yeasted dough can rise and puff pastry can puff.

As with many discoveries, the domestication of wheat and the making of risen bread was as much accident as intent. A truly remarkable series of fortuitous, mutually beneficial interactions between wheat and humankind helped to guarantee the success of both species.

DOMESTICATION

Today's wheat is descended from wild grasses. Our hunter-gatherer ancestors certainly supplemented their diets with large-seeded wild wheat grasses for thousands of years, perhaps even cultivating the stands sporadically. Necessity, however, seems to have been the impetus for domestication of these wild grasses. A climatic shift about 10,000 years ago in the southern Levant (modern Jordan and Israel) brought warm, dry summers. Heat-resistant adaptive grasses thrived as other vegetable food sources diminished. Humans harvested the grasses more frequently, especially favoring the large-seeded, nutrient-packed wild wheats like einkorn and emmer.

Wild wheats are self-sowing. That is, the upper portion of the grass stem that bears the seeds, the rachis, becomes brittle upon maturity. It breaks apart easily in a good breeze or upon contact, scattering the seeds that will become next year's plants. Archeologists and agricultural scientists theorize that when humans gathered the wheat, most of the seeds fell to the ground. The seeds that made it home, attached by an unusually tough rachis, were mutants. Inadvertently, humans selected wheat that would not have survived natural selection: If the stem and kernels remain stubbornly intact, the grass is no longer self-sowing. Perhaps this new wheat was easier to transport back to camp in quantity, meaning a bit of leftover grain could then be planted conveniently close by. In a span of what archeologists estimate to be less than thirty years, humans and this now co-dependent strain of wheat set up housekeeping. Hunter-gatherers became farmers.

TRANSFORMATION

Further selection by the farmer, combined with accidental crosses with wild grasses and new mutations, soon produced new wheat varieties. Selection continued to occur not only for obvious boons like bigger kernels and greater yields but also for ease of processing. The advent of a free-threshing wheat, where the seed or kernel separates relatively easily from the husk by mere agitation, was a critical step in the evolution toward bread wheat. Previously, parching—or heating the grain on a hot stone—was a favored method for removing the tightly attached husk from the kernel. The more palatable naked kernels were then softened in boiling water and the resulting gruel was eaten plain or baked later into flatbreads. And flat was most likely the name of the game: Parching at least partially denatures or cooks the gluten-forming proteins in wheat, as well as destroys critical enzymes that help yeast convert sugar into starch. With free-threshing wheat, raw wheat kernels sans husk could be dried and ground, and the resulting "flour" had the potential to consistently produce risen loaves.

Wild yeasts had probably colonized grain pastes on occasion, but it was the availability of a wheat flour that could form a gluten network which made leavened bread feasible. The baker could replicate yesterday's loaf by saving a bit of the old risen dough to use as leavening for the next day's batch. The risen loaves had an appealing texture and aroma, as well as providing a more easily digestible form of nutrients. The Egyptians were using baked loaves of risen bread to start the fermentation process in beer by 5000 B.C.E. The brewery's use of malted grain (usually barley or wheat, sprouted and then lightly toasted) in the beer ferment (wort) attracted the species of yeasts and their symbiotic bacteria that produce bread humans find most appealing. The yeasty dregs of the beer provided bakers with a reliable, predictable yeast variety that is the ancestor of commercial yeast used today. The species of wheat we refer to as bread wheat, *Triticum aestivum*, was the most favored grain throughout the Roman Empire. During the Dark Ages and up until the nineteenth century, wheat waned a bit, perhaps because it required more effort and time than its more self-sufficient cousins like rye and oats. Wheat returned to preeminent stature early in the twentieth century.

MODERN WHEAT

Wheat is the second largest cereal crop in the United States; corn, with its myriad uses in industrial food and even nonfood applications, ranks first. Worldwide, however, wheat or rice, depending on the region, is the dominant food grain. It is wheat's gluten-forming proteins, so inextricably linked with the development of baking, that, when combined with a willingness to adapt to new environments and new demands, help to explain its enormous popularity. It grows well over a wide range of moderate temperatures. It is relatively easy to cultivate and consistently produces high crop yields. The wheat kernel has high

FIGURE 1.1 Emmer wheat.

FIGURE 1.2 Modern wheat.

nutritional value and good keeping qualities. Wheat can be processed with very little waste; what is not sold as flour is used for animal feed.

Genetically, wheat carries seven chromosomes to a cell. In diploid wheats like einkorn, there are two sets of chromosomes per cell. In tetraploid wheats—durum wheat being the best known example— there are four sets of chromosomes per cell. Hexaploid wheats have six sets of chromosomes and include bread wheat (*Triticum aestivum*), club wheats, and spelt wheats. *Triticum aestivum* accounts for 92 percent of the American wheat crop. Of the remaining percentage, about 5 percent is *Triticum durum*, or durum wheat, and 3 percent is *Triticum compactum* (red and white club wheats). Durum wheat is used almost exclusively in pasta making, and the club wheats are used in crackers and other products requiring flour with a low protein content.

CLASSES OF BREAD WHEAT

Of the types of bread wheat grown here in the United States, 5 primary classifications are of major importance: **hard red spring wheat, hard** red winter wheat, soft red winter wheat, hard white wheat, and soft white wheat. Hardness, growing season, and color are the three criteria used to draw the distinctions among these classes.

Hard and *soft* refer not only to the actual hardness of kernel of wheat (i.e., how hard it is to chew) but more specifically to the kernel's protein content: The hardest wheats genetically contain more protein and fewer starch granules. Hard wheats contain a layer of water-soluble protein around the starch granules; in soft wheats this trait is far less prominent. For the baker, this means that hard wheat flours produce doughs capable of the greatest gluten development. These hard or "strong" flours are ideal for bread. Hard wheats are grown where rainfall is low and the soil is more fertile, generally west of the Mississippi River and east of the Rocky Mountains up into Canada. Hard wheats account for about 75 percent of the American crop, but only a tiny amount of the Western European crop. This factor requires some juggling of flours when, for instance, adapting a classic French baguette recipe for American flour.

Generally, soft wheats have a high starch yield on milling and a low protein content. They are grown in areas of high rainfall and lower soil fertility, primarily east of the Mississippi River. Low-protein southern flours are deployed to their best advantage in their growing region's specialties—biscuits, pies, and cakes where tenderness is prized over strength. Beyond wheat's given genetic quotient of hardness or softness, environmental conditions determine the hardness of any given crop. Not only the overall protein content but also the quality and specific amounts of each protein present can be affected by seasonal variations.

Winter and *spring* refer to the two growing seasons for wheat. Winter wheats are planted in the fall. They grow for a very short period of time, become dormant during winter, resume growing in the spring, and are harvested in early summer. They are usually grown in areas that have relatively dry, mild winters, like Kansas. Winter wheat is generally higher in minerals. Spring wheats are planted in the spring and harvested in late summer. They are usually grown in areas with severe winters, such as Minnesota and Montana. Spring wheat usually contains more gluten than winter wheat of the same variety.

Color is the final determining criterion in classifying wheat. A slightly bitter red pigment is present in the seed coat of red wheats,

WHEAT COMPARISON CHART (UNITED STATES)

Hard red winter wheat (HRW)	Largest percentage (40 percent) of U.S. crop; moderately high protein content, generally used for all-purpose flours; 11–12 percent average protein content.
Hard red spring wheat (HRS)	20 percent of U.S. crop; highest protein common wheat class, primarily used in bread flour and high gluten flours; 13–14 percent average protein content, up to 16 percent. Subclasses are dark northern spring, northern spring, and red spring.
Hard white wheat (HW)	Newest class of wheat grown in U.S.; used in artisan breads, similar to hard red winter wheat, but with red pigment bred out, used to make mild-tasting whole wheat products; 11–12 percent average protein content.
Soft white wheat (SW)	10 percent of U.S. crop; protein content of about 10 percent, grown primarily in Pacific Northwest, preferred for flatbreads, cakes, pastries, crackers, and noodles. Subclasses are soft white, white club, and western white.
Soft red winter wheat (SRW)	Low-protein wheat usually grown in warmer, southern climates, primarily used in cake and pastry flours, crackers, and snack foods; 10 percent average protein content.
Durum wheat	Very hard, high-protein wheat used to make semolina flour for pasta; 15 percent average protein content. Subclasses are amber (pasta) and red (poultry and livestock feed).

similar to the tannins in tea; this trait has been bred out of white wheats. Hard white wheats are used primarily in whole wheat products where the bitter taste is undesirable, but a relatively strong flour is desired. Tortillas and bulgur are examples. Hard white wheat flour is also becoming popular with artisan bread bakers. Its higher mineral (ash) content makes it ideal for long fermentation periods, and it has a slight natural sweetness. Red wheat generally has more gluten than white wheat.

COMPONENTS OF THE WHEAT KERNEL

A wheat kernel consists of three basic parts: the bran, the germ, and the endosperm. The **bran** consists of several layers of protective outer coverings. The aleurone layer of starch-free protein that surrounds the endosperm is not truly a part of the bran, but usually comes off with it during the milling process. The bran, comprising 13 to 17 percent of the weight of the wheat kernel, contains relatively high amounts of celluloses (fiber), protein, and minerals. The **endosperm**, the part of the kernel beneath the bran covering, acts as a food reservoir for the growing plant. It composes 80 to 85 percent of the grain's weight, including the aleurone layer removed with the bran. The endosperm consists of starch granules embedded in a matrix made up of gluten-forming proteins. In its center, near one end, is the germ. The **germ**, composing 2 to 3 percent of the kernel's weight, is the embryonic wheat plant. It contains high levels of proteins, lipids, sugars, and minerals.

GRIST MILLING

Milling is the mechanical process in which wheat kernels are ground into a powder or flour. Beginning with simple crushing in a mortar

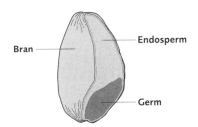

FIGURE 1.3 Components of the wheat kernel.

and pestle, humans rapidly devised more and more efficient ways to accomplish this feat. The ancient Egyptians advanced to grinding the grain (grist) between two large flat stones (grooved or dressed to let the fine flour particles escape), moving in opposite directions and driven by animal power. Grist mills soon employed the power of running water to drive wheels. Stone-ground flour is de facto whole-grain flour; only when the flour is bolted or sifted will it become white stone-ground flour. The finer the sieve, the whiter the flour will be; it will, however, always contain some of the finely crushed wheat germ. Flour was usually produced in just one session of grinding—only with the advent of new harder wheat varieties was it necessary to pass the grist through again, this time with the stones set closer together. Stone-ground flour is generally produced without generating excessive heat, which is thought to be beneficial to both flavor and performance of the flour in breads. Also, the presence of small amounts of finely ground wheat bran (with its relatively high amounts of pentosans) is believed to increase moisture content in breads and helps prevent staling. Wheat germ provides a nutty, pleasant taste and aroma to the baked loaf.

Flour must be oxidized before it is ready to use (see oxidizing and bleaching, pages 14–15). This can be done by adding a chemical to the flour or it can be done naturally by letting the flour age. Natural aging, or oxidizing, takes three to six weeks. In whole-grain or stone-ground white flours, natural aging of flour can be problematic since both the thiol groups and the fats (wheat germ oils) oxidize. When fats oxidize, they become rancid; therefore, the aging must be done at a cool temperature. Once purchased, naturally aged whole-grain flours must be stored in the refrigerator if they are not used in a timely fashion. Use freshly milled whole-grain flours promptly—or, even better, grind the grain as needed if you work on a very small scale—to prevent off flavors from developing.

Roller Milling

For the past hundred years, roller milling has been used to produce the majority of flours. It is especially suited for producing white flours.

Roller milling, in addition, creates the capability to produce hundreds of "streams" of flour from one single grain stock. Flour producers can combine various streams to produce flours of a desired protein content or particular makeup.

In either grist or roller milling, the kernel is first cleaned in a series of operations designed to remove dust and any foreign particles. In roller milling, the wheat kernel is then dried and rehydrated to a specific moisture content designed to optimize the separation and grinding processes that follow. At this point, different strains of wheat can be blended to produce a stock with the desired characteristics. The first pass between heavy ridged metal rollers revolving toward one another serves to break the kernel into its component pieces; this first **break roll** produces some flour, chunks of endosperm (termed variously "shorts," "overtails," or "overs"), bran, and germ. The process is repeated another four or so times, using rollers with successively smaller grooves that are set closer and closer to one another. These are all break rolls, designed to separate the endosperm from the bran. The germ is quite plastic owing to its high oil content and is easily flattened into a single plug on the first couple of passes. It is usually removed by the third break roll (despite its high nutritive content of lipids or fats) because it easily becomes rancid and will cause spoilage in the resulting flours. The bran is somewhat flexible and progressively detaches from the endosperm in large flakes. After each break roll, the stock is sifted or bolted to remove the flour, the smaller and smaller pieces of endosperm (or **middlings**), and bran pieces. After about the sixth break, practically all that remains is bran. Bran is removed from white flours since its particles have sharp edges that can disrupt gluten formation.

Flour Grades

At this point all the middlings (endosperm fragments) plus minute amounts of germ and bran are sifted and then ground into flour between smooth rollers in a series of seven to nine reduction rolls. Flour, middlings, and bran are again produced every pass, separated out by bolting, with the middlings continuing through further rolls.

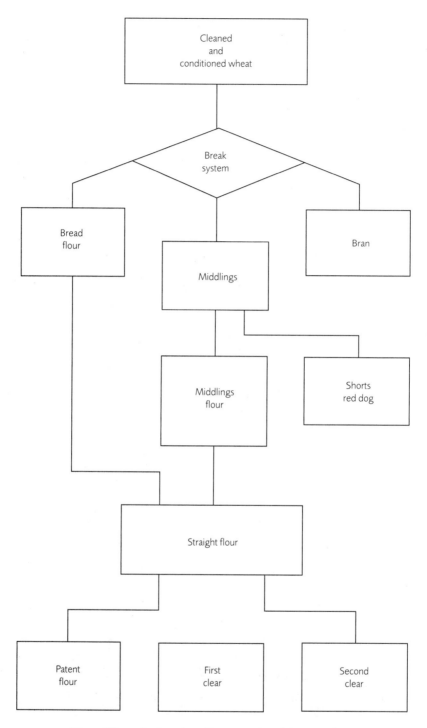

FIGURE 1.4 **The milling of wheat into flour.** Reprinted from *A Treatise on Cake Making,* by permission of Standard Brands, Inc., copyright owner.

Different streams of flour may be separated out at any point to be sold. All flour streams contain individual starch grains, small chunks of the protein matrix in which the starch is embedded, and bigger chunks of the protein matrix with some of the starch granule still attached. Different streams of flour will have different ratios of starch to protein, however, and may be kept and packaged separately for this feature. The first flour streams separated out in the breaking process contain the least bran and germ; they are more "refined." These are sold as patent flours. Within this class are further grades ranging in refinement (or absence of bran and germ) from fancy to short to medium to long. Subsequent streams of refined middlings produce flours known as clear flours. These also have grades from fancy clear to first clear to second clear. Lower grades of flour are usually quite dark and are most frequently used in combination with other flours, particularly in rye bread baking.

EXTRACTION RATE

From a given batch of 100 pounds of grain, only 72 pounds of straight flour result. A straight flour is one in which all the various streams of flours are combined. Of the remaining 28 pounds, the separated bran or germ may be added back in varying percentages to make "whole wheat" flour. The final shorts—a mixture of bran bits, plus some pulverized endosperm and germ—is sold as animal feed. The 72 pounds of flour from 100 pounds of grain is referred to as a 72 percent **extraction rate**, meaning there is little or no bran or germ in the finished flour. European flours generally have a slightly higher extraction rate—between 75 and 78 percent. The inclusion of more bran and germ, along with the fact that European wheat is softer, means that French bread flour has about 2 percent less protein than American bread flour. Many artisan bread bakers making hearth breads prefer a higher extraction flour (one with more residual bran and germ) for its flavor and baking quality. Home bakers can achieve roughly the same substance by adding a small percentage of sifted whole wheat to their bread flour.

FRACTIONATION

Since the 1950s a technique has existed called fractionation that can produce flours that are significantly higher or lower in protein content than the parent stock. Flours with different ash contents, particle size, or amylase activity (see page 20) than the parent stock can also be produced. It's a complicated process involving air streams and centrifugal force, but it basically uses particle size and density to sort for the desired characteristics.

FLOUR AND OXIDATION

Flour that is freshly milled, or green, does not make great bread. The dough is lacking in extensibility, and is slack and difficult to handle. The resulting baked loaves tend to have coarse crumb and poor volume. Aging the flour over a period of several months with repeated stirring so that fresh flour is continually exposed to air corrects this problem. The process of oxidation thus occurs naturally; as the flour sits and is repeatedly exposed to air, many of the thiol groups on the protein molecules oxidize, or give up their free sulfur to an oxygen molecule. If not oxidized, these thiol groups can disrupt the sulfur-to-sulfur protein bonds that help give a dough elasticity as gluten is developed; these are the bonds that allow a dough to snap back into shape after being stretched. In unaged flour, thiol groups grab onto the free sulfur when the dough is stressed, the original sulfur-to-sulfur bond is broken, and the dough becomes slack.

BROMATION AND ALTERNATE METHODS OF OXIDIZING

As in any business, a period of waiting such as for oxidation is viewed as a hindrance to profit. And natural oxidation results are not always completely uniform. Large milling operations since the early 1900s have been sidestepping this process by the addition of inexpensive chemical oxidants. A few parts (75) per million of potassium bromate was generally thought to strengthen the dough throughout the handling process as well as allow for shorter fermentation times, reduced mixing times, and faster processing. Any flour that has potassium bromate added is known as bromated flour. However, since the early 1990s, potassium bromate has been suspected as a possible carcinogen; in 1991, California began mandatory labeling of all products containing potassium bromate. Although potassium bromate is still legal, the following substances have also been FDA approved as alternate oxidizing agents in flour: ascorbic acid (vitamin C), azodicarbonamide (ADA), iodate of calcium, and iodate of potassium. In Germany and France, the only oxidizing agent for flours allowed by law is L-ascorbic acid. Ascorbic acid is frequently used in the United States along with other oxidizing agents to improve gluten quality.

BLEACHING

Bleaching flour with one of several agents removes the xanthophyll, a carotenoid pigment that causes the flour to be slightly yellow in color. Some, but not all, bleaching agents can also perform the function of aging or oxidizing the flour. Chlorine dioxide, chlorine, and acetone peroxide are used to both bleach and age flour (see Pyler, p. 353). When bread flour is bleached it is usually done for color purposes alone: The bleaching agent, usually benzoyl peroxide, does not oxidize the flour. All-purpose flours are available bleached or unbleached, and cake flour is always bleached with chlorine. Bleaching with chlorine oxidizes both the starches and protein present in flour at the relatively low levels employed in cake flour. This oxidation improves dough strength, which seems antithetical to the idea of soft cake flour.

Chemically bromated and/or bleached flours are designed to perform particularly well in industrial-scale breadmaking where their abilities to minimize fermentation and mixing times and make the dough withstand high-speed mixing are viewed as a bonus. Artisan breadmaking, with its long fermentation periods and relatively gentle handling of the dough, usually does not employ bromated or bleached flours. The bleach residues may also adversely affect the balances of yeast and bacterial cultures in wild yeast starters. Debate continues over whether the chemicals used in bleaching and bromating pose any sort of health risk. Many experts contend that bromating agents, especially, are reduced to iodine salts upon baking; the same salts are found in very small quantities in sea salt, and are closely related to iodized or table salt, and thus, harmless.

Bleaching affects the behavior of starch in flour much more advantageously than it affects the behavior of protein. Cake flour, milled from soft red winter wheat with a low-protein, high-starch content, profits from a certain degree of bleaching in several aspects. Chlorination makes the wheat starches in cake flour able to absorb more water, resulting in moister baked goods. (In bread flours, on the other hand, protein rather than starch is primarily responsible for flour hydration. The high protein content [needed to build gluten structure] of bread flour ensures adequately hydrated dough. Bleaching bread flour would be superfluous and counterproductive.)

Cake flour is traditionally bleached with chlorine gas and is left a bit acidic. Fat will stick to chlorinated wheat starch, but not to unchlorinated starch. Air bubbles in creamed cake batters are dispersed primarily in fat; distribution of bubbles is thus more regular and a finer texture is produced when bleached (cake) flour is used. The acidity will cause the structure of cakes to set faster as the starch gelatinizes sooner in the oven, reducing baking time and keeping the cake moister. Acidity also discourages the development of gluten, important in making tender cakes.

OTHER ADDITIVES/IMPROVERS/ CONDITIONERS

Some flours can be deficient in enzymes, particularly beta amylase, that convert starch into sugars. Since yeast feeds on sugar, not starch, this can be a problem. To correct an enzymatically unbalanced flour, either malted barley flour (from germinated grain) or fungal amylase is added at the flour mill. To perform this correction on your own, add

$^1/_2$ teaspoon of enzymatically active (diastatic) malted barley flour per 1 cup of flour. If bread doughs are fermenting sluggishly or have poor volume, the flour may not be enzymatically balanced. Too many enzymes produce a slack, sticky dough that results in gummy bread.

Calcium phosphate may be added to bolster the leavening action of baking powder in doughs or batters that contain significant amounts of acidic ingredients like buttermilk.

Mold inhibitors like vinegar or other acids can discourage microbial action. Certain bacteria form thick-walled spores that are not killed by baking; they form sticky, yellowish patches in the bread that pull apart into ropelike strands. The addition of propionates (salts of propionic acid) inhibits the growth of both mold and rope-forming bacteria.

Most of the vitamins present in wheat (particularly B-vitamins and vitamin E) are concentrated in the bran, the germ, and the aleurone layer of the endosperm that is removed with bran during milling. Whole-grain flours, flours with higher extraction rates, and the end streams of flours will contain more vitamins. Cake flour, with its lower extraction rate, contains the fewest vitamins. To offset the loss of these vital nutrients, the government dictates that flour be enriched with iron, B-complex vitamins, thiamin, riboflavin, niacin, and folic acid. Vitamin E is volatile, subject to oxidation and rancidity, and so it is not added to the flour. Flour is usually fortified by the miller.

COMPONENTS OF FLOUR

The wheat grain is characterized by a high carbohydrate content (about 70 percent), relatively low protein content (9 to 13 percent), low moisture content (11 to 13 percent), small amounts of lipids, a number of enzymes, and fiber, minerals, and vitamins. The carbohydrates are primarily starch and cellulose. The proteins include, of course, glutenin and gliadin, the gluten formers, as well as minute amounts of other proteins. Lipids are present primarily in the germ and bran of the wheat kernel and are not a significant factor in white flours. Minerals make up what is known as the **ash content** of the flour. The ash refers to the amount of mineral residue left behind in a controlled burn of a flour sample. Vitamins, predominantly the B-complexes and vitamin E, are again present most significantly in the bran and germ, but are removed during milling and may be added afterwards.

CARBOHYDRATES

Starch, dextrins, cellulose, pentosans, and various free sugars make up the carbohydrate content of wheat. Milling removes almost all the cellulose as well as most of the pentosans. Most fiber in wheat is in the cellulose. Damaged starch granules (altered during the process of milling) play an invaluable role in structural development in leavened breads and batters. In yeast doughs, the amylase enzymes attack damaged starch first, producing sufficient simple sugars (carbohydrates) to feed the yeast during fermentation. Damaged starch also affects the formation of dextrins during baking and the moisture level of the finished product. Ratios exist for the optimum level of damaged starch found to be beneficial in flour, directly correlating with the protein content of the flour. Flour contains a small amount of sugar; melbiose is converted by an enzyme in yeast, melbiase, to produce simple sugars directly available to the yeast as food. The pentosans in flour may amount to 2 to 3 percent, primarily in the tailings or end runs in milling. Pentosans can aid in producing bread with a higher moisture content and reduced staling.

PROTEIN

Flour is produced from the endosperm of the wheat. The endosperm contains about 80 percent of the total amount of protein in the whole kernel. **Gliadin** and **glutenin** make up most of this and are usually present in almost equal proportions. Variations in their relative proportions may significantly affect gluten formation. Gliadin seems to be a key player in the volume attained in breadmaking, imparting viscosity and extensibility. Glutenin provides elasticity and strength to the dough. Both of these proteins are directly affected by both environment and genetics. Environmental conditions influence protein quantity while genetics seem to determine protein quality. In other words, even low-quality wheat can produce some high-protein flours.

The quality of wheat is determined, rather tautologically, by how well it performs in the task it has been given. Good cake flour will rely upon the same factors to produce lovely tender cakes that would produce horrible, flat, gummy bread. American hard wheat flours, with their high protein content and ability to absorb large amounts of water, may make it difficult to produce a European hearth bread with crisp, brittle crust and open crumb. Just remember that each type of flour was created with a specific purpose in mind—how well it lives up to that promise determines how "good" it is. Quality flours perform well over a broad range of protein contents.

GLUTEN FORMATION

When wheat flour is mixed with water and stirred or kneaded, the glutenin and gliadin proteins not only bond with the water but also link and crosslink with one another to eventually form sheets of a flexible, resilient film called gluten. Gluten can trap air and gases formed by yeast, causing bread to rise. As the yeasts feed on the sugars, they produce a liquid containing both alcohol and carbon dioxide. The carbon dioxide is released upon contact into the air bubbles, enlarging them. In baking, the alcohol converts to gas, enlarging the bubble even more—producing ovenspring. Flexible starch granules held in place by the gluten network also bend around the air bubble. The gluten protein eventually cooks, releases its water into the starch, and begins to firm. This provides the structural framework for the loaf of bread. As the starch gelatinizes, it also becomes semi-rigid, giving even more support. In cakes or quick breads, however, too much gluten can be detrimental. The efficacy of chemical leaveners can be compromised when gluten prevents them from bubbling through a batter. Protein content determines how much water a flour can absorb—the greater the amount of protein, the more hydration is possible.

ENZYMES

Enzymes are biochemical proteins that act as catalysts, meaning they have the ability to instigate chemical changes without themselves being changed. Flour naturally contains small amounts of enzymes called **amylases** and **diastases** that can break down starch into simple sugars needed by yeast. Wheat flour does not contain sufficient sugar for optimal yeast growth and gas production, but the enzymes break down damaged starch into maltose and glucose. Frequently wheat flour is deficient in these enzymes. As a corrective measure, additional enzymes are introduced. The resulting flour is enzymatically balanced. The first source of these enzymes was malted wheat flour, then malted barley flour, and most recently fungal amylase. Sprouted, or malted, grain increases the presence of diastase enzymes and is particularly beneficial to naturally leavened doughs. Enzyme activity confers a number of boons. Crust color improves from **Maillard reactions** (browning reactions) enhanced by increased amount of sugars. Flavor is improved by the same Maillard reactions. Reactions induced by the addition of small amounts of certain heat-stable amylases present, for instance, in rye flour or in fungal amylase can continue well into baking, producing sweetness without the detrimental effects of added sugar on yeast fermentation and gluten structure of a dough. An excess of these enzymes, however, will cause too much of the starch to be converted to sugar and result in a flat loaf. One other class of enzymes, the proteases, is significant. An excess of protease enzymes, which prefer to digest gluten proteins, will result in slack, sticky dough.

LIPIDS

Only 1 to 2 percent of lipids make it past milling into flour. The glycolipids seem to aid the gluten-forming proteins in retaining the carbon dioxide gas produced in fermentation. In effect, they seem to be sealing the burst gas cells as the proteins denature during baking, preserving volume. Lipids can also bind glutenin to starch to gliadin; this very thin lipid layer increases plasticity and ovenspring. They may also help in preserving freshness in the baked bread for the same reason. Other lipids—free fatty acids such as lineoleic and linolenic acids and the monoglycerides—are oxidated by the enzyme lipoxygenase, naturally present in wheat, during the process of dough mixing. This causes a natural bleaching of the carotenoids, brightening the crumb, imparting a pleasantly nutty flavor, and binding those troublesome thiol groups that cause poor dough performance.

MINERAL CONTENT/ASH

Minerals are the inorganic substances present in wheat that are derived from the soil. Wheat flour contains anywhere from 1 to 2 percent minerals. Ash content (see page 17) is affected by the soil itself, rainfall, type and amount of fertilizer, and so on. Once again, during milling most of the wheat kernel that contains significant proportions of minerals is removed with the bran and germ. The minerals that remain in white flour are actually in excess of what minerals occur in the endosperm. Thus, the ash content of the flour is directly related to the amount of bran particles in the flour. High-extraction flours generally have a high ash content. A level of at least .44 to .48 percent of ash in bread flour is viewed as favorable, and many artisan bread bakers prefer higher values. High ash content ensures the presence of minerals that cause the gluten formed to be more tensile.

FLOUR VARIETIES AND HOW TO CHOOSE

Flour performs a number of functions in baked goods: It provides structure; it binds and absorbs; it affects keeping qualities; it affects flavor; it imparts nutritional value. Not every flour is going to do the same job well, so over the years "flour" has become many, many "flours." Pastry chefs today are presented with a bewildering array of flours tailored to meet specific requirements in different products. The big variable at the heart of this proliferation is protein content (and quality) and its consequences for gluten development. Modern milling practices can further modify the inherent ability of a specific wheat through choices in blending, milling, and processing.

MILLING TERMS

These terms are how millers define their flours to the baking trade. Patent, clear, and straight flours all have their own subgrades (fancy, short, long, first, and second) that refer to the percentages of various streams they may contain. All of these terms refer to hard wheats.

PATENT FLOUR Single streams of flours from early on in the milling process; considered more refined as they contain less bran and germ residuals; low in minerals (low ash content); more expensive.

CLEAR FLOUR Also called common flour, less refined and higher in protein than bread flour; milled from extreme outer layer of wheat endosperm; slightly darker in color; 16 percent protein content causes it to be frequently used with rye flour to alleviate its lack of gluten.

STRAIGHT GRADE FLOURS Combination of all streams of flour created during milling process; protein content around 11.5 percent is ideal for hearth bread; higher ash/mineral content good for long fermentation processes.

HIGH EXTRACTION FLOUR Flour from the end runs or streams at the mill containing more of the residual wheat bran and germ; light tan in color; highly flavorful; extraction rate anywhere from 75 to 95 percent; protein content is usually lower due to the inclusion of the fractions of flour that do not contain the gluten-forming proteins. Flours with an extraction rate between 75 and 78 percent are ideal for artisan breads. Very high extraction flours are used with other flours.

BAKER'S TERMS

Bakers use the following terms to describe the standard blends of flour they would ordinarily employ for a specific purpose. Most of these flours are available in some form to the retail buyer; the home consumer may not be able to find one quite so specific, but can usually blend a decent concoction from the other flours.

ALL-PURPOSE FLOUR Available bleached or unbleached; blend of hard spring wheat and soft winter wheat; protein content between 9 and 11 percent.

BREAD FLOUR Available bleached or unbleached, bromated or not; hard red spring wheat; protein content between 11.5 and 13 percent; usually includes enzymatic corrective; slightly granular to the touch.

HIGH GLUTEN FLOUR Unbleached; dark spring northern wheat; 14 percent protein content; used in combination with bread or all-purpose flours; good for highly machined doughs or in combination with grain flours lacking gluten.

WHOLE WHEAT FLOUR Unbleached; contains all of the wheat grain including bran, germ, and endosperm; several types are available: soft whole wheat flour with low protein content used in chemically leavened batters like muffins and pancakes, protein content around 11 percent; whole wheat from hard red winter wheat used primarily in bread, protein content around 13 percent.

PATENT DURUM FLOUR Fine silky grind of extremely hard cold weather wheat; unbleached; pale yellow in character; protein content of around 12 percent; particularly good in hearth breads.

PASTRY FLOUR Available bleached or unbleached; soft winter wheat; protein content around 9 percent.

COOKIE FLOUR Soft wheat flour; protein content between that of pastry flour and cake flour; usually only a bakery item.

CAKE FLOUR Always bleached and enriched; soft winter wheat, particularly from warmer growing regions; protein content around 7.5 to 8 percent; ideal for cakes and biscuits.

SPECIAL FLOURS

ARTISANAL BREAD FLOUR Unbleached; lower protein content of around 11.5 percent; performs in hearth breads much like lower protein European flours; equivalent to U.S. flours with higher extraction rate (75 to 78 percent).

VITAL WHEAT GLUTEN What is left over when starch has been removed from wheat flour in a washing process; protein content about 40 percent; used in breads prepared with other grains that lack gluten-forming proteins.

GRAHAM FLOUR Similar to whole wheat flour, but the bran particles have been very finely ground; for use in cookies or soft rolls and breads.

ORGANIC FLOUR Always unbleached and unbromated; growing conditions are not yet standardized; expensive, up to twice the cost of regular flour; good for beginning naturally fermented starters for bread due to high content of microflora.

WHEAT BRAN Removed in milling, sold separately; contains all of the cellulose in wheat that provides fiber; used extensively in health breads and in muffins.

WHEAT GERM Removed in milling, toasted and sold separately; is a wonderful addition in pancakes, cookies, and muffins; provides nutty, pleasant taste in bread; spoils quickly, especially if not properly refrigerated.

SELF-RISING FLOUR Available as cake flour or as all-purpose flour to which baking powder and salt have been added in ratios ranging from $1/2$ teaspoon to $1 1/2$ teaspoons double-acting baking powder and $1/4$ teaspoon to $1/2$ teaspoon salt per cup of flour.

SOUTHERN ALL-PURPOSE Includes White Lily brand with a very low protein content approaching that of cake flour; usually bleached; protein content around 9 percent.

(*continued*)

INSTANT FLOUR Includes Wondra brand, a low-protein pregelatinized (partially precooked) wheat flour with added malted barley flour; used in pie crusts for tenderized effect and to thicken sauces without clumping.

STRONG AND WEAK Terms used by bakers to describe the ability of a particular flour to form gluten, akin to the hard and soft description of the wheat kernel. Both sets of terms are directly related to the protein content of the wheat endosperm that allows the flour to form gluten. Strong flours can form the good-quality, elastic gluten that makes for great bread. Weak flours have less gluten-forming capacity and are best suited to cakes and pastry.

STORAGE

Flour should be stored in a cool, dry, well-ventilated area free of odors. Flour can readily absorb odors that spoil the taste of the finished baked product. A storage temperature somewhere between 60 to 70°F is ideal. Wheat germ, wheat bran, or flours that contain significant amounts of them should be refrigerated as they quickly become rancid.

NON-WHEAT FLOURS

RYE FLOUR

Rye is another member of the wild grass family whose cultivation stretches back into antiquity. Rye is hardier than wheat in challenging climates and is frequently grown either side by side or in rotation with wheat to ensure some sort of grain crop. More rye than wheat was grown during the Middle Ages, and it is still a favored grain in the colder European climates, especially the Scandinavian countries.

Whole rye flour does not have enough of or the right kinds of gluten-forming proteins to make light bread by itself. Rye does contain a roughly similar amount of protein, even both of the gluten-forming proteins, glutenin and gliadin, but in proportions smaller than in wheat. The gliadin in rye, however, doesn't interact with the glutenin in the same way as wheat gliadin does in forming gluten. Most of the structure provided by rye flour in bread comes from the interaction of its proteins with **pentosans** (gumlike substances) and the gelatinization of its starch. Rye doughs containing more than 20 percent rye flour rely on the viscosity of starches and pentosans to trap carbon dioxide gas and provide structure. Any air trapped in the dough is not enclosed in gluten cells that can expand, but in an unstable foam. As the loaf of rye bread enters the oven, in the absence of gluten, the gelatinized starch on the outside of the loaf forms a sort of skin that aids in gas retention. Wheat flour is added in varying amounts to compensate for the gluten deficiency in rye.

Another problem in making light, well-shaped rye loaves arises in the heat-stable nature of an enzyme, amylase, that breaks down starch. During baking, the starch granules in both wheat and rye uncoil from their crystalline structure and are basically dissolved in the water. This process creates a kind of gel that sets as it cooks, providing structure to the baked bread. In wheat breads, the amylase enzyme is denatured or made inactive before starch gelatinization takes place. In rye bread, however, this enzyme is far more heat-stable. This means the amylase is free to attack not just the initially available damaged starch, but the starch made available by gelatinization. The result is that way too much starch is converted to sugar and the bread flattens, sags, and becomes heavy as the loaf undergoes hydrolysis. The action of rye amylase is inhibited, however, in an acid environment, especially in conjunction with salt. Traditional rye breads are made with sour starters; the low pH slows down enzyme action and protects the starch until the rye amylase is finally denatured during baking. Long fermentation also makes the rye more digestible. (The word *pumpernickel* has its rather humorous roots in two German words, *pumpern*, "intestinal wind," and *nickel*, "demon" or "sprite.")

Rye flour comes in a wide variety of styles and sizes. Commercial rye flour is usually not made from the whole grain; instead, different parts of the endosperm are separated out during the milling process. Most of the mineral content, and hence the ash percentage, of rye is contained in the outermost layer of the endosperm, just inside the bran coat. Ash content is significant in breadmaking as it can appreciably affect the vigorousness of natural fermentation. White rye flour is milled from the center of the endosperm. Cream or light rye flour is from the next layer of the endosperm. Dark rye flour comes primarily from the outer portion of the endosperm. Rye is also available as a meal: ground from the whole kernel. Rye meal is available in various particle sizes, ranging to fine, medium, or coarse. The coarse grade of rye meal is what is commonly referred to as pumpernickel flour. Rye chops are the equivalent of cracked wheat. Rye bread is traditionally strongly flavored with caraway seeds. Its baking quality is dependent on its enzyme content, which can vary widely from one batch of grain to another. Wholegrain rye flours are particularly sensitive to deterioration in storage; not only do they smell rancid but their performance in doughs is compromised as well.

Rye flour is extremely hygroscopic, meaning that it will absorb moisture from the environment. For this reason, rye breads have an extremely high moisture content that translates to very good keeping qualities. It also means that the baking breads take longer to set. Occasionally rye breads are not sold until the following day.

RICE FLOUR

Rice flour is produced by grinding uncoated rice. It is used like pastry flour and is a good substitute for wheat flour in food allergy cases as long as the appropriate changes are made in the recipe to accommodate the lack of gluten. Rice flour is traditionally used in some shortbread recipes owing to the fine, sandy texture it produces.

CORNMEAL AND CORN FLOUR

Cornmeal is available in two colors, yellow and white. Yellow cornmeal is a good source of vitamin A; white cornmeal is not. Either color of cornmeal is available in either a fine or coarse grind. Old-process cornmeal is prepared by grinding the whole corn kernel with the exception of the outer bran coat. New process, or degerminated cornmeal, has the germ and all the bran removed. Degerminated cornmeal keeps better, as the fats in the germ do become rancid quickly. Old-process cornmeal, however, has superior flavor and food value. Cornmeal is used in some hearty breads, in muffins, and, of course, in cornbread. Corn flour is very finely ground degerminated cornmeal. It is used in crepes, cakes, muffins, and breads in combination with wheat flour.

TRITICALE

An extremely hardy and nutritious hybrid of wheat and rye cereal grasses, triticale is used primarily for animal feed in the United States. Triticale flour does not make good bread unless it is used in combination with wheat flour; it performs similarly to rye. Bread made from triticale alone will have poor volume and a gummy texture. The gluten formed by triticale is of poor quality; doughs are more extensible, but less elastic.

SOY FLOUR

Soy flour is made from soybeans, a member of the legume family. Soybeans are cultivated worldwide, but only as a primary food crop in Asia. Elsewhere, soybeans are more frequently used to produce oils, both edible and industrial, and as animal feed. Since soybeans contain high levels of easily digestible protein and oils and are an excellent source of amino acids, their popularity and use in other forms are beginning to increase in Western culture. Soy flour is frequently used in creating baked goods for those people who have allergies to wheat protein. Soy flour is usually defatted to prevent spoilage and heat-treated to remove the beany taste. When added to wheat bread in a percentage below 3 percent, defatted soy flour does not have any appreciable effect on the dough's performance or taste, other than a slight increase in water absorption (see Pyler, pp. 401–403). Beyond this rate, it begins to disrupt gluten formation and good structure; soy flour has no elastic properties whatsoever. It is used in small quantities as a replacement for milk in breadmaking to improve texture and decrease staling. In doughnut making, up to 15 percent soy flour can be used to reduce oil absorption and improve shelf life. It can be added to chemically leavened baked goods in a higher proportion than to yeasted products.

BARLEY

Barley cultivation most likely began at the same time as wheat. Barley has two advantages over wheat: a short growing season and an extremely hardy nature. Flatbreads made from barley, a grain that has no gluten-forming proteins, were popular until the Roman era, when wheat was favored. During the Middle Ages, especially in the Scandinavian countries, barley was a staple food of the lower classes. In Middle Eastern countries today, barley is still widely used. Western countries use barley primarily as animal feed and to make malt—pulverized, sprouted grain. Malted grain contains more of an enzyme that converts starch to sugar and is used to supplement wheat flour to ensure a good fermentation rate in yeasted breads. Malt is also used, of course, to transform grain mashes into beer or liquor.

Barley is available in a number of forms for use in soups, pilafs, and breads. Hulled barley has been husked, but retains most of its bran; it is the most nutritious form of barley. Scotch or pot barley is triple-polished to remove the bran (and many of its nutrients). Pearled barley is polished even more and in the process loses not only its bran but its germ as well. Most of the vitamins, minerals, and fiber are also removed by this point. Barley flakes are made from the flattened whole seed and used like rolled oats. Barley flour is available in a range of whole-grain composition; whole-grain barley flour has a darker color and pronounced nutty flavor.

OATS

Oat products are available in a number of forms for the baker: rolled oats, quick oats, steelcut oats, and oat flour. Oats are processed differently from wheat and rye; an adherent husk must be removed from the grain before it can receive further processing. Once the oat berries or groats are hulled, they are heat-treated to both soften the groats and to inactivate the enzymes that would eventually cause the fats to become rancid. Rolled oats are groats that have been flattened by passage between two rollers. They are used primarily in cookies, whole-grain breads, streusels, and granola. For quick oats, the groats are cut into pieces before being flattened; they require shorter cooking than rolled oats, but are used almost interchangeably in baking. Steelcut oats are quick oats that have not been flattened; they are used in specialty breads for their nutty flavor and nubby texture. Oat flour is either a by-product of the above processes or is milled intentionally as an end product from the whole groat. Oat flour is most frequently employed in chemically leavened products such as pancakes, waffles, and muffins. Since it has almost no gluten, it is not a primary bread ingredient.

MILLET

Millet is an umbrella term for several unrelated cereal grains, including common millet, pearl millet, sorghum or milo, and teff. All of these grains have been cultivated for many thousands of years, throughout the world. Generally, all millets are small in size, but are very high in protein, around 16 to 22 percent. Millet grows well in hot, arid climates and even thrives in poor soils. In parts of Asia it is an important food source, usually consumed as a porridge, unleavened bread, or beer. Western cultures tend to use cooked millet as an ingredient in healthy, high-nutrition wheat breads.

POTATO FLOUR

Potato flour (ground dried potatoes) or dehydrated potato flakes can be added to wheat flour in low percentages (typically around 3 percent). It can aid in moisture retention, act as an extender, and help to keep bread soft as it ages. Potato flour contains 8 percent protein and is higher in thiamin, riboflavin, and niacin than wheat flour.

BUCKWHEAT

Buckwheat is not a cereal grain at all, not even a grass. It is a member of the same family as rhubarb and sorrel. Its kernels are actually achenes, or dry fruits, similar to the "seeds" in strawberries. Buckwheat grows well in cold climates and in poor soils. Eastern European cultures (especially Russian) and the Japanese use buckwheat most frequently. Buckwheat flour is used in a number of breads and pancakes, or blinis, as well as noodles. The whole buckwheat grain may be cooked in the same way as rice and is most familiar in the preparation known as kasha, a type of pilaf.

MISCELLANEOUS SEEDS/LEGUMES

Peanut flour and cottonseed flour are high in protein with good amounts of vitamins, particularly the B-complexes. They are added in small percentages (under 5 percent) to increase the nutritive content of bread produced on a large commercial scale without changing the texture or flavor greatly.

SPELT

Spelt wheat is one of the ancestors of modern bread wheat. It is not free-threshing wheat; its hull requires considerable effort to remove. Hulled spelt wheat can be prepared like rice. It has a mellow, nutty flavor and a higher overall protein content than common bread wheat. Spelt protein, however, is seemingly tolerated better by people with wheat allergies. Spelt flour can be substituted for wheat flour in recipes.

QUINOA

Quinoa is an annual plant of a family that includes beets, chard, and spinach. It is native to South America and has been grown in the Andes for over 5,000 years. It is very hardy, resistant to both cold and drought. Quinoa's many tiny seeds resemble a cross between millet and sesame seeds. Quinoa provides more nutrients than cereal grains; it is high in protein, magnesium, iron, and potassium. Quinoa can be used whole, cooked or soaked, in wheat health breads. Ground quinoa can be substituted for a small portion of the wheat flour in breads, cookies, and muffins. It is usually not used alone since it does not form gluten.

AMARANTH

Amaranth is an herbaceous plant native to the Americas. It was farmed extensively in Mexico before the Spanish conquest. The seeds are rich in nutrients with a distinctive, slightly spicy flavor. Amaranth can be used whole, cooked or soaked, in health breads and is also available as a flour. Amaranth has no gluten-forming proteins; it could conceivably be used alone only in waffles, pancakes, or perhaps cookies. Any instance when some gluten formation is needed for structure, however, as in breads and cakes, it should be used in combination with wheat flour.

CHAPTER 2

YEAST AND CHEMICAL
LEAVENERS

Yeast is alive, baking soda and other chemical leaveners are not, but both release carbon dioxide into doughs and batters, causing them to rise and expand in the oven. Beyond that, however, yeast and chemical leaveners have nothing in common. They are grouped together in this chapter because their function in baked goods is the same: to make things rise.

YEAST

The wonder of risen bread results from the activity of millions of individual yeast cells, yet few people have a good understanding of the yeast products available and how best to utilize them. Because they are living organisms (and if they aren't the bread won't rise), knowing how to make yeast flourish is paramount.

Yeast is living, yes, but is neither plant nor animal. Yeasts belong to a separate kingdom in taxonomy, the fungus kingdom. There are many, many species of yeast, and they are everywhere. Undoubtedly, you are covered with some now. How and why did humans harness these unseen microorganisms to make risen bread? Most likely by accident. A piece of dough, presumably to be used for flatbread, may have been left unattended longer than normal by a distracted baker. Wild yeasts, present in the grain or perhaps the clay bowl, began to multiply and ferment in the dough. Imagine the surprise caused by the lighter texture and interesting flavor of the baked bread—all from a dough that may not have looked much larger before going into the oven! This was a serendipitous discovery, but one that forever changed how we eat.

Leavened bread followed the domestication of wheat, and has been in our cooking repertoire for at least 6,000 years. In Egypt and throughout the Middle East, baking and the brewing of barley ale were closely linked—indeed, it was the same yeast doing the fermenting. The barm, or ale leaven, could be used to inoculate dough with yeast. This relationship continued into the nineteenth century in England, where yeast left over from making ale could be purchased from local brewers and used at home to make bread.

Romans used what the French now call a "chef" to leaven bread: They saved a piece of dough that possessed an active yeast population for the next day's baking. This is sometimes also termed a starter, since it starts the next bread, but the word *starter* has other connotations we'll discuss later.

It was not until the second half of the nineteenth century that yeasts were identified by Louis Pasteur as the cause of fermentation. The Carlsburg Laboratories in Denmark were soon able to isolate and develop pure strains of yeast for commercial use, increasing its availability.

A single strain of the species *Saccharomyces cerevisiae* originally served both brewers and bakers. Later, genetic strains were developed to better suit either brewing or baking. Today, the major types of bakers' yeast (compressed fresh yeast, active dry, instant active dry, and osmotolerant instant active) are all different strains of *Saccharomyces cerevisiae*.

FERMENTATION

Fundamentally, yeast feeds on sugar and converts it to carbon dioxide, also producing lesser amounts of substances such as alcohols, ketones, and aldehydes. "Convert" is a nice way of saying "digest and expel." If there is no oxygen present, the yeast produces primarily alcohol, as is the case in wine and beer production, and in bread doughs where the oxygen has been depleted. The carbon dioxide bubbles are trapped in the gluten network (formed when wheat flour is moistened with water and stirred), making the dough rise as it proofs on the counter and causing the dough to expand further in the heat of the oven. The remaining chemicals contribute to the complex flavor of yeasted bread. In general, a long, slow, cool fermentation makes a tastier bread with better textural and keeping qualities. If dough is overproofed and the yeast begins to run out of food, the flavor turns from pleasant to acrid. Additionally, the structure of the dough is compromised, resulting in a loaf with poor volume.

Yeast breaks down the starch present in flour into sugars, using an enzyme called invertase. Quality flour usually contains enzymes (amylases) that also break down the carbohydrates in starch to sugars. Bacteria present often work in conjunction with yeast, breaking down starches into simple sugars. This is particularly the case with sourdough breads, where bacteria play an essential role in developing flavor and contributing even to the rise of the dough (see "Wild Yeast Leavens," page 41). Diastatic malt powder (see "Malt Syrup," page 58) can be added to poor flours to improve the dough. It contains active enzymes that will break down starch, and the malt sugar (maltose) provides food for the yeast and bacteria. Diastatic malt syrup can be added to bread doughs to improve enzyme activity, add moisture, and contribute sugars and caramel flavors. The powder is preferred in bread doughs, since the syrup makes the dough sticky. It is not necessary to add granulated sugar (sucrose) to a recipe, as food for the yeast (see "Active Dry Yeast," page 38).

TYPES OF YEAST

FRESH OR COMPRESSED YEAST is the most traditional form of yeast used by bakers, and many consider it the most reliable, since it has undergone minimal processing. Fresh yeast produces the most carbon dioxide gas per cell, giving it superior dough-raising capability. A gram of compressed yeast contains a whopping 25 billion cells. Sold either solid in blocks or crumbled in bags, fresh yeast is slightly dehydrated (about 30 percent) but requires no hydration time, unlike active dry yeast. Cakes of yeast can be dissolved with the liquid portion of the dough, and the crumbled form may be incorporated with the dry ingredients. Fresh yeast will not be damaged by cool liquids (see below). Naturally, fresh yeast has a shorter shelf life than dry yeast. Keeping the yeast in a cold refrigerator (32° to 42°F) will maximize shelf life. In this range, the yeast will suffer only a 10 percent loss after four weeks. Fresh yeast will not freeze until below 30°F. To prevent dehydration while in storage, wrap partially used blocks of compressed yeast in waxed paper, then seal in plastic wrap. Remember, at room temperature yeast cells are very active—a block of fresh yeast left on a kitchen work table will quickly run out of food and die.

ACTIVE DRY YEAST came onto the market around the time of World War II. Developed from a strain of *Saccharomyces cerevisiae* that could withstand dehydration (down to 5 percent moisture content), active dry yeast became popular because of its long shelf life. Essentially dormant until rehydration, a jar or envelope that is hermetically sealed with an inert gas or vacuum-packed will last a year. After opening, tightly sealed active dry yeast will keep a month at room temperature, but at least two months in the refrigerator. Repeated opening of the jar, which exposes the yeast to warm, humid air, may cause the yeast to lose some of its potency.

Active dry yeast must be hydrated in warm water, ideally 110°F, for 5 to 10 minutes. (Very hot water should never touch yeast directly; it is killed instantly at 140°F.) Adding a small amount of sugar to the warm water, a common practice with older recipes, is unnecessary. Sugar, an immediate source of fuel for yeast, stimulates the yeast to ferment quickly and give off gas bubbles—a surefire way to prove that the yeast is active. "Proofing the yeast," as the practice is called, is needed only if you have doubts about the freshness of your yeast. The time dry yeast requires for rehydration is called the lag time.

Warm water for rehydration not only increases the rate of fermentation but also prevents damage to yeast cells. Cool water causes the cell walls to rupture easily. This not only kills the yeast but also the damaged cells release glutathione into the dough, which interrupts gluten formation.

Active dry yeast produces less gas per cell than any of the other forms of commercial yeast.

INSTANT ACTIVE DRY YEAST is preferred by most bakers over active dry yeast. Developed to have porous cells that instantly absorb water, this yeast gets to work faster by eliminating the rehydration or lag time. Since instant yeast does not require hydration in water, it can be mixed directly with the flour. The exception to this rule is a water-poor dough; to prevent the yeast from competing for moisture with flour, sugar, and starches, mix it first with a little of the warm water called for in the recipe. When the yeast is mixed directly with the flour, the ideal dough temperature should be between 70° and 90°F for the cells to hydrate. Naturally, the water temperature must be quite warm, warmer than 110°F, to achieve this.

Instant dry yeast has been available to both professionals and home cooks for some time, but because yeast companies market it differently to each group, there is much confusion. Quick-Rise and Rapid-Rise, both trademarked brands, are instant active dry yeast. Their brand names have given consumers the impression that these yeasts make dough rise faster than regular active dry yeast. Actually, instant yeast produces more gas per cell, which means *less of it* is needed to ferment a dough. Since both the regular active dry and the instant active dry yeasts are packed in $\frac{1}{4}$-ounce foil envelopes (the same amount), the instant yeast will appear to make bread rise faster. The bottom line is that fast-rising and instant are the same yeast, as are several brands of bread machine yeast, which contain added dough enhancers. Instant yeast, or any yeast packaged as rising fast, will work fine for long, slow fermentation so long as the proper amount is used. See the chart on page 40 for how to substitute one type of yeast for another.

OSMOTOLERANT INSTANT ACTIVE DRY YEAST is used principally in rich sweet doughs, where sugar, milk, egg, and perhaps fat are in abundance and water is not. To compensate for the sluggish performance of yeast in this environment, great amounts of yeast are usually called for in such recipes. Osmotolerant yeast will not require such bolstering, as they have been specifically selected for low-moisture, high-sugar doughs. *Osmotolerant* is a big word, but the concept is very simple: Osmosis is the process of how a solution (here, water) moves through a semipermeable membrane (the cell walls of yeast). In a moisture-poor dough with added sugar, the yeast must compete with the proteins and starches in the flour and the sugar for what little water is available. This exerts osmotic pressure on the yeast cells, which have trouble maintaining moisture equilibrium.

Osmotolerant describes the special yeast that will withstand (is tolerant of) the osmotic pressure.

There is no rule of thumb for how much yeast to use, since that is determined by the length of fermentation time desired (for development of complex flavors) and whether lots of sugar and fat are in the dough. Yeast will multiply as long as good conditions prevail, so even a pinch will leaven several loaves—if you give them time. In a straight-rise dough with no sugar or fat, like pizza dough, ½ ounce fresh yeast will leaven between 5 and 6 cups of flour in one to two hours at room temperature.

FREEZING YEASTED DOUGH

Extra care must be given to any yeasted dough that will be thawed, proofed, and baked at a later time. Though many bakers insist that choice of yeast influences how well a dough performs after being frozen, scientists believe that how the dough is handled is the most important factor.

Ice crystal formation poses the greatest threat to yeast cells, as the asymmetrical hard edges can rupture the cell walls. Fast freezing dough at 20°F is best for symmetrical crystal formation and for the yeast. Remember that pure water freezes at 32°F, but it must be colder to freeze dough. Obviously, keeping the freezer at a steady temperature will preserve yeast cells, while slight variations could destroy them. All frozen doughs should be thawed gradually, in the refrigerator, before being brought to room temperature.

If you know you will be freezing a batch of dough, keep it as cool as possible and freeze immediately after mixing. If the freezing time is longer than four days, increase the amount of yeast by as much as 10 percent to compensate for possible loss. Where applicable, increase the amount of gluten in the dough to bolster gas retention.

HANDLING YEAST

Yeast should not come into direct contact with salt or sugar, which damage it. This applies to measuring those specific ingredients together, for example. If all the dry ingredients in the recipe are combined, there is no danger, as the flour buffers the yeast.

When a dough is going to have a long fermentation time, salt can be used to slightly inhibit or control the action of the yeast and prevent overfermentation.

Many believe that if milk is not scalded it will harm the yeast. However, only raw milk must be scalded before it can be used in bread recipes, as it contains enzymes that have a negative effect on fermentation, resulting in poor loaf volume. Pasteurized milk does not pose this danger, since the heat processing denatures these inhibiting proteins.

WILD YEAST LEAVENS (SOURDOUGH STARTERS)

Sourdough starters, also known as wild yeast starters, do not contain commercial yeast. Instead, whole-grain flour and nonchlorinated water are combined and, it is hoped, become inoculated with yeast spores and bacteria present in the grain and environment. Other ingredients, such as organic raisins, grapes, and potato water, are unnecessary. Whole-grain flour (wheat or rye) is preferable owing to its high mineral content and enzyme activity, which encourage these organisms to thrive. Heavily chlorinated water may initially inhibit bacterial growth. If you can smell the chlorine, consider using a different source of water, or at least let the water stand until the chlorine gas dissipates (see page 134).

Though most bakers are familiar with the concept of developing a wild yeast starter, few realize the importance of bacteria. Flavorful sourdough breads are a collaboration between yeasts and bacteria. The bacteria feed on maltose, a sugar that yeasts use as a second choice, and break it down into glucose. Bacterial fermentation results in carbon dioxide, which means that sourdough breads are leavened by the action of bacteria as well as yeasts. But the most important contributions of the bacteria are lactic and acetic acids, which give the breads their distinctive tang and complex flavor.

Wild yeast starters usually contain several yeast and bacteria strains at first, but over time a well-maintained starter will eventually have only a few dominant ones. Unless you send out your starter for analysis, you won't know which species to thank.

Starters can be thick or thin, but keep in mind that thin starters cannot be stored as long without refreshment. Thin starters run their course faster and have a tendency to develop more acid. Other than that, both are equally proficient at leavening bread doughs. The hardest part of developing the starter is having the patience to tend it until it has a yeast population active enough to leaven bread. It can take a few weeks to build a powerful, flavorful wild-yeast starter. Beyond that, it is simply a matter of keeping the yeast and bacteria alive by frequently discarding a portion of the old starter and refreshing it with more flour and water. Wild-yeast starters stored in the refrigerator can be refreshed weekly, but at room temperature they will need to be fed daily.

Only recently refreshed starters should be stored in the refrigerator to prevent the yeast population from being depleted. Though wild yeasts don't mind cool temperatures or a fair amount of acetic acid, they do not fare well under both conditions. A refreshed starter is less acidic and provides plenty of food for a week in cold storage. The starter will require several refreshments at room temperature before it regains its previous vigor. Care should be taken to keep the starter at a moderate temperature. Warm temperatures, such as over 80°F, favor bacterial growth over yeast growth and thus alter the flavor and leavening profile of the starter.

Even when active, doughs made with wild yeast starters require a longer fermentation than those made with commercial yeast—at least eight hours. Commercial yeast can be added to a questionable starter to ensure a good rise, but it should never be part of the actual starter. A healthy starter is usually too acidic for long-term survival of commercial yeast, and in any case the dominant yeast strain usually remains dominant for the long term.

The (bio)chemistry behind sourdough starters and breads is amazingly complex, and scientific progress continues to be made. Baking naturally leavened breads requires knowledge that is beyond the scope of this book. Anyone interested in pursuing this type of artisan bread should consult specialized books such as *The Bread Builders: Hearth Loaves and Masonry Ovens* by Daniel Wing and Alan Scott.

CHEMICAL LEAVENERS

BAKING SODA is one of the few alkaline ingredients used in the pastry kitchen (the other examples are egg white and some alkalized, or Dutch-process, cocoa powders). It is a powerful leavener that readily reacts as soon as it comes into contact with an acidic batter or dough, often causing bubbles and visible thickening in liquid batters. Baking soda reacts at room temperature, rather than in the oven, and many books stress the need to immediately place a baking soda–leavened batter into the oven to prevent collapse. However, unless the batter is very thin or continually stirred after being initially mixed, the bubbles remain and the batter will rise. Muffin, pancake, and waffle batters rely heavily on baking soda for leavening, and it is not uncommon to find chefs who let these batters rest after mixing.

For layer cakes, muffins, and quickbreads, the typical amount of baking soda to use per cup of flour is $1/4$ teaspoon. Heavier batters, such as for fruit cake, may use greater amounts, but beware of recipes that call for more than $1/2$ teaspoon soda per cup of flour. Drop cookies may contain more; here, however, the soda is to facilitate browning by reducing the pH of the dough (see Chapter 17) rather than acting as extra leavening (see Corriher, p. 129).

When a batter is unusually acidic, from ingredients such as buttermilk or molasses, the baking soda may exceed the $1/4$ teaspoon per cup of flour ratio. This added baking soda not only affects the leavening action but it also alters the flavor by neutralizing the batter's acidity. If you want to preserve the pleasant tang of buttermilk in a cake, use the minimal amount of baking soda. Or add cream of tartar to the baking soda (one part soda to two parts cream of tartar), which neutralizes it, forming carbon dioxide without changing the pH of the batter.

Baking soda is used to leaven cakes with unalkalized cocoa powder, whose natural acidity it neutralizes. It turns the medium brown color of natural cocoa a deep mahogany. Earlier in the century it was popular to put enough baking soda into devil's food batter to turn the cake reddish in color. This much soda leaves an aftertaste. If more acid is added to natural cocoa, it turns yellowish brown. Dutched, or alkalized, cocoa is used in conjunction with baking powder, since it has already been neutralized by an alkali.

Baking soda has a limited shelf life, since moisture in the air reduces its strength over time. Active baking soda should hiss, or give off carbon dioxide, when mixed with acidulated water.

CREAM OF TARTAR (potassium acid tartrate) is derived from tartaric acid, a by-product of wine production. It is not a leavener per se, but when combined with an alkali such as baking soda, the two substances are neutralized, giving off carbon dioxide. When combined with baking soda in this way, the two may be called a single-acting baking powder (see below). Cream of tartar is added to egg-white foams, since the presence of an acid helps stabilize the beaten eggs. It is also added to sugar syrups, either to produce invert sugar or to prevent crystallization of sucrose molecules.

BAKING POWDER is a combination of several different leaveners. The leaveners react only with each other, giving off carbon dioxide in the process. Since the ingredients neutralize each other, they do not alter the pH of the batter or leave an aftertaste.

An example of a **single-acting** baking powder is the combination of cream of tartar with baking soda, discussed above. Not only is this combination single-acting but it is also **fast-acting**, since the two ingredients react as soon as they encounter the liquid of the batter. If the leaveners did not react until they were exposed to the heat of the oven, they would be **slow-acting**. Large commercial and industrial bakeries use highly calibrated baking powders for specific applications and have more access to purely slow-acting baking powders. Cornstarch is added to baking powders to keep the ingredients dry and separate.

Most recipes assume the baker is using **double-acting** baking powder, so called because it reacts both at room temperature and in the heat of the oven. Once the initial reaction takes place when the leavening is stirred into the batter, a second reaction follows when the batter heats up, effectively bolstering the batter and preventing collapse until the cake sets. Double-acting baking powder uses baking soda for its alkaline component and two different acid ingredients. The common acid ingredients are sodium acid pyrophosphate (both slow and fast), monocalcium phosphate (fast), anhydrous monocalcium phosphate (slow), sodium aluminum phosphate (slow), and sodium aluminum sulfate (slow). Since baking soda is more powerful than the acids, less of it is used. About $\frac{1}{4}$ teaspoon of baking soda is in each teaspoon of baking powder.

To test the activity of baking powder, stir a small amount of it into very hot water. It will fizz or hiss if it is still good.

AMMONIUM BICARBONATE is a leavener called for in older, European recipes for cookies and crackers. It does not require an acid or alkaline substance to react; it will automatically break down into a gas in the heat of the oven. It cannot be used for all baked goods, however. The gas smells unpleasantly of ammonia, and only the low height and large surface area of cookies guarantee that all of the gas will evaporate before the cooking is complete.

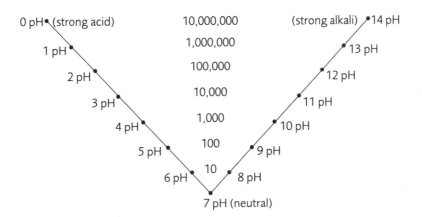

FIGURE 2.1 The pH scale.

pH LEVELS OF COMMON INGREDIENTS

Following is a list of the pH levels of common foods. When formulating cake recipes, it is helpful to consider the acidity of the ingredients when choosing a leavener.

pH VALUES OF FOODS USED IN BAKING

FOOD	pH VALUE
Apples	3.3–3.9
Apricots	3.3–4
Baking powder	7
Baking soda	8.4–8.8
Banana	5
Blackberries	3.8–4.5
Blueberries	3–3.4
Bran, wheat	5.6
Buttermilk	4.4–4.8
Cane sugar	6.5–7
Carrot, raw	5.3
Cream cheese	4.1–4.8
Cream and milk	6.4–6.8
Cream of coconut	5.5–5.9
Dutched (alkalized) cocoa	6.8–7.8
Eggs	6.6
Egg white	7.9
Egg yolk	6
Evaporated milk	5.9–6.3
Figs	5–6
Fruit preserves	3.5–4.5
Glucose	4.8–6
Honey	4
Invert sugar	2.1–4.5
Lemon juice	2.2–2.4
Lime juice	2.8
Malt syrup	4.7–5.2
Maple syrup	5
Molasses	4.9–5.4
Nectarines	3.9–4.2
Peaches	3.3–4
Pineapple, canned	3.2–4
Plums	2.8–4.3
Prunes	3.4–4
Pumpkin	5
Raspberries	3.2–3.9
Rhubarb	3.1–3.4
Vinegar	2.2–3.4
White wheat flour, bleached	5.7–5.9

CHAPTER 3

SUGARS AND OTHER SWEETENERS

Т

he word *sugar* can mean many different things. Often equated with sucrose, or granulated white sugar, the word usually refers to common table sugar, a substance refined from sugarcane or beets. But as any baker knows, sugar comes from many plant sources and takes many forms. Honey, maple sugar, and corn syrup are all sugars. In this sense, the word *sugar* no longer refers only to granulated sugar; it defines a specific type of substance. Ultimately sugar is a chemical designation for specific molecular structures.

As dull as it sounds, the easiest way to understand the similarities and differences between honey and granulated sugar, as they apply to a pastry chef, is to start with chemistry. Nutritionally speaking, humans require six basic substances for survival. Water, carbohydrates, proteins, fats, vitamins, and minerals. Sugars, or **saccharides,** as they are called, are a subgroup of carbohydrates. When many sugar molecules are joined together in long chains, they are no longer technically a sugar— they are a starch. So sugars are the building blocks of more complex types of carbohydrates; many saccharides joined together are a **polysaccharide,** the prefix *poly* meaning "many."

The human body requires carbohydrates, but the process of digestion breaks carbohydrates (starchy foods like bread, pasta, and potatoes) down into the simplest form possible. Polysaccharides become saccharides. There are two major types of saccharides: **monosaccharides** and **disaccharides.** The prefix *mono* means "one," so monosaccharides are the smallest elemental sugars. *Di* means "two"; it takes two monosaccharides to form a disaccharide. In the body, all carbohydrates are essentially broken down into glucose (also known as dextrose), the monosaccharide our cells use for fuel.

So if all carbohydrates are broken down into sugars by the body, why aren't sugars considered a primary food source? When we look at the food pyramid, sugary sweets are always relegated to the tiny box of things we should minimize; meanwhile, complex carbohydrates are exalted. Though sugar is fuel, it has no other nutritive value for the body. Starchy, complex carbohydrates like oatmeal or potatoes provide vitamins, minerals, fiber, and even protein in addition to fuel. Sugar-rich fruits and vegetables provide vitamins, minerals, fiber, and water.

This discussion isn't meant to slander sugar in any way. After all, this is a book devoted to pastry. If there is any hidden message, it is to also eat your vegetables. Why not get the essentials over with and move on to a glorious chocolate mousse?

MONOSACCHARIDES AND DISACCHARIDES

Whether we are talking about honey or corn syrup, the foods we commonly use as sweeteners contain varying compositions of the same basic sugars. These sugars can be classified as monosaccharides (single sugars) or disaccharides (double sugars).

Glucose (dextrose) and **fructose** (levulose) are monosaccharides—basic sugars that are also building blocks for more complicated sugars. They share the same chemical formula, but the arrangement of their atoms differs. The terms dextrose and levulose describe the direction the sugar molecules rotate (the prefix *dext* means "to the right" and *lev,* "to the left") as seen under a beam of polarized light—an important designation, since it is their molecular arrangement, not their formula, that differentiates these sugars. Galactose is another monosaccharide, one of the two molecules that join to form lactose, the sugar in milk.

The disaccharrides include sucrose, maltose, and lactose. Each has two parts: **Sucrose** is one molecule of glucose joined with one molecule of fructose; **maltose** is two molecules of glucose, and **lactose** is one molecule of glucose joined with one molecule of galactose.

Each monosaccharide and disaccharide has a markedly different level of sweetness. Sucrose is the standard against which all others are compared, perhaps because granulated sugar has dominated baking and candymaking for so long. Glucose is less sweet than sucrose, having about 75 percent the sweetness. Fructose, on the other hand, is almost twice as sweet as sucrose. Both maltose and lactose are less sweet than granulated sugar, at 30 percent and 15 percent, respectively.

CANE AND BEET SUGARS

Historically, pure white granulated sugar was the final goal of sugarcane refining. The process created many other flavorful by-products, such as molasses, the intensely flavorful syrup that is left over, and brown sugars, which are all essentially granulated sugar with remnants of molasses still present.

White sugar beets were later discovered to be an excellent source of sucrose, and today they are the other major source of granulated sugar. Though the process of refining sugar beets is similar to that of refining cane sugar, no other sweet by-products are created. Unlike sugarcane molasses, the syrup drawn off sugar beets is not the least bit appetizing to humans and is used for animal feed.

Sugarcane was grown throughout the Middle East, India, and even China in ancient times. Alexander the Great may have sent some back to Europe, but it was probably the Moorish invasions of Spain that brought greater knowledge of sugarcane. The plant was brought to the New World by Christopher Columbus, where it flourished in the ideal climates of islands such as Haiti and the Dominican Republic. Production quickly expanded throughout the Americas and coastal Africa. Unfortunately, the liberation of the sugar market from Middle Eastern dominance was darkened by its New World association with the slave trade.

GRANULATED SUGAR

The production of granulated sugar from sugarcane begins with boiling the juice extracted from the pulpy plants with lime, which partially purifies and clarifies the sugar syrup. This syrup is then further evaporated and concentrated before being seeded. (The introduction of sugar crystals to a sugar syrup encourages continuous crystal formation. Using crystals to control the formation of more crystals is called seeding.) This mixture is centrifuged to draw off the liquid, which later becomes molasses. The raw sugar that remains is redissolved, stripped of color, and filtered for impurities using granular carbon. A final crystallization occurs that is controlled to yield granules of a specific size.

SUPERFINE SUGAR

Superfine sugar, or castor sugar, is simply a finer-grained granulated sugar. Since the individual grains of sugar are smaller, they dissolve faster. For this reason, superfine sugar is perfect for making angel food cakes and meringues, where the dissolved sugar will become part of the egg foam, stabilizing it by absorbing moisture. By providing more sharp-edged crystals than the same weight of regular sugar, superfine sugar is superior for creaming with butter to aerate batters. It is preferred for cold liquids as well, where regular granulated sugar resists dissolving.

CONFECTIONERS' SUGAR

Also called powdered sugar, confectioners' sugar is granulated sugar that has been pulverized into a powder. To prevent lumping and caking, a small amount of cornstarch is added, less than 5 percent by weight. This makes confectioners' sugar helpful in baked meringues, where the added cornstarch can absorb moisture and help prevent weeping. Confectioners' sugar dissolves instantly. However, because it is easily dissolved and has no sharp edges, confectioners' sugar is inefficient for creaming with butter to aerate batters.

COARSE SUGAR

Coarse sugar, known as crystal sugar or decorating sugar, is large-grained granulated sugar used as a decorative topping for cakes and cookies.

DARK AND LIGHT BROWN SUGAR

Softer and more moist than granulated sugar, brown sugars retain a small portion of molasses-like syrup, giving them their characteristic caramel flavor. (Molasses is the by-product of sugar production; see below.) Darker sugars are generally more intensely flavored, as the color relates to the amount of molasses present.

Historically, brown sugar is cane sugar in which the refining process is incomplete. Because it preceded granulated sugar in stages of refinement, and because the molasses-syrup residue on the sugar originally contained minor amounts of minerals, brown sugar has been considered more healthful and less refined than granulated sugar. Today, brown sugar is produced after granulated sugar: A caramelized syrup with a specific color and flavor profile is added to dissolved sucrose and then recrystallized.

Brown sugar is no longer synonymous with raw sugar, the granules present in the early stages of refining sugarcane syrup. Raw sugar, which may contain dirt, mold, fiber, and bacteria, is not approved for human consumption in the United States. Many sugars that are labeled "raw" have actually been steam cleaned, and the term is meant to convey minimal, and supposedly more natural, processing. Read the label carefully; much sugar labeled "raw" is actually refined white sugar with added coloring and flavor.

Glucose and fructose are present in the molasses-like syrup that coats the brown sugar crystals. Because these monosaccharides are more hygroscopic than sucrose, meaning that these molecules attract and absorb moisture from the environment, brown sugar will remain moist if kept in an airtight container. It also means that products baked with brown sugar will stay moist longer than sucrose-based goods. Unlike granulated sugar, which is over 99 percent pure sucrose, brown sugar ranges from 85 to 92 percent sucrose, along with small amounts of glucose and fructose. Still, the sweetness level of brown sugar, particularly the light ones, mimics granulated sugar.

Brown sugar should be tightly packed when measured. It can be substituted for granulated sugar for its distinctive flavor, but its added moisture and lower browning temperature should be considered. Granulated light brown sugar is now available, which is pourable and dry and thus a closer equivalent to granulated white sugar.

MOLASSES

After the juice of the sugarcane has been boiled, evaporated, and centrifuged to yield sucrose, the residual syrup is called first molasses. Usually this cane syrup will be processed a few more times to extract as much sucrose as possible, and each of these steps will yield a separate grade of molasses. As the syrup is repeatedly boiled and processed, the flavor becomes more concentrated and caramelized, so that a darker and harsher-flavored molasses is associated with the last stages of production.

The last molasses product, and most strongly flavored, is called blackstrap molasses. Blackstrap molasses has been touted as healthful for its calcium, iron, potassium, and B-vitamin contents, but many of these are minute or not in a form easily assimilated by the body. The process of purifying the molasses removes still more nutritive value.

The higher grades of molasses, called light and dark, are used in baking. They have been blended with clarified cane syrup to achieve a balanced and uniform product. In general, molasses contains approximately 35 to 50 percent sucrose, about 15 to 30 percent invert sugar (invert sugar is a mixture of glucose and fructose), about 20 to 25 percent water, and from 2 to 5 percent mineral matter, along with a small amount of protein and other constituents. The significant portion of invert sugar is the result of repeated processing under high heat.

Molasses is added to recipes for its strong distinctive flavor, rather than for sweetness. The presence of invert sugar, in addition to its water content, means that products made with molasses will retain moisture well. Molasses, and to a lesser extent all brown sugars, is slightly acidic, making it particularly responsive to the alkaline leavener, baking soda.

Look for molasses that has not been treated with sulfur dioxide, which leaves an unwanted residual sulfur taste.

GOLDEN SYRUP

Also known as light treacle, golden syrup is a product of refining sugarcane. Treacle is often used as a synonym for molasses, and in England dark treacle corresponds to molasses. As the name suggests, golden syrup is pale gold in color and imparts a delicate toasty flavor.

DEMERARA SUGAR

Originally produced in the Demerara region of Guyana, this light brown sugar with hard crystals was also once truly a raw sugar. Today it is usually made by adding a molasses syrup to white sugar crystals. Because it is less moist than typical light brown sugar and possesses coarser crystals, Demerara sugar is often used to decorate cookies and cakes. It can be creamed with butter in batters, but its larger crystals make it less efficient at aerating. Exercise caution using this mild-flavored sugar as a primary sweetener. After being baked in a muffin, for example, the flavor will be the same as that of regular light brown sugar. Shortbread, on the other hand, has so few ingredients that the delicate flavor of the sugar may shine through.

TURBINADO SUGAR

This pale brown sugar was once sold raw, but today it is purified and cleaned with steam before being dried into coarse-grained crystals. All sugars marketed as raw or less refined carry a heavy price tag. Be sure to check the label—many brown sugars that claim to be less refined are actually granulated sugar with added color and flavor.

MUSCOVADO SUGAR

Also known as Barbados sugar, where it was once made, muscovado was originally a raw, very dark brown sugar. The name *muscovado* is derived from the Spanish words for "more finished," *mas abacado*, meaning that it is more finished than molasses. Muscovado sugar sold in the United States has been purified. It is fine, moist, and dark, imparting a lovely molasses-like flavor to baked goods. It compares closely with dark brown sugar.

INVERT SUGAR

Invert sugar syrup is made from a sucrose-water solution that is heated with the addition of an acid. The heat and presence of the acid breaks down the sucrose molecules into their constituent parts, glucose and fructose. The process is called inversion because the optical rotation of the now divergent molecules inverts, or changes, direction.

Invert sugar syrup does not crystallize under normal conditions, and is used either to prevent the formation of sugar crystals or to control it. It is preferred over sucrose for making fondant, candy, glazes, and sorbets where a fine, nongrainy texture is desired. Fudge and caramel sauce are two examples of candies that would be less palatable with a sandy texture. Aside from the water content in the syrup, the large amount of fructose present in invert sugar gives baked goods better moisture retention, as fructose is more hygroscopic than sucrose. Also, it is the fructose in invert sugar syrup that makes it sweeter than granulated sugar.

Though invert sugar can be purchased commercially and in specialty stores, you can make your own by boiling granulated sugar with water (about one-third water by weight) and adding a small amount of acid, such as citric acid. If 5 pounds of sugar is used, only a tenth of an ounce of acid is necessary. Remember that the boiling point of a concentrated sugar solution is higher than 212°F; in this formula it will be between 220° and 225°F.

Invert sugars that have not been neutralized are slightly acidic. This does not significantly affect the flavor; however, a small amount of baking soda ($^1/_4$ teaspoon for the 5 pounds sugar used above) can be used to neutralize the syrup.

Corn Syrups and Related Products

CORN SYRUP

After sugarcane and sugar beets, corn is the next largest food crop used for sugar. But unlike sugarcane and beets, corn is predominantly starch, not sucrose. The presence of an acid or, more commonly, an enzyme, is required to convert the starch slurry into glucose, maltose, and other higher sugars. This conversion can be controlled in order to produce syrups of varying sweetness: The more complete the conversion, the sweeter the syrup. The corn syrups most commonly available approximate the sweetness of sucrose.

The viscosity of corn syrup depends on how complete the starch conversion is. The more long-chained starch molecules present (less conversion), the thicker the syrup. Long-chained molecules, such as dextrins (see below), get tangled up easily, slowing down the movement of even small molecules like glucose. For this reason corn syrup is valuable in making glazes and candies, where it prevents graininess. The longer molecules simply get in the way of crystal formation.

GLUCOSE SYRUP

Glucose syrup is a corn syrup that yields a high amount of glucose, meaning that the starch conversion is more complete. Glucose syrup also contains a significant amount of dextrins, which give the syrup additional moisture-retaining properties. Dextrins are another product of starch-to-sugar conversion. Long chains of glucose (dextrose) molecules joined together, dextrins are larger than sugar molecules but smaller than starch molecules.

DEXTROSE

Granular glucose is usually called dextrose. It is produced by dehydrating high-glucose corn syrup. It is less sweet than sucrose, is less soluble in water, browns at a lower temperature, and crystallizes slower.

HIGH FRUCTOSE CORN SYRUP

High fructose corn syrup is made by introducing the enzyme glucose isomerase to a glucose-rich corn syrup. The enzyme effectively converts glucose molecules to fructose molecules. Like other syrups, the final amount of fructose can be controlled. Corn syrups with 42 percent fructose will have a similar sweetness to sucrose. Anything higher will be sweeter.

LIGHT CORN SYRUP

Light corn syrup is a mixture of regular corn syrup and high fructose corn syrup. It is completely clear with little discernible flavor. Salt and vanilla flavor are common additions.

DARK CORN SYRUP

Dark corn syrup combines light corn syrup with refiner's syrup, a syrup derived from sugarcane refining. Caramel color and flavor have been added, giving dark corn syrup a vague molasses aroma. A small amount of salt is present.

MALT SYRUP

Malt and malt syrup can be made from a variety of grains, though barley, corn, wheat, and triticale are commonly used. The first step in making malt syrup is to make malt, by steeping the grain in water until it sprouts. At germination, amylase-type enzymes (amylases are enzymes that act on starch molecules), such as diastase, are released and convert the grain starch into a sugar, maltose. The green malt is dried in kilns at gradually increasing temperatures and then ground into a mildly sweet, vaguely toasty powder. At this point, malt powder may be used to brew beer, condition bread doughs, and make malt vinegar or malted milk powder. The natural application for malt is in breadmaking and the fermentation of alcohol because yeast feeds on maltose.

Malt syrup is the result of a second phase of production. The malt powder is combined with water and agitated at elevating temperatures until the amylase enzymes have broken down all the starch into maltose and dextrins. The insoluble malt husks are filtered out and the extract is made into a syrup. This syrup is less sweet than sugar and has an earthy, toasty flavor.

Malt syrups generally have a higher starch conversion than malt powders, which accounts for their greater sweetness but lessens their enzymatic activity. If you are adding malt syrup or powder to yeasted doughs, check to see if the product is labeled "diastatic" or "nondiastatic." Diastatic malt syrup (or powder) will still possess enzyme activity, which enhances yeast productivity and improves loaf grain and volume. Though nondiastatic syrup lacks diastatic and amylolytic enzyme activity, it will still improve loaf texture by the action of other types of enzymes, which condition the dough and aid in gluten formation, and by the moisture-retaining properties of the syrup.

HONEY

The sweet nectar from flowers collected by honeybees is primarily sucrose. Enzymes in the bees' saliva break down the sucrose into its constituent parts, fructose and glucose, making honey similar to invert sugar. Sucrose, maltose, minerals, and other higher sugars are also present in small amounts, as are the flavoring agents derived from the nectar's plant source. In the hive, evaporation creates the concentrated substance we know as honey.

At this point the honey is under 20 percent water, over 70 percent glucose and fructose, and less than 10 percent other sugars and solids. Glucose crystallizes more readily than fructose (but both are less prone to crystallize than sucrose); and because the glucose level in honey is close to the saturation point (a given amount of water can only suspend so much of any sugar), honey taken from the hive is slightly grainy. Honey is usually filtered and treated before being sold. This treatment consists of heating the honey to at least 140°F to kill any wild yeast present that would ferment the sugar. Heating the honey provides the added bonus of dissolving the glucose crystals and allowing uniform distribution of moisture, which forestalls crystallization in the future.

The flavor of honey, naturally, is dependent on the plant source of the nectar. Bees may visit a huge range of plants, or a single crop may be the dominant source. Orange blossom and clover honey are delicately flavored, while mesquite, buckwheat, and chestnut honeys are distinctively, even strongly, flavored. What is interesting about these honey varietals is that the ratio of fructose to glucose differs in each one. The higher the fructose level, the more resistant to crystallization the honey. Tupelo honey has the highest ratio of fructose to glucose, and it remains smooth the longest.

Honey is $1^1/_4$ times as sweet as granulated sugar. The wonderful flavor of the bolder honeys, such as mesquite and lavender, is currently in vogue, however, they are very costly. The best way to showcase their flavor is in glazes, honey-butter for scones, and ice creams.

FRUCTOSE (LEVULOSE)

Often called fruit sugar, fructose has been embraced as healthful by many because it is perceived to be a natural, unrefined sweetener.

Fructose is not the only sugar present in fruit, nor is it more natural than sucrose or glucose. The granulated fructose available today is commonly produced by dividing sucrose—plain old granulated sugar—into fructose and glucose. Because fructose is half of a sucrose molecule, it has half the calories. This feature, coupled with its intense sweetness, makes fructose a good sweetener for people trying to reduce their caloric intake. It takes almost twice the sucrose to provide the same degree of sweetness.

MAPLE SYRUP (AND SUGAR)

Maple syrup is derived from the sap of maple trees, particularly in the northeastern United States and Canada, where environmental conditions favor a long, sweet sap run, collected from the first real spring thaw until the leaves start to emerge, at which time the flavor of the sap becomes unappealing. The sap is only mildly sweet, and it is the long process of boiling the sap that concentrates the sweetness and brings out its characteristic flavor. The primary sugar in maple syrup is sucrose, though small amounts of glucose and fructose are present. Maple syrup is graded, ranging from fancy or Grade AA, Grade A, to Grade B, progressing from mildly flavored light-colored syrups to more distinctively flavored amber ones. Grade C syrup, harder to find, has a robust flavor that resembles molasses in intensity.

Maple syrup is sweeter than sugar, and usually the heartier flavored grades do better as a flavoring agent in baked goods. Delicately flavored syrups are fine for pancakes or glazes, but the mild maple flavor doesn't come through as a flavoring agent in cakes and breads. Read labels carefully to avoid maple-flavored syrups, which are artificially flavored high fructose corn syrups and contain no maple syrup.

Maple sugar is created when maple syrup has boiled long enough (evaporating and concentrating the sugar) to force the sucrose to crystallize as the syrup cools. Remember that a given amount of water can keep only a limited amount of sugar in solution at room temperature, even though the same amount of sugar will stay dissolved at higher temperatures. Maple syrup is a costly ingredient, and maple sugar even more so.

PALM SUGAR

Palm sugar, also known as jaggery, can be made from palm trees or from sugarcane. When it is made from palm trees, it is often called gur. This sugar, used in India, has a complex flavor—more like wine than caramel. It can be found in block form, or in a soft, whipped honeylike consistency.

DATE SUGAR

Date sugar is not actually sugar at all, but is dehydrated and finely ground sweet dates. The high fructose content makes it an efficient sweetener, but it cannot be used to replace sucrose without radically changing the finished flavor and texture of the recipe.

SUGAR SUBSTITUTES

Sugar substitutes are not commonly used in smaller bakeries or restaurants, but they are becoming more available owing to increasing demand. You may need to look into sugar substitutes if you prepare food for people on restrictive diets, such as diabetics. Here is a brief list of common sugar substitutes.

Sugar alcohols include **sorbitol, mannitol, isomalt,** and **xylitol.** Here, the term *alcohol* is a chemical designation for a specific family of organic compounds; it does not refer to a fermented or distilled alcoholic beverage. Sugar alcohols are absorbed more slowly in the body than are regular sugars, a plus for those with heightened sensitivity to glucose. With the exception of xylitol, the sugar alcohols are half as sweet as sucrose. They have nearly the same calories as sucrose, so to achieve the same sweetness more calories are used. Thus, baked goods made with sugar alcohols are not low in calories. Sugar alcohols do not promote tooth decay like sucrose, but in large amounts cause diarrhea. Of these, isomalt is the least likely to cause intestinal upset. Isomalt is also heat-stable, unlike many artificial sweeteners.

Artificial sweeteners as a group have no caloric value. Most of them leave a slight aftertaste. **Aspartame**, sold under the brand name NutraSweet, is much sweeter than sugar, so its 4 calories per gram are negligible because so little is needed to sweeten. Aspartame is not heat-stable, and thus not helpful to bakers except in frostings and some fillings. **Alitame**, a sweetener loosely related to aspartame, awaits FDA approval. It is heat resistant. Aspartame is currently used in most sugar-free soft drinks and sweets because it tastes the most like sugar. Many fears that aspartame causes headaches and even brain tumors have been put to rest, but it does pose a health threat to people who suffer from the rare disease phenylketonuria. Saccharin, once a common soft-drink sweetener, is now less widely used than aspartame. It is sweeter than sugar and has a stronger aftertaste than aspartame. It is not heat-stable.

Two heat-resistant sweeteners, **acesufame-K** and **sucralose**, are more recent alternatives to sugar. They are unabsorbed by the body and thus pass through unchanged. Acesufame-K compares to NutraSweet in sweetness (200 times that of sucrose), and sucralose (sold under the brand name Splenda) is a whopping 600 times more sweet.

THE ROLE OF SUGAR IN BAKED GOODS

Sugar imparts sweetness, of course, and depending on the type used in the recipe, it can contribute flavor. Beyond sweetness, the presence of sugar brings certain physical properties:

BROWNING

Sugar in any form will contribute to crust color and browning in the oven, as the sugar along the hot surface caramelizes. Even a small amount of milk or milk powder in a bread dough will improve crust color. Glucose and fructose brown at lower temperatures than sucrose, so ingredients like honey or corn syrup will produce a darker product if the recipe and baking temperature are not adjusted.

AERATION

Granular sugars, including brown sugars, creamed with butter or any solid fat will aerate a batter. This is an essential step in many recipes. The presence of chemical leaveners such as baking powder will expand the air bubbles present, but creaming the sugar and fat is the most effective way to guarantee a light, evenly textured product.

TENDERNESS

In batters and doughs, sugar competes with the starches and protein in flour for available water. By doing so, it interferes with gluten formation, thereby "shortening" or tenderizing the product. The presence of sugar also tenderizes structure by interfering with starch gelatinization (see Chapter 7 for more on gelatinization).

MOISTURE RETENTION

The sugar in baked goods allows them to retain moisture. A roll made with sugar will stay fresh and moist longer than one without. This is even more apparent with syrups containing fructose, corn syrup, or honey. Though the syrup contributes moisture, it is the hygroscopic aspect of fructose that gives the baked goods superior keeping qualities. Not only does fructose retain moisture, it attracts and holds moisture from the environment. Cakes made from honey or molasses, such as lebkuchen or gingerbread, have remarkable keeping qualities. The hygroscopic quality of sugar, especially fructose, is accentuated on rainy, humid days, which are detrimental to candymaking. As the candy cools and sits in the kitchen, the sugars attract moisture from the air, causing hard candies like toffee to become sticky and chewy.

EGG FOAMS AND STRUCTURE

Sugar whipped with eggs or egg whites dissolves, melting into the foam's air cell structure where it can absorb moisture and prevent weeping, thereby making the whipped egg foam more stable. In batters, the presence of sugar raises the coagulation temperature of eggs, giving the batter more time to rise before it sets.

SPREAD

Sugar contributes to batter spread in the oven. This is most noticeable in cookie doughs. Confectioners' sugar with its additional cornstarch spreads less than granulated sugar, and brown sugar spreads more. Any sugar in syrup form causes greater batter spread.

FERMENTATION

The presence of small amounts of sugar in bread dough (1 teaspoon of granulated sugar, for example) aids in yeast fermentation. Yeast will consume the simple sugars available in a dough before breaking down the starch in the flour into sugar. (The addition of sugar is not necessary in quality flours.) The opposite is true for doughs with a lot of sugar. In this case, the sugar seems to make fermentation sluggish.

EGGS

Eggs rarely get the attention deserving of one of the pastry chef's most versatile ingredients. No staple food excels in so many supporting roles: thickener, emulsifier, leavener, and structural foundation. The egg is ubiquitous. Custards, sauces, meringues, buttercreams, cakes, and cookies all rely on eggs to contribute to their texture. And, of course, the egg takes center stage for soufflés, its most glamorous role.

Nutrient Composition of Eggs and Function in Egg Cookery

Eggs are considered a complete protein, containing all the essential amino acids humans use to build other proteins used in the body. Eggs also contain a significant amount of B vitamins, vitamin E, and other vitamins and minerals, all for just over 70 calories per large egg. A large egg provides 6 grams of protein, which creates structure in baked goods and thickens custards. Each large eggs contains 4 to 5 grams of fat. The fat is laced with lecithin and cholesterol, the substances that give eggs the ability to emulsify oil-and-water solutions. (You may recognize lecithin as a common ingredient listed on food labels. Often the source of this lecithin is soy, not egg, based.) The yolk contains all the fat and half the protein. A whole egg has a moisture content of close to 75 percent. The white is 86 percent water, and the richer yolk around 50 percent.

PROPERTIES IN COOKING

The specifics of egg cookery, as they relate to meringues, custards, and cake baking, are covered in subsequent chapters. Below is a brief summary of how eggs function in the pastry kitchen.

The protein in eggs coagulates when heated, giving eggs the ability to **thicken** sauces, fillings, and custards. Both the yolk and the white contain protein, so whole eggs or their separated components may be used to set liquids. Whole eggs, with twice the protein of each single component, have greater thickening power than yolks alone. However, using all or mostly yolks to thicken provides a richer, smoother texture. Yolks impart a rich, creamy mouthfeel to custards owing to their fat content and emulsifying abilities.

An **emulsifier** stabilizes a mixture that inherently wants to separate into its two parts, like oil and water. An emulsifier acts as a go-between, preventing direct contact between the two opposing types of molecules. Usually, one liquid is suspended in another. Mayonnaise, for example, is an oil-in-water emulsion that relies on eggs for stability. Whipping oil with water will never produce a fluffy, creamy mixture; the addition of eggs stabilizes the two, creating a remarkable mouthfeel. Though the chemistry of emulsion is not central to pastry work, fat separation can occur in rich dessert sauces. Slowly whisking the barely warm sauce into an egg yolk can restore smoothness. Since the emulsifiers in egg yolks also inhibit the formation of sugar crystals, egg yolks are used to prevent graininess in some frostings and candies.

Beaten whole eggs, egg whites, and yolks are used as the primary **leavening** agents in many types of cakes and soufflés. The air cells trapped in the egg foam expand in the oven to leaven the batter. Egg whites have the greatest leavening capacity by volume, as the fat in the yolk inhibits foaming.

In baked goods, the egg's key role is to provide **structure**, although it also contributes a significant amount of moisture and richness from its inherent water and fat content. As the batter cooks, the heat slowly sets the egg protein, adding to the cake or bread's structure (the protein and starch in flour create structure also; see Chapters 1, 7, and 14).

Egg washes are brushed on many baked goods to create a golden, shiny top. The egg white provides luster and the egg yolk color. Beating the egg with a small amount of water and salt makes a smooth, lump-free wash that is easy to apply with a pastry brush.

Egg proteins begin to coagulate, or set, well under the boiling point of water. Thus, sauces and custards containing eggs are heated gently to avoid scrambling the egg proteins, which destroys their thickening ability. Egg whites begin to set at 144° to 149°F, and egg yolks at 149° to 158°F. A custard sauce that contains no starch, such as crème Anglaise, will scramble just over 180°F. The presence of sugar, water, or starch will raise the temperature of coagulation. A custard thickened with starch must be brought close to a boil to kill alpha amylase, an enzyme present in egg yolks that will break down the starch, causing the custard to thin. For more information, see Chapters 7 and 15.

CHARACTERISTICS OF QUALITY FRESH EGGS

Clean, quality eggs are the industry norm. Because egg flavor, yolk color, and shell quality are directly related to diet, hens are fed a nutritionally balanced feed. This ensures uniform quality. It is extremely rare that an inferior egg, or a rotten one for that matter, finds its way into the kitchen.

Shell color is determined by genetics and is not related to nutritional value. Brown eggs are no more nutritious than white eggs.

The shell eggs used by chefs and consumers are **Grade AA** or **Grade A**, Grade AA being the highest. The grading system is based on the textural qualities of the egg white and yolk. A sample egg is broken onto a flat surface, and the amount of spread and height is measured. A compact, thicker white and plumper yolk indicate a high grade. Be aware that as the egg ages, its white becomes thinner and its yolk more prone to breaking.

Blood spots in the yolk and the twisty, opaque strands of egg white called chalazae are not cause for alarm. Blood spots do not indicate fertilization, nor contamination, and are perfectly safe to consume. The knotty, ropy chalazae (plural) are anchored to the shell and hold the yolk in place. The more prominent they are, the fresher the egg. They do not interfere with cooking, and straining custards after cooking en-sures they do not interrupt smooth sauces and fillings.

As an egg ages, its texture and pH change. Freshly laid eggs have a pH of 7.6, but the pH increases to 9 as the egg ages, making it more al-kaline. The textural changes of eggs as they age have consequences in the kitchen. Since fresh eggs are thicker, eggs for poaching should be as fresh as possible. Separating shells from boiled eggs is easier with older eggs, however. Egg white foams are more stable if made with fresh eggs, but fresh eggs will not whip as quickly or to as great a volume as slightly older eggs.

Farmers are developing eggs for specific consumer concerns. By changing the hen's diet, some egg producers have created alternatives to standard eggs. **Organic eggs**, for example, are laid by hens fed only organically grown feed. Organic eggs often come from uncaged hens (check the label), offering peace of mind to animal rights enthusiasts. Eggs rich in **omega-3 fatty acids** come from hens fed a diet rich in flax, the primary vegetable source of this heart-healthy fat. Organic eggs, eggs from uncaged hens, and omega-3 rich eggs are more expensive to produce and, hence, cost more.

Proper Storage and
Salmonella Prevention

Fresh eggs are cleaned, inspected, and sorted by size before being packed. Egg shells are porous. An egg emerges with a protective cover-ing, or cuticle, that prevents moisture loss and contamination. Wash-ing the egg removes this protective coating, so a thin coating of food-grade mineral oil is applied as a sealer. Therefore, shell eggs should not be washed again after purchase or delivery unless they will be used immediately. Ideally, eggs should remain in the carton or a similar container, which protects them from refrigerator odors and rapid moisture loss. Of course, this is not a serious concern in a high-volume production kitchen, since the eggs are used so quickly.

If you suspect you have some elderly ova on your hands, there is a test to determine freshness. A small air cell exists at the large end of the egg. Eggs are packed large-end-up to keep the air cell in place. As the egg ages and moisture slowly evaporates, the air cell grows larger. Thus the air cell can be used to determine an egg's freshness. A freshly laid egg has the smallest air cell, and will lay on the bottom of a water-filled glass. Within a few days, the egg will stand on end at the bottom of the glass. If the air cell is large enough for the egg to float, the egg is old. This test must be taken with a grain of salt, because higher grade eggs have smaller air cells.

Proper storage ensures a long shelf life. Eggs kept in the coldest part of the refrigerator, usually near the back where the temperature is steady at 40°F, keep the longest. Stored this way, eggs are good for up to five weeks after they've been packed. Because of frequent door opening, the convenient space at the front of the refrigerator is rarely at 40°F. The motto "use them or lose them" comes to mind. An egg left out at room temperature overnight has lost a week of its shelf life.

Though proper storage prevents growth of salmonella bacteria, the primary causes of food poisoning are cross-contamination and poor hygiene. Salmonella can be found on many animal products, such as chicken and fish, and it is easily transferred by human hands. A cloth, knife, or board can unwittingly harbor bacteria. Frequent hand washing is essential, also, in preventing bacterial spread; hence, the warning signs in employee restrooms. Very few eggs arrive contaminated—the figure according to the American Egg Board is 1 in 20,000. Still, few professionals are willing to take the risk of using raw eggs in desserts.

Bacteria do not rapidly multiply at temperatures below 40°F, and they are killed instantly when cooked to 160°F. Minimizing the time food is in the danger zone between the two temperatures is key in preventing food poisoning. For custards, such as crème Anglaise, this means rapid cooling of the cooked sauce over an ice bath or in a cold refrigerator, and for egg dishes like quiches, it means careful reheating to 160°F. Recipes for cakes and meringues almost always call for room-temperature eggs (see Chapters 14 and 15). This can be accomplished in seconds by placing the eggs in a bowl of hot water, or warming a bowl of shelled whole eggs over another bowl of hot water. It should go without saying that cracked eggs are likely to be contaminated and should be discarded.

At the end of the day, after assembling many component recipes, a pastry kitchen is likely to have excess yolks or whites. Raw whites keep in the refrigerator for as long as four days, and unbroken yolks, covered with water, for two days. Both should be kept in tightly sealed containers. Beyond storing eggs for a few days, you can freeze them. Only perfectly separated eggs whites should be frozen—that is, egg whites with no trace of yolk or foam-inhibiting fat. Whites can be frozen as is, in a single container or individually in ice cube trays. Egg yolks, when frozen, thicken into a gluey gel that is hard to make smooth. To prevent this, stir $\frac{1}{8}$ teaspoon salt or $1\frac{1}{2}$ teaspoons sugar or corn syrup into every four yolks. Whole eggs, when lightly beaten to distribute the yolk evenly, can be frozen as is. Frozen, eggs last for a few months. Any egg product should be thawed in the refrigerator overnight or in cold running water rather than at room temperature. To measure thawed eggs, remember that 3 tablespoons equals a large whole egg, 2 tablespoons is a large egg white, and 1 tablespoon equals a large yolk.

EGG SIZES

Eggs in the shell come in many sizes, jumbo, extra-large, large, medium, small, and even, really, pee-wee. Jumbo eggs are 30 ounces per dozen in the shell and pee-wee are half that much at 15 ounces. Large eggs, at 24 ounces per dozen, are the standard, and when a recipe calls simply for an egg, it is more than likely a large one.

Large eggs weigh 24 ounces a dozen, but that does not mean each egg is precisely 2 ounces; some are more, some less. There is only so much you can ask of a hen. Below is a chart of approximate volume and weight measurements for eggs. It looks good on paper, and it comes in handy in the kitchen, but it is far from exact.

EGG MEASURES

One large egg, out of the shell, is about 1.75 ounces. The white accounts for about 1.15 ounces and the yolk for around .60. On digital scales that can measure only in increments of .25 ounce, this comes out as 1.25 ounces for the white and a half ounce for the yolk.

1 CUP = 4 X-LARGE EGGS = 6 X-LARGE WHITES = 12 X-LARGE YOLKS

1 CUP = 5 LARGE EGGS = 7 LARGE WHITES = 14 LARGE YOLKS

1 CUP = 5 MEDIUM EGGS = 8 MEDIUM WHITES = 16 MEDIUM YOLKS

Note that medium eggs are the easiest to measure because 2 table-spoons, or 1 ounce, is a white, and 1 tablespoon, .50 ounce, is a yolk. You should also notice that in the section on freezing eggs, this is how to measure *large* thawed eggs. Not perfect, but close enough.

OTHER EGG PRODUCTS

FROZEN WHOLE EGGS, EGG WHITES, AND SUGARED YOLKS are available in both cardboard cartons and large containers. They have been pasteurized. For large-volume kitchens, they are one of the few conveniences that do not compromise quality. Thaw containers of frozen eggs under cool running water, or in a tub of cold water, if waiting twenty-four hours for them to defrost in the refrigerator is out of the question. The yolks are sugared to preserve their texture. Usually this has little effect on recipes, but you can decrease the amount of sugar called for in a recipe if needed. Though raw pasteurized eggs are themselves safe, the same guidelines for storing and handling eggs and egg-based foods, discussed above, must be followed.

POWDERED EGG WHITES are dried pasteurized egg whites. They can be used for uncooked meringue-based buttercreams and royal icing recipes that normally call for raw egg whites. Recipe directions for rehydration vary slightly from brand to brand, so follow package directions. Most dried pasteurized egg whites have a lower pH than typical egg whites, ranging between 6.5 and 7.5.

PASTEURIZED FRESH SHELL EGGS are becoming more and more available. Milk is pasteurized by heating it to 160°F for 15 minutes, or holding it at a lower temperature of 144°F for 30 minutes. Eggs are fully cooked at 160°F, so pasteurization occurs by holding the eggs at a lower temperature for several minutes. As a consequence of this process, the egg appears slightly cloudy and thickened. Beating time, particularly for egg white foams, is lengthened considerably. Again, though raw pasteurized eggs are themselves safe, the same guidelines

If you run out of pasteurized eggs, follow the method below, recommended by the American Egg Board, to use in recipes that call for raw eggs:

For each raw yolk, stir in 2 Tbs. liquid, preferably the one called for in the recipe, and cook, stirring, in a double boiler until the mixture thickens enough to coat the back of a spoon or registers 160°F. Chill rapidly by stirring over an ice bath.

For each raw egg, stir in $^1/_4$ cup liquid or sugar or any combination thereof, and cook in a double boiler, stirring, until the mixture thickens enough to coat the back of a spoon or registers 160°F. Chill rapidly by stirring over an ice bath.

For each 2 raw egg whites called for, stir in $^1/_4$ cup sugar, 2 tsp. water, and $^1/_8$ tsp.

cream of tartar. Cook in a double boiler, whisking constantly, until the temperature registers 160°F. The mixture will be ready to beat into an egg white foam (a meringue, really, because of the sugar) immediately.

Although precooking the egg usually won't change the end product much, some just don't work with cooked eggs. Homemade mayonnaise, for example, calls for oil and other flavorings to be whisked into raw egg yolks. If the oil is gradually whisked into the yolk, it remains emulsified—a single yolk can "hold" close to $^3/_4$ cup oil. A precooked yolk, however, will hold much less oil and will be less shelf stable. Egg foams tend to be heavier when cooked this way.

for storing and handling eggs and egg-based foods, discussed above, must be followed.

EGG SUBSTITUTES have become popular for people on low-cholesterol diets because they contain egg whites, but no cholesterol-rich yolks (one egg yolk supplies almost an entire day's worth of cholesterol, according to USDA dietary guidelines). They are adequate for muffins and pancakes, but cannot be used in place of egg whites in meringues or cakes. Egg substitutes contain gums and other additives that prevent foaming.

SEPARATING EGGS

Eggs are easiest to separate when cold, but recipes often require room-temperature or even warm eggs, since eggs beat to better volume when warm. Some chefs claim, rightfully, that cold eggs just take longer to beat to the same volume. However, the height of a cake baked with a warm egg white foam will be greater than a cake leavened with cool egg white foam (see Pyler, p. 1005).

There are two ways to approach the situation. One, you warm the eggs in a bowl of hot water and then very carefully separate them; or two, the longer but surefire method, you separate the eggs first before warming them over a bowl of hot water.

For the sake of speed and ease, pastry chefs tend to separate eggs with their hands, though the officially sanctioned method is with an egg separator. If you are a frequent hand-washer, the danger of cross contamination is minute. Squeaky clean hands and bowls are essential, anyway, to ensure that no grease or oil touches the egg whites. The presence of any fat will prevent the whites from whipping to maximum volume, so never use plastic bowls, which harbor grease, and never break an egg directly over the precious bowl of whites. A single piece of broken yolk means significantly reduced volume.

Instead, break eggs one or two at a time into a bowl, then use two or three fingers to gently scoop out the yolks, letting the whites drain off. Place the yolks in another bowl, then pour the whites into a third bowl. Repeat. Separating warm eggs requires more care, as the yolks burst easily. Breaking the egg directly into your hand (over a bowl), with fingers opened enough to let the white slip through while retaining the yolk, is even faster.

EGGS AND METAL COOKWARE

One of the proteins present in egg white, conalbumin, reacts with untreated metal cookware. This has a definite benefit with **copper**. When egg whites are beaten in a copper bowl, copper-conalbumin is formed.

The egg foam is more stable than one mixed in a stainless steel bowl, and though the volume of beaten whites appears the same, the volume of the finished product containing the copper-bowl beaten whites will be greater.

Copper has the unique property of making egg whites resistant to overbeating. Egg white foams beaten in copper bowls lose less water while standing (weep less) than other foams.

Cast-iron cookware can turn eggs a reddish brown color. Cooking eggs in untreated **aluminum** pans discolors eggs, turning them an unappetizing gray.

CHAPTER 5

FATS AND OILS

Fats and oils are both **triglycerides,** a class within the larger chemical designation of **lipids.** All fats are lipids, but not all lipids are fats. A triglyceride is composed of three (tri) fatty acids linked by a molecule of glycerol. There are also diglycerides and monoglycerides, having two and one fatty acid attached to a molecule of glycerol. Lecithin, the emulsifier in egg yolks and soybeans, for example, is a diglyceride. Hence, lecithin is a lipid, but not a fat.

Lipids themselves are not soluble in water, the prime example being oil, which stubbornly refuses to associate with water. Thus, oils and fats are termed hydrophobic. But individual fatty acid molecules that are not joined with glycerol are polar: They are water soluble at one end and fat soluble at the other. The diglyceride lecithin is unusual because it retains the polar nature of its fatty acids: it has the capacity to act as a go-between in an oil-water solution, since one side of each molecule of lecithin is attracted to water and the other side to the oil. Such substances are called emulsifiers, since they can create a stable emulsion from two substances that inherently do not want to mix.

METABOLISM

Like carbohydrates, fats are made up of carbon, hydrogen, and oxygen atoms, and both fats and carbohydrates provide fuel for our bodies. Energy is released when molecular bonds are broken between weaker carbon-to-carbon or carbon-to-hydrogen bonds and are replaced by stronger carbon-oxygen and hydrogen-oxygen bonds. This is also called **oxidation**, which describes any chemical reaction where an electron is taken from a molecule. Sugars (simple carbohydrates) have fewer calories than fats, making them less efficient as fuel, or, from the opposite point of view, less potentially fattening. Fat molecules are primarily chains of carbon atoms with bonds to hydrogen, and they have a great amount of potential energy since those weak bonds can easily be oxidized. Carbohydrates already have some of their bonds given over to oxygen, so they provide less caloric fuel since they are not able accept as many oxygen atoms, which means they cannot undergo as extensive an oxidation as a fat can.

SATURATION LEVEL OF COMMON FATS

(listed in order of low to high saturation: % saturated, % polyunsaturated, and % monounsaturated)

Canola oil	**7**, 26, 67
Safflower oil	**9**, 78, 13
Sunflower oil	**12**, 72, 16
Corn oil	**13**, 58, 29
Olive oil	**14**, 10, 76
Soybean oil	**15**, 62, 23
Peanut oil	**18**, 34, 48
Shortening	**25**, 25, 50
Cottonseed oil	**27**, 55, 18
Lard	**43**, 10, 47
Beef tallow	**48**, 3, 49
Cocoa butter	**60**, 5, 35
Butter	**68**, 4, 28
Palm kernel oil	**83**, 5, 12
Coconut oil	**90**, 4, 6

PLASTICITY AND SATURATION

Fats and oils are differentiated by whether or not they are solid or liquid at room temperature. Thus, shortening is a fat, and corn oil an oil. Bakers usually refer to both fats and oils simply as fats, since they serve practically the same function in baking. In general, animal-derived fats are solid at room temperature (butter, lard, beef tallow), and vegetable ones liquid (corn oil, safflower oil, olive oil). One notable exception to this rule is cocoa butter, a plant-derived fat that is solid at room temperature. Vegetable oils that have undergone hydrogenation become solid at room temperature (see below).

Animal fats are usually more **saturated** than vegetable fats. A fully saturated fat has as many hydrogen atoms

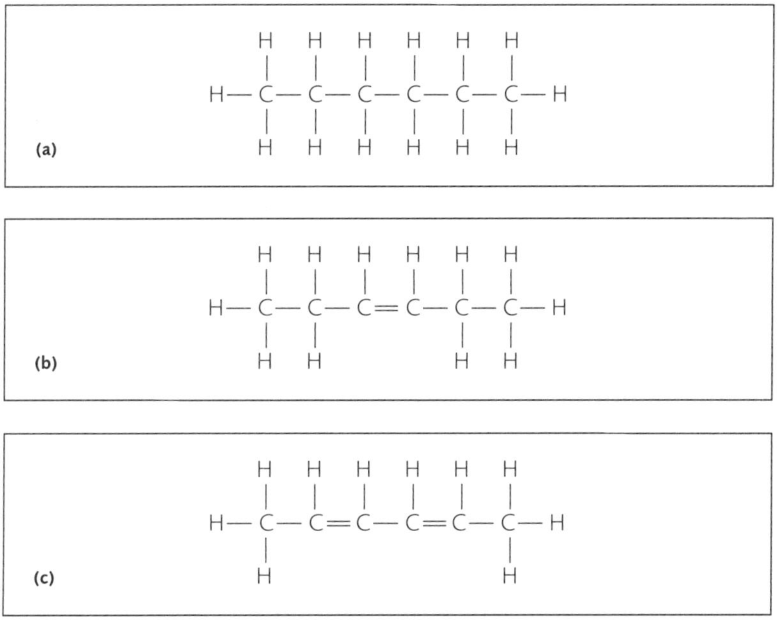

FIGURE 5.1 (a) Saturated, (b) monounsaturated, and (c) polyunsatured molecules.

attached to the carbon chain as possible (see Figure 5.1a). A **monoun-saturated fat** has one double bond between two of the carbon atoms in the carbon chain, and a **polyunsaturated fat** has several of these bonds (see Figures 5.1b and 5.1c). Those weak double bonds are unstable and can be easily oxidized, which leads to rancidity in unused oils. Another way to think of oxidation is that it is the process of aging or decaying in organic substances.

OXIDATION AND HYDROGENATION

That one type of process, oxidation, describes both the biochemical metabolism of energy in the body (good) and the process of aging and rancidity (not so good) may seem impossible. This presents a dilemma. An oil can oxidize during storage, which makes it rancid and unhealthy to consume, but when we consume fresh oils, our body oxidizes them to use them for energy. How is it that one type of oxidation is harmful and another good? The answer is many variables cause oxidation. Several factors contribute to rancidity, a far more random chemical process than metabolism. Metabolism is conducted by a series of catalyzed reactions completely controlled by enzymes—very specific processes for very specific results.

Oxidation can be forestalled in fats by hydrogenating them. Introducing hydrogen atoms to monounsaturated or polyunsaturated fats makes them more stable by replacing the weak double bonds with a carbon-hydrogen bond, and this increases the shelf life of the fats. If hydrogen atoms take up the space left open by the double bond, the bond is no longer open for other atoms or molecules to use. This is how margarine and shortening are made, and it is called **hydrogenation**. Both margarine and shortening begin with vegetable oils (though sometimes animal fat is used) that are converted from liquid unsaturated fats to solid and more fully saturated fats. In general, saturation corresponds with plasticity, so that saturated fats are likely to be solid at room temperature. The so-called tropical oils—coconut and palm kernel oil—are dramatic exceptions to this rule: despite being fluid, they are more saturated than even butter or beef tallow (see Figure 5.2).

Since margarine and shortening are solid at room temperature, they have the ability to incorporate air when beaten with sugar. In the earlier part of this century, both were advertised as inexpensive replacements for butter in baking. Margarine, which originated in France in the nineteenth century, has a low water content, as does butter. It also

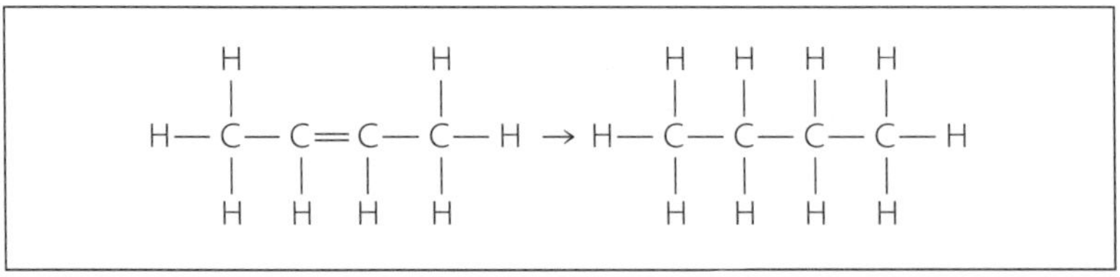

FIGURE 5.2 Hydrogenation. All of the carbon atoms in the second molecule have been bonded to hydrogen atoms. The first molecule is unsaturated; the second is saturated.

contains coloring and flavors to make it appear as appealing as butter. Margarines may be soft or hard, depending on the extent of saturation (from hydrogenation) and how much air has been whipped into them.

Shortening does not contain any water, and it usually contains around 10 percent air by weight. This air contributes to the overall aeration of batters and doughs, which is usually manually accomplished by creaming sugar with fat or beating air into egg foams. Shortenings are sophisticated fats: They have a high melting point, but are pliable even when cool, making them excellent for creaming with butter or blending with flour for pie dough because they will not melt as easily as butter. The incorporated air makes shortening a better and more consistent fat for aerating batters. Many shortenings also contain added emulsifiers. Emulsifiers act at the boundary between fat and water molecules, keeping them evenly dispersed. When emulsifiers are added to shortenings, they contribute to better aeration of batters and a finer crumb and tender texture. They can accomplish this because the air in batters usually is within the fat, and since emulsifiers disperse fat better, the cake is moister and well aerated.

"TRANS" AND "CIS" FATS

Hydrogenated fats are under intense scrutiny by nutritionists. By now everyone is aware that they often have more saturated fat than unsaturated, and saturated fat elevates serum cholesterol levels and can contribute to heart disease. Over the past twenty years, the concern about the effects of "trans" fats in the body has put hydrogenated fats in a

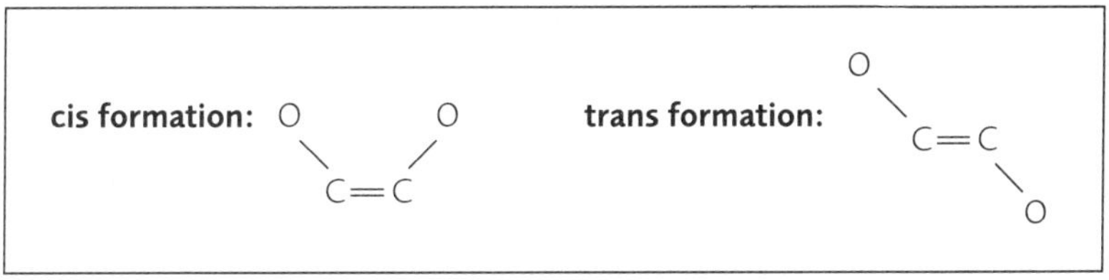

FIGURE 5.3 "Cis" (same side) and "trans" (across) formation of fat molecules.

negative light. Naturally occurring fats have a particular shape or configuration that reflects the angles at which the atoms are connected to one another. Hydrogenation changes this configuration, creating what is called an optical isomer. Optical isomers have the same atoms, but are shaped differently. Hydrogenation creates "trans" fats rather than the naturally occurring "cis" fats (see Figure 5.3). This change of shape affects biochemical processes in the body, which are specific chemical reactions carried out by exacting proteins (enzymes). When a fatty acid changes shape, an enzyme may fail to recognize it. Or it may treat the unfamiliar substance differently. Scientists suspect this results in an elevation of LDL cholesterol in the body, the type of cholesterol that adversely affects the heart and arteries.

SMOKE POINT

When choosing a fat for deep frying or sautéing, it is essential to consider its smoke point. Fats have a very high boiling point, far beyond water, and this high heat means that fried foods cook quickly. Each oil or fat will begin to break down at a different temperature based on the composition of its triglycerides. The temperature at which a triglyceride begins to change into an unpleasant gas is called its **smoke point**. The intense heat not only forms an unpleasant odorous gas (smoke) but also creates substances in the oil itself that impart an off taste to foods.

Some of the substances created as the fats break down are unhealthy, toxic, and even carcinogenic. As a fat is exposed to heat over time, its smoke point is steadily reduced as its fats break down. An oil's smoke point can fall by 100°F after a single use, which may inadvertently lead to spontaneous combustion and take the chef by surprise. The temperature at which an oil can combust is called the **flash point**, which is not far above the smoke point. If the smoke point is reduced, so too is the flash point.

Fats suitable for frying will have a high smoke point and be resistant to breakdown during extended heating. The temperature range for frying is generally 365° to 390°F, so the smoke point of the fat used should be well above those temperatures, around 410°–450°F. Though the oil should be maintained near the bottom of the range, it is necessary at times to raise the frying temperature before adding a large volume of food to the oil, since the addition of cooler dough rapidly reduces the temperature.

Even a stable frying oil with a high smoke point will slowly break down as it is heated. Continuous heating will lower the smoke point. Because time and expense require that oil be used as conservatively as possible, most serious bakeries employ special equipment for deep frying. This not only makes frying safer but the machines are better at maintaining a constant temperature. Also, the small particles of food that drop to the bottom of the fryer will not burn and contaminate the rest of the oil quickly, as they would if fried in a pot of oil over direct heat, since commercial fryers often place the heat source just above the bottom level of the fryer.

Food can be fried in any nonreactive pan on a stove top. Reactive metal pots, such as iron or copper, lead to oxidation (aging, breakdown) of the oil. Choose a stainless steel pot with sides that are high enough to provide 4 inches of clearance above the level of the oil. The wider the diameter of the pot, the more quickly the oil will be exposed to the air, an often forgotten source of oxidation that can lead to flavor deterioration.

Choosing a suitable frying fat is complex. In general, vegetable fats have a higher smoke point than animal fats. The presence of free fatty acids (more common in animal fats), emulsifiers, and preservatives reduces the smoke point. See the chart on page 80 for a fat comparison. Saturated fats are more stable. Coconut oil and palm kernel oil have been popular frying oils in the past; however, they have fallen out of favor because their high level of saturated fat corresponds to an increase in serum cholesterol.

Butter, which contains protein and carbohydrates in addition to fat, has a very low smoke point that makes it inappropriate for high-heat cooking. The smoke point of butter is increased if it is **clarified**. To clarify butter, it is melted and cooked over medium-low heat until foam rises to the top and the whey falls to the bottom of the pan. The foam is skimmed off, and the butter strained through cloth or a fine sieve, leaving the whey behind. The butter is now translucent and resists rancidity because the milk solids have been removed. Even clarified butter is not a choice for deep-fat frying, but it is an especially flavorful medium in which to sauté fruit or nuts.

The healthiest oils for the human heart are usually monounsaturated or polyunsaturated oils, especially ones that have undergone minimal processing. But these oils are not necessarily suitable for frying. Cold-pressed extra-virgin olive oil, for example, has a smoke point lower than minimal frying temperatures by almost 100°F. But regular olive oil, which has been refined differently, has a higher smoke point. Nevertheless, monounsaturated, and especially polyunsaturated, oils will breakdown much more easily than saturated fats. Wholesale distributors carry a wide range of fats and oils for different uses, giving professional bakers a range of oils especially made for deep frying. Currently, soybean and corn oils have been specially developed and refined to create stable frying oils.

Many books include charts listing the smoke points of common oils. Research for this edition found that temperatures do not correspond in different sources, however. The reason for a lack of consensus is the effects of refining processes on an oil's smoke point. Four different corn oils could have four different smoke points, making any list of good frying oils tenuous at best. A fat's saturation level is a good indicator of frying stability, but remember that many shortenings, which are quite saturated, contain other ingredients, such as emulsifiers that are not suitable for high-temperature cooking.

THE TEXTURE OF FAT IN BAKED GOODS

The creamy smoothness of ice cream, pudding, mousse, or chocolate illustrates how fat contributes a pleasing texture to desserts. Though not creamy in texture, the mouthfeel of baked goods such as frosted cakes and Danish depends significantly on their fat content.

The choice of fat influences the finished volume, texture, and flavor of baked goods. Cookies made with butter are likely to spread more than cookies made with hydrogenated vegetable shortening, for example. How the choice of fat affects the texture of laminates, pies, cookies, and cakes is addressed within specific chapters.

THE BAKER'S DILEMMA

Though food faddists may look at sugar with disdain, fat is universally regarded as the primary threat to heart health and weight mainte-nance. Pastry chefs find themselves with the dilemma of trying to make a great-tasting and textured product, often with ingredients that, when consumed in excess, are unhealthy.

Animal fats such as lard and butter contain cholesterol, as well as saturated fat, but they create baked goods with a wonderful mouthfeel. Butter is the single most important fat in baking, and its flavor is asso-ciated with quality and richness. Shortening makes pie dough flaky, cookies taller, and cakes tender, light, and moist. It also is easier to work with at a wide range of temperatures, and is much more shelf stable. When it is used in conjunction with butter, a perfect balance of texture and flavor can be achieved. But all hydrogenated fats affect heart health adversely.

Oils can be heart healthy. Minimally refined, cold-processed mono-unsaturated and polyunsaturated fats still contain beneficial fatty acids, but they are not shelf stable or heat-stable. However, oils are not appro-priate for every recipe. The oils that are best for deep frying are saturated fats—perfectly shelf stable, but not heart healthy. Cocoa butter is an in-teresting fat. Though it contains a significant amount of saturated fat, the human body breaks it down into a heart-healthy monounsaturated fat.

Pastry chefs with clients who want reduced-fat food will have to work hard at adapting recipes. Though it is not easy to commit to preparing diet-specific food, the population seeking vegetarian (no meat), vegan (no animal products), healthy (whole-grain, healthy fats), organic, low-cholesterol, and even

HOW TO REDUCE FAT IN BAKING

Replace some of the whole eggs with egg whites.

Increase moisture to compensate for fat loss in baked goods, such as with buttermilk or corn syrup.

Use fruit purées when possible.

Dried apricots can be softened in hot water and puréed for a minimally flavored fat replacer.

Starches, gums, and gelatin can compensate for fewer eggs used in custards.

Reduced-fat dairy products perform well in baked goods, but fat-free do not.

more specialized foods for gluten allergies and diabetes is steadily growing. In the future, it may be profitable to pursue such customers. However, it is harder to convert pastry products to be low in fat than savory food, since the chemistry of baking can be toyed with only so much. Fat is often the source of flavor and texture in pastry products.

CHAPTER 6

MILK AND DAIRY
PRODUCTS

The consumption of milk and dairy products may be ubiquitous in America; however, it is not a worldwide phenomenon. While mother's milk is the primary food for newborns, the digestive enzyme lactase, necessary to break down milk sugar lactose, begins to wane in children by age three. Most of the world's populations find milk, if not all dairy products, not only difficult to digest but also repugnant. The use of milk from other mammals is recent on the human timeline, dating back to around 10,000 B.C.E. About this time, herds such as sheep and goats were domesticated, the development of agriculture began, and beer and bread became a part of our diet.

Unlike milk, cream, and butter, fermented dairy products such as yogurt and cheese continue to be consumed into adulthood because they have little, if any, lactose present. Lactose is consumed by bacteria during fermentation. Fermented dairy products also keep better than fresh ones, making them more convenient in warmer climates. These products are more likely to be consumed worldwide. For reasons scientists are still trying determine, northern Europeans as a population never lost the ability to produce lactase. Thus, the love of fresh milk, cream, butter, and cheese is peculiarly Western. (See Kiple and Ornelas, sections III.9 and IV.E.6.)

PASTEURIZATION AND HOMOGENIZATION

Fresh milk is highly perishable, and only with the recent advances in preservation has milk been regarded as a safe, pure form of nourishment.

Pasteurization of milk in the United States occurred around 1900 but was not enforced until the middle of the century. **Pasteurization** is the process of heating a substance to kill bacteria that contribute to spoilage and disease. Milk products can be pasteurized at 143°F for 30 minutes or at 161°F for less than a minute. After heating, the milk is rapidly cooled. Pasteurization denatures enzymes inherent in the milk that break down milk fats, thus preventing the milk from developing an off flavor.

Homogenization was developed to prevent the milk and cream from separating into two layers. The days of the milkman delivering milk jugs with delicious cream at the top are part of America's past. Many consumers found the cream, which is lighter than milk and rises to the top, absolutely delicious. However, the cream resists being stirred back into the milk, a problem solved by homogenization. Homogenized milk is forced through minute openings, under pressure, which breaks the fat globules into a much smaller and uniform size. These small particles resist joining together and rising, thus keeping liquid milk uniform. Homogenized milk can be described as an emulsion, since the small, evenly sized particles of fat are held in a stable solution.

Pasteurization and homogenization made milk consumption safe, but even though its shelf life has been extended, milk is still a very perishable product. Sunlight and warm temperatures cause rapid spoilage and souring of dairy products.

FRESH MILK AND CREAM

Both freshly pasteurized and raw milk will quickly separate into two layers upon standing. The cream rises to the top and the milk remains beneath. The longer the milk stands, the higher in fat the cream layer and the lower in fat the milk. Modern dairies use centrifugal force to efficiently separate milk and cream into various categories based on fat content. These products are then homogenized to prevent any further separation. Below is a list of basic milk and cream products used in pastry kitchens.

MILK

If a recipe calls simply for milk, it is referring to **whole milk.** Whole milk has 3.5 percent fat, and is called whole because it resembles the milk taken straight from the cow, before any cream has been removed. It is the richest and most flavorful of the fresh milk products. Milk is highly nutritious, containing protein, carbohydrates (sugars), vitamins, and minerals, and yet it is 87 percent water. Milk is just slightly acidic, with a pH of about 6.6.

Reduced-fat milk can be either 2 percent fat, 1 percent fat, and rarely, $1/2$ percent fat. **Skim milk,** also known as nonfat milk, is so named because all the cream has been skimmed from the top of the milk (before the machine age). Obviously, it has only trace amounts of fat. Modern dairies often add nonfat milk solids to skim milk to give it more body and flavor. Milk solids increase the amount of protein present.

CREAM

Half-and-half is half milk and half cream, with a fat content near 12 percent. **Light cream,** also known as coffee cream, is usually 20 percent fat, though it can range anywhere between 18 and 30 percent. Neither of these two creams has enough fat to be whipped.

Whipping cream, also known as light whipping cream, ranges between 30 and 36 percent fat. Technically, any cream with over 30 percent fat can be whipped, but chefs prefer **heavy whipping cream** for its reliability and stability. It ranges between 36 and 40 percent fat, though 37 percent is the average. It is also known simply as heavy cream. Cream, like butter, easily absorbs the odors of other food in the refrigerator, which can cause desserts to have an off flavor.

Ultra-pasteurized heavy cream has been heated to a very high temperature, about 280°F, to extend its shelf life. Home cooks are unlikely to use cream quickly, and high-heat pasteurization allows the cream to be used more gradually. Even though the cream is held at the high temperature only for a second, the flavor often tastes "cooked." The greater concern with ultra-pasteurization is its negative effects on whipping.

Heat destroys the enzyme that allows fat globules to clump together, and ultra-pasteurized cream has been exposed to a higher temperature than regular cream. Since the fat molecules must stick together for cream to be whipped and hold air, ultra-pasteurized cream requires a longer beating time. Indeed, some chefs have found ultra-pasteurized cream to be unreliable, if not downright resistant, to whipping. Ultra-pasteurized cream is less stable when whipped, leaking more water than other creams. See more about whipping cream, below.

BUTTER

Cream is fat dispersed in a water solution. During the making of butter, agitation reverses (or inverts) the solution, causing the butterfat to join together in a continuous phase and the water to be squeezed out.

Sweet butter is made from sweet cream, meaning cream that has not been soured. It must have a butterfat content of at least 80 percent to be labeled butter; otherwise, it is designated a spread.

The bakery standard is **unsalted sweet butter.** Much butter is salted to extend its shelf life, but most chefs want to control the amount of salt added to food. **Salted butter** may mask odors, so that spreading it on bread may taste fine, but baking butter cookies with it intensifies any off flavors. The opposite of sweet cream butter is not salted butter but butter made from cream that has been soured. This means that sweet cream butter is not synonymous with unsalted butter, and a package that says sweet cream butter may also be salted. Check the label.

European-style butter is made from cream that has been thickened and slightly soured by bacterial fermentation, much like crème fraîche, sour cream, and yogurt. This cream has a fuller, riper flavor that imparts a nutty richness to the butter. European butter also has less water and more fat (82 to 86 percent) than American butters. European-style butter is made by several dairies in the United States, as part of a premium product line.

Buttermilk was once the by-product of churning butter from cream, full of whey proteins high in lactose milk sugar. Those who grew up near small dairy farms remember the tangy sweet taste of fresh buttermilk with nostalgia, since modern buttermilk is too harsh to be a beverage. Today, it is made with low-fat milk, usually 1.5 percent, that has been thickened and acidified by bacteria. It is the same process as for yogurt, and, like yogurt, can be made at home. Even though it is low in fat, buttermilk seems rich and thick. Salt and even tiny flakes of butter are common additives. Buttermilk adds a rich buttery flavor to baked goods. Like all soured dairy products, it has a tenderizing effect on baked goods.

Canned and Dry Milk

Canned and dry milks are more economical and easy to store than fresh milks.

Evaporated milk is just what it sounds like—milk that has water removed from it (60 percent), concentrating its sweet flavor and thickening it slightly. It can be made from whole, low-fat, or nonfat milk. Evaporated whole milk must have at least 7.5 percent fat, though it often has much more. Evaporated milk must be sterilized at a high temperature, which imparts a flavor that some find slightly caramel-like and others regard as tasting "cooked."

Sweetened condensed milk also has 60 percent of its moisture removed, but a large amount of sugar has been added to the milk, about 20 percent by weight. Because the high sugar content prevents microbial growth, sweetened condensed milk doesn't have to be sterilized. It is extremely viscous. Anything labeled "unsweetened condensed milk" is simply evaporated milk. Sweetened condensed milk stars in many notable recipes, such as key lime pie, ice cream, and fudge. Dulce de leche, a smooth caramel sauce, is made by boiling the sweetened milk until it turns golden.

Dry milk is milk with all of its water removed. Dried whole milk, nonfat dry milk, and powdered buttermilk are the most common types available. With its fat content, dry whole milk must be refrigerated. Even though the flavor of dry whole milk is superior, nonfat dry milk is preferred in bakeries because it is shelf stable. It adds richness to baked goods and encourages browning. Dry milk comes in both powder and flake form.

OTHER DAIRY PRODUCTS

Sour cream is a thickened light cream, having around 20 percent butterfat. Much like yogurt and buttermilk, sour cream is thickened by an acid-producing bacteria culture. Creamy and tangy, it is the closest thing we Americans have to the milder and creamier European crème fraîche. Sour cream adds moisture and richness to baked goods, in addition to a delightful tanginess.

Yogurt is pasteurized milk that has been inoculated with bacteria. The bacteria ferment the lactose and create tangy lactic acid, thickening the milk in the process. At one time, this fermentation occurred naturally in unpasteurized milk. Today the process is carefully controlled. Many brands advertise the use of "live cultures" that make yogurt easier to digest than other dairy products. The more lactose that has been fermented, the easier to digest. In the United States, yogurt is made from cow's milk. Plain yogurt is made from whole milk, and low-fat and nonfat yogurt are made from reduced-fat and skim milk, respectively. Yogurt is seldom called for in baking, but it adds a pleasant flavor similar to buttermilk. Low-fat yogurt can be used in place of buttermilk in recipes, and higher fat yogurt in place of sour cream. Yogurt can be further concentrated and thickened by placing it in cheesecloth and letting the moisture drain.

Authentic French **crème fraîche** is made from unpasteurized cream that is allowed to ferment or thicken, thanks to lactic-acid-producing bacteria native to the cream. Crème fraîche may be soft, like sour cream, or firmer like mascarpone. In the United States, pasteurized cream is used, so fermenting agents must be added to it. Chefs can make their own by stirring a small amount of buttermilk into heavy cream and leaving the mixture to thicken at room temperature overnight. It is common in Europe to make ganache with crème fraîche rather than heavy cream.

Cream cheese, now synonymous with the brand name Philadelphia, is a soft, spreadable cheese made from whole milk and cream. It is slightly tangy and smooth, and should have at least 33 percent butterfat. Artisanal cheeses will have a more complex flavor and creamier texture. Neufchâtel is a slightly reduced-fat version that may be substituted for regular cream cheese. Cream cheese is the star of American cheesecakes. Whipped and fat-free versions will not perform well in baked goods.

Mascarpone is an extremely rich Italian cow's milk cheese made from acidulated heavy cream. Technically, it is not a true cheese, since it involves no rennet or curds. The acid thickens the cream and causes moisture to separate from the butterfat. Butter is at least 80 percent butterfat, and mascarpone is not far behind at over 70 percent butterfat. Usually, the thickened, acidulated cream is set over a cloth, allowing the liquid to drain. Well-made mascarpone is silky, sweet, and slightly nutty, and it is highly perishable. Though acid had been added to it, mascarpone is not as tangy as yogurt or sour cream. It is used for tiramisù, Italian tortas, and cheesecakes.

Other dairy products of interest to pastry chefs are **farmer's cheese,** a smooth and slightly tangy cheese that is firmer than cream cheese, and quark. **Quark** is a mild, rich, and creamy unripened soft cheese that resembles sour cream in texture.

BAKING WITH DAIRY PRODUCTS

When altering recipes or developing new formulas, the major factors concerning the choice of dairy product are fat and sourness. If canned milks are involved, their increased sugar becomes a consideration. A pound cake formula that calls for a small amount of whole milk will be richer with the added fat of sour cream. Substituting buttermilk for sweet milk in a muffin recipe may require a change in leaveners.

CASEIN

There are many different proteins present in milk products, but most people are familiar with two of them, thanks to nursery rhymes: curds and whey (see McGee, p. 11). The curds in the nursery rhyme are coagulated casein, the protein of import to pastry chefs. Casein is what causes milk to curdle at high temperatures, particularly if an acid or fierce agitation is added to the equation. Fat can act as a buffering agent, preventing curdling. Adding low-fat milk to hot caramel curdles the milk instantly, but adding cream will not. High-fat dairy products used in sauces will not form a thick skin as quickly as those made with regular milk.

Casein affects pastry chefs because it is responsible for the skin that forms on dairy-based sauces, like pastry cream and crème Anglaise. The only way to prevent the skin from forming is to create a barrier between the casein and the air. Generally this is accomplished by placing plastic wrap directly against the surface of the sauce, or by letting a tablespoon of butter melt on the surface of the sauce while hot. Though the casein skin can be skimmed from the surface, a new skin will form. Since removing the skin also removes nutrients, creating an air-free seal is more efficient.

WHIPPED CREAM

When beaten vigorously, foam will appear on the surface of even low-fat milk. The composition of milk foam is similar to that of an egg white foam, since both foams are made by linked protein molecules. When the milk is agitated, the proteins coagulate slightly and join one another to form the surrounding structure that holds the trapped air. In milk, however, that structure is not stable and the foam quickly dissipates. Cream, on the other hand, will form a stable foam thanks to its fat content.

The butterfat globules in cream will begin to stick together when the cream is beaten. They form a more stable structure to support the foam. Beginning at about 20 percent fat, creams can be whipped, but only creams above 30 percent create foams with any longevity.

Perfect whipped cream should double in volume. If the cream is to be sweetened, the sugar should not be added until the cream is almost at the soft peak stage. The cream should be very cold to hold its shape when whipped, since the butterfat it contains melts at room temperature. Remember that the same fat is in both cream and butter, just in varying amounts, so just as butter is hard when cold, cold cream is thicker. The old trick employed by home cooks of chilling the beater and mixing bowl before whipping is impractical in pastry kitchens, where the bowl may weigh over 30 pounds. Still, keeping everything as cool as possible is essential, and that includes the air. Cold cream may refuse to whip in a hot kitchen, since beating hot air into the cream simply melts the fat and collapses the foam.

Unlike egg whites, heavy cream that is slightly overwhipped and appears grainy can be brought back to a smooth state by beating in more heavy cream. If the cream is overwhipped to the point that small globs of hardened butterfat have formed, the emulsion has inverted and nothing can be done save for beating the cream until all of it has turned to butter.

Though whipped cream will hold its shape for two days if kept cold, most bakeries stabilize whipped cream that is used as a topping. Stabilized whipped cream holds its shape longer at room temperature. Usually, commercial stabilizers available from wholesale distributers are added, or unwhipped cream with the stabilizers already added is purchased. Gelatin works equally well, but it must be softened and warmed in a small portion of cream before it can be used. The gelatin mixture should be cooled to just warm before being beaten into the rest of the cold whipped cream. Food scientist Shirley Corriher simply melts a few marshmallows into her cream, since they contain gelatin already. A softer stabilized cream can be made by thickening cornstarch with a portion of cream, but it will not be as stable at room temperature.

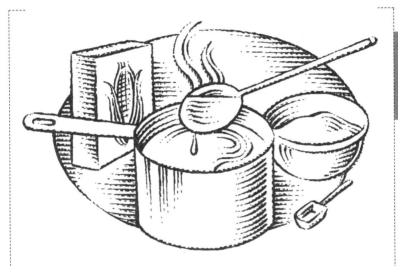

CHAPTER 7

THICKENERS: STARCHES, GELATIN, AND GUMS

T hickeners are what turn sweetened cream into panna cotta, make crème anglaise into a molded Bavarian, and gel fresh fruit juices in pies. Starches, gelatin, and gums are also used in low-fat recipes to replace eggs, a higher-fat source of thickening power. Thickeners provide structure and stability to foods that are ephemeral, such as whipped cream and meringue. Since thickeners come from many different sources, each type has different properties that make it suitable—or not—for one dish or another.

STARCHES

Starches have many functions in baked goods, puddings, and sauces. They help stabilize the delicate structure of soufflés, and they prevent egg custards from curdling (see Chapter 15). The starch present in flour, when broken down, serves as food for yeast in bread doughs, thus aiding fermentation (see Chapter 2). Starch gelatinization in bread doughs and cakes forms an important part of the supporting structure of baked goods (see Chapters 12 and 14). Starch can also be used to moderate the protein strength of flour, since adding starch to flour reduces the percentage of gluten-forming proteins. Thus, substituting starch for a small portion of strong flour can make a more tender crumb. Not only does this reduce the ratio of protein to starch but also the crumb becomes more tender because the starch competes with gluten-forming proteins for water (Chapter 14).

This section, however, is concerned with the thickening property of starches. Starches are used to thicken fruit-based desserts such as pies, cobblers, and crisps, as well as for thickening custards, such as pastry cream. Not all starches behave the same way. Some are best for dishes that will be frozen and thawed; others are better for giving fruit fillings a clear shine. It is up to the chef to determine which starch to use in a specific application.

GELATINIZATION

Gelatinization describes in one word what starches do: When heated, they absorb moisture, swell, and thicken liquids, forming a gel-like structure. Some starches can absorb 100 times their weight in water.

Starches are found in the seeds of grains and in the roots of plants. Plants create starch as a form of energy reserve. Through photosynthesis a plant produces glucose, which fuels its cells, and extra glucose is converted to starch for storage. Starches are very long chains of glucose molecules. In Chapter 3 sugar was defined as a simple carbohydrate compared to starch. Granulated sugar, sucrose, is composed of one molecule of glucose and one molecule of fructose. The starches described below range roughly from 10,000 to 50,000 glucose molecules each, varying according to their plant source. To be botanically correct, what cooks refer to as "root starches" are usually tubers. A tuber is a thick part of the root or rhizome that stores plant food, or starch.

Starches are considered semicrystalline in structure and are discussed as *granules*. They can vary in shape as well as length. Straight molecules are called **amylose**, branched ones are called **amylopectin**. Each shape behaves differently when heated and cooled, providing different thickening characteristics. Grain seeds and roots vary in their ratios of amylose to amylopectin. In general, grain-derived starches are higher in amylose and root-derived are higher in amylopectin. Grain starches have at most 30 percent amylose, and tubers, with the exception of potatoes, have much less.

Unlike sugars, starches do not dissolve in water at room temperature but must be heated before they can swell and thicken. As a starch-thickened sauce slowly heats, the starch granules absorb water and be-

GRAIN STARCHES VS. ROOT STARCHES

The serving temperature, storage conditions, and desired finished appearance of the product will determine whether you thicken with a grain starch (wheat flour, rice flour, or cornstarch) or a root starch (arrowroot, tapioca, or potato).

FILLINGS THICKENED WITH GRAIN STARCHES	FILLINGS THICKENED WITH ROOT STARCHES
Will weep when frozen	Will freeze and thaw without weeping
Will appear opaque when cooled	Will thin if reheated
Will thicken into a firm gel as they cool	Thicken at a lower temperature (around 170°F)
Gelatinize just below a boil and can be brought to a boil	Will be thickest when hot and slightly thinner when cool
Can be reheated without danger of thinning	Range from clear to translucent and shiny when cool
Can tolerate moderate stirring while hot (before it is cool and set)	Will thin if stirred too much

gin to swell. If the sauce has been thickened with flour or cornstarch, the starch granules reach the gelatinization range beginning at 140° and 145°F (lower for root starches). At this point, the granules are so swollen with water that they no longer resemble granules but gels. All of this is invisible to the naked eye, of course, since sauces seem to be either thin or suddenly thick. The greatest viscosity is reached when the overloaded starch granules burst. For grain starches, this will occur between 175° and 205°F, but for root starches, such as potato, this can occur under 170°F. When the starch granules burst, more starch leaks into the sauce and contributes to thickening. The empty starch shells are the primary source of thickening: Their size prevents quick and easy movement through the sauce. So long as they are not deflated by vigorous stirring as the mixture cools, the sauce remains thick. Amylose, which is straight, has better thickening ability than the branched amylopectin. Its long shape, when swollen, makes amylose more likely to collide with other molecules and get tangled up. Amylopectin, though branched, moves with the ease of a round object through liquid. Amylose, on the other hand, is more like a long swollen caterpillar that gets in the way.

Below is a list of common thickeners. Keep in mind that starch and flour are not interchangeable terms. Corn flour, for example, will contain protein and minerals in addition to starch. Potato starch is derived from potatoes, but potato flour is the whole peeled potato, dried and pulverized. Tapioca and arrowroot are referred to as flours, however.

WHEAT FLOUR is not pure starch, usually having around 10 percent protein. Naturally, low-protein flours have more starch and are better thickeners. The presence of protein makes flour less efficient as a thickener than pure starches. Pure wheat starch, though less available, can be used as an alternative. In general, it takes almost twice as much flour to thicken as any of the other grains or roots listed below. Flour, though, is the standard since it is universally available in pastry kitchens, so all other starches are compared to it. Flour, like all grain starches, must be well cooked or it will leave a raw cereal aftertaste.

CORNSTARCH is the preferred starch in American recipes, probably because it is readily available. In Europe it may be called cornflour, a term in the United States that refers to finely ground cornmeal. Fruit juices in pies thickened with it are translucent rather than opaque, unlike flour, though not as clear as root-based thickeners. Cornstarch must be fully cooked or it will leave an unpleasant pasty, raw taste behind. Cornstarch used to thicken custards is usually mixed with a small amount of liquid to form a paste to prevent it from forming lumps.

WAXY CORNSTARCH is almost 99 percent amylopectin, and thus behaves more like a root starch than a grain starch. It has little of the cereal taste of regular cornstarch, and pies made from it will not weep after being frozen.

RICE STARCH is derived from rice flour. It is less commonly used in this country than other grain starches, though rice flour, which has no gluten, is sometimes added to cookies such as shortbread to create an even more tender, crumbly texture. Rice starch has almost twice the thickening power of flour.

POTATO STARCH is widely used in European cooking. Though American bakers have also adopted the tradition of using mashed potatoes, starchy potato cooking water, and even instant potato flakes (with additional water) in baked goods for tenderness and added moisture, pure potato starch comes after flour, cornstarch, and tapioca as a preferred thickener. European chefs, however, prefer potato starch since it has no cereal flavor, and because it swells and gels at a lower temperature than flour or cornstarch. In cakes, potato starch can be substituted for a portion of flour to "soften" it, since starch has no protein. A cake batter with potato starch will finish cooking at a lower internal temperature, which keeps the cake moist by reducing cooking time, and has none of the raw taste it would have if cornstarch had been used. Since cornstarch requires higher gelatinization temperatures, the cake would have cooked longer and potentially lost more moisture. Potato starch falls in between the grain and root starches in temperament: It has a little less amylose than flour (23 percent) and has more amylopectin than the other roots. Potato starch has over twice the thickening power of flour.

TAPIOCA, derived from the cassava plant, is the thickener of choice for juicy berry pies, since it does not cloud the color of the fruit and thickens beautifully. Tapioca flour and the instant tapioca granules both work well; however, the instant granules take on a noticeable globular texture if there is not enough liquid provided by the fruit juices. Because instant tapioca granules require moisture to dissolve, they remain hard on the surface of lattice-topped pies where they are directly exposed to the dry air of the oven. Tapioca flour, since it is finely ground, dissolves more easily and evenly. It has twice the thickening power of flour.

ARROWROOT FLOUR comes from the starch of a tropical tuber believed to be native to South America. It has almost twice the thickening power of flour, and is perfectly clear and tasteless.

INSTANT STARCHES are specially processed (basically pre-cooked) so they have the ability to swell and thicken cool liquids. One instant starch sold under the brand name Clearjel is made from waxy cornstarch, which makes it particularly useful for fillings and pies that will be frozen and thawed. This starch is more indifferent to acidic fruit or liquids than other starches.

Other ingredients that affect starch gelatinization are:

RAW EGGS contain an enzyme called amylase that will break down starch amylose. Sauces and custards containing eggs must be brought almost to a boil (when bubbles appear) to inactivate this enzyme. The presence of the starch makes it possible to bring the egg to such a high temperature without curdling it. The custard may thicken properly at first even if the enzyme is not destroyed, but it will slowly destroy the amylose and thus also the set gel. A classic example is cream pie: If the amylase is not destroyed, a filling that set beautifully when poured into the pie shell will be soup the next morning.

ACIDS, such as wine, vinegar, or lemon juice, inhibit the ability of starch to swell and thicken. If the recipe is very acidic, the acid must be added last, letting the starch do its job of thickening first. It must be added while the mixture is still hot, or the thickness will be destroyed by the added liquid.

SUGAR competes with starch for water, and thus slows the swelling of starch granules. High amounts of sugar can prevent the starch from being able to swell and thus thicken adequately. Sugar also increases the temperature of starch gelatinization. Sucrose and lactose are the two sugars that affect starches the most. Though almost all milk products contain lactose, remember that concentrated products like evaporated milk have even more.

GELATIN

Gelatin is used to set chiffon pies or Bavarians and to stabilize whipped cream and glazes. It is also an ingredient in marshmallows. Gelatin has no real flavor, so it lets the other flavor components shine. Like some starches, gelatin can hold 100 times its weight in water. Liquids set with gelatin will hold their shape when unmolded. Used in moderation, gelatin is a wonderful stabilizer, but too much makes mousses and chiffon pies rubbery. A perfect Bavarian, for example, should just barely hold its shape. The moment it hits the tongue it should dissolve into a light creaminess. If it does not melt immediately, the tongue registers the resistance as a rubbery sensation, indicating too much gelatin.

Gelatin is an animal protein derived from the collagen in skin and the connective tissues, such as tendons and cartilage. Most gelatin is processed from pig skin. For those who avoid animal or pork products, a gum (see below) is the most suitable replacement.

There are two forms of gelatin: **leaf** (or **sheet**) and **powdered**. Powdered gelatin comes both in .25 ounce envelopes (about $2^1/_4$ teaspoons each) and in bulk containers. One teaspoon of Knox brand powdered gelatin is the equivalent of two sheets of gelatin. The sheets are standardized, so that one sheet has the same gelling capacity as another despite differences in thickness or dimensions. Powdered gelatins are not equal; each has a bloom rating to express gelling power.

HOW GELATIN WORKS

Powdered gelatin must be sprinkled over a small amount of cool water or liquid, such as cream or an alcohol like bourbon or rum (but preferably not highly acidic juices, which inhibit gelatin), for a minute or two to soften—$^1/_4$ cup liquid for 2 teaspoons gelatin is sufficient. The liquid is then gently heated until the gelatin dissolves. It is advisable to check with your fingers to ensure that the gelatin is completely dissolved, since even small granules will form larger rubbery spots when set.

Sheet gelatin is soaked in cold water for 10 minutes to soften. It is then squeezed to drain it of the soaking water and gently melted in the liquid called for in the recipe.

The gelatin mixture should be cooled until it just begins to set before it is folded into delicate egg-white foams or cold whipped cream. If you are diligent about frequent stirring, this can be done quickly over an ice water bath, or more slowly in the refrigerator. Gentle stirring prevents the mixture against the side of the bowl from setting faster than the rest. If the gelatin sets too quickly, creating lumps, simply reheat it until it is completely dissolved, providing the beaten whites or whipped cream have not been added. Gelatin can be reheated with no ill effect so long as it is not boiled. High heat reduces its thickening power.

Large amounts of sugar and acidic fruits have an inhibiting effect on gelatin's ability to gel, but when a dessert completely refuses to set, an enzyme in the fresh fruit may be the culprit. Enzymes in fresh pineapple, figs, papaya, kiwifruit, honeydew melon, mangoes, and ginger interfere with gelatin. However, cooking these fruits to 185°F will destroy the enzyme. Canned fruit is not a problem, since its processing denatures any inhibiting enzymes.

GUMS

Gums have several different functions in a bakery. They can be used as thickeners or stabilizers, much like starches or gelatin. In certain icings, the addition of gum will prevent cracking or stickiness. Gums may be used in reduced-fat baked goods to improve texture and prevent moisture loss. The addition of gum can retard the crystallization of sugar, and it can function as an emulsifier. Gums prevent weeping (called syneresis—the release of liquid from a gel) of egg-based custards and fruit pie fillings. And finally, gums are used to make gum paste, a malleable substance that can be formed into decorative flowers or shapes for wedding cakes.

Gums fall into three categories: those derived from terrestrial plants, alginates (seaweed), and those commercially produced by microbial fermentation. There are many gums used in commercial baking today (see Table 7.1), and the list below covers just a few that might be accessible for commercial bakeries.

TERRESTRIAL PLANTS

GUM TRAGACANTH is derived from an Asian plant. Usually sold in powder form, it is used in combination with confectioners' sugar,

TABLE 7.1 COMMERCIAL GUMS			
Marine Plants	**Terrestrial Plants**	**Microbial Polysaccharides**	**Polysaccharide Derivatives**
Agar	Guar gum	Dextran	Carboxymethyl cellulose
Alginates	Gum arabic	Gellan gum	Methyl hydroxy-propyl cellulose
Carragheen	Gum tragacanth	Rhamsan gum	Hydroxypropyl cellulose
Furcellaran	Karaya gum	Welan gum	Hydroxyethyl cellulose
	Locust bean gum	Xanthan gum	Propylene glycol alginate
	Pectin		Hydroxypropyl guar Modified starch

Xanthan: Natural Biogum for Scientific Water Control, third edition. Rahway, N.J.: Merck and Co., 1988. (Kelco is a division of Merck and Co.)

water, shortening, and food colors to make gum paste flowers and decorations for specialty cakes.

ALGINATES

AGAR-AGAR, also called Japanese gelatin, is a powdered, tasteless derivative of seaweed. It is often used in place of gelatin for those who keep kosher or are vegan. If substituting for gelatin, less agar-agar will be needed as it has greater thickening capacity.

CARRAGHEEN comes from dark seaweed off the coast of Ireland and is sometimes called Irish moss. It may be used much the same way as agar-agar.

MICROBIAL GUMS

These gums are important to large-scale industrial food production but are rarely used by the typical pastry chef. The names of some of these gums, such as **Xanthan** and **Dextran,** may sound familiar since they are common ingredients in packaged mixes, candies, and snack foods.

CHAPTER 8

CHOCOLATE

Native to tropical America, the cacao tree produces beans that have been cultivated for at least 3,000 years. Though Columbus sent cocoa beans back to Spain, the first anecdotal evidence of Aztec reverence and consumption of cocoa beverages was given by members of Cortez's expedition. Crew members witnessed the emperor Montezuma drinking cup after cup of a bitter drink made from ground cocoa beans and water. The emperor claimed chocolate to be an aphrodisiac. The conquistadors were surprised to discover that cocoa beans were prized almost as much as gold. Indeed, they served as currency and were given to the emperor as tribute payment.

At first, Europe did not hold chocolate in the same esteem as the New World. The Aztec drink recipe of unsweetened chocolate and ground dried chiles just didn't take off, despite its promotion among the upper classes as an exotic novelty. However, when the European colonists began adding sugar to their chocolate, its popularity spread across class lines and continents. A perfect combination was born.

CACAO CULTIVATION

Today, cacao cultivation extends around the globe, limited to countries near the equator where the necessary rainfall and warmth prevail. Central and South America, Africa, and Indonesia dominate production worldwide. In 1737, Linnaeus, the famed Swedish botanist, classified the species as *Theobroma cacao*, literally "food of the Gods," referring to an ancient Aztec legend. Three varieties of the cacao tree are recognized: **criollo**, the most rare and difficult to grow; **forastero**, the most common and hardy; and **trinitario**, a hybrid of the first two varieties.

Most chocolates are blends of the three types, with each type contributing its own strengths. Like many wines, great chocolate is the result of skilled blending to achieve complex, but balanced flavor. For example, forastero lacks the delicate flavor of the criollo, but it gives body to the chocolate. And, as in wine or coffee, the soil in which the trees are grown imparts its own distinctive flavor. Sweetness, acidity, and smokiness are all geographically linked characteristics.

Harvesting and Producing Chocolate

Cocoa beans are harvested year-round. The cacao trees are rather fragile, necessitating that the pods be harvested by hand. Within each pod, up to forty seeds (beans) nestle in a sticky pulp. The pods are split open immediately and the beans are scooped out with the pulp, covered, and

FIGURE 8.1 **Cacao plant with pods.**

left to ferment. This first step of fermentation is essential in developing chocolate flavor. Next, the beans are dried in the sun or in a gently heated room, then graded and packed for export.

The beans are processed at individual chocolate company locations, usually far from the country of origin. Each company jealously guards its specific "chocolate" recipes and has developed a characteristic style of manufacturing. Generally, however, the first step is careful roasting of the beans to bring out flavor. At this point, the bean skins slip easily from the kernels, or **nibs**, which are then ready to be made into chocolate or cocoa powder.

If cocoa powder is the desired end product, the nibs are ground and pressed to extract the cocoa butter. The nibs retain a little of the cocoa butter, but are now dry enough to be pulverized and sieved into cocoa powder. The separated cocoa butter (about 54 percent of the nib by weight) may be used later for the manufacture of bar chocolate, or sold to confectioners and other industries.

To make chocolate, the nibs are first ground into a paste. This paste, or **chocolate liquor**, contains only the cocoa solids and cocoa butter inherent in the beans. The term *liquor* does not refer to alcohol. Specific recipes for individual chocolates then add varying proportions of ingredients such as sugar, milk solids, vanilla, lecithin, and extra cocoa butter to the chocolate liquor. **Conching** is the next step. Named for the shell-shaped machine first used for this process, a conching apparatus uses paddles to create a rolling-churning action, making the chocolate silky smooth. The action of conching, which aerates the mixture, encourages any remaining bitter volatile acids to be expelled. After conching, the chocolate is cooled, molded into blocks or coin-shaped pastilles, and packaged.

TYPES OF CHOCOLATE AND COCOA

UNSWEETENED CHOCOLATE, also called bitter and baking chocolate, is pure chocolate liquor. It must contain 50 to 58 percent cocoa butter. Depending on the brand, other flavorings such as vanilla or salt may be present.

BITTERSWEET AND SEMISWEET CHOCOLATE both must contain at least 35 percent chocolate liquor. Sugar, added cocoa butter, lecithin (usually derived from soybeans), and vanilla are other typical ingredients. Strangely, there is no official distinction between the two chocolates. Some assume that bittersweet is less sweet than semisweet, but one company's semisweet may be less sweet than another's bittersweet. Over the past decade, many bittersweet chocolates have come on the market that contain 50, 60, even over 70 percent chocolate liquor. These chocolates are intensely "chocolaty" and less sweet than typical bittersweet chocolates, and recipes may need adjustment to accommodate them.

MILK CHOCOLATE contains at least 12 percent milk solids and 10 percent chocolate liquor. The sweetest of the chocolates, it is also the most popular plain eating chocolate. Milk chocolate also contains lecithin, vanilla, and, of course, sugar.

WHITE CHOCOLATE, made from cocoa butter, contains no cocoa solids, and hence lacks the characteristic chocolate flavor. At the time of this writing, the FDA does not recognize (or regulate) the label "white chocolate." Sugar, vanilla, milk solids, and lecithin are added to cocoa butter to create white chocolate. Read labels carefully. If another vegetable fat has been substituted for cocoa butter, you are dealing with **confectionery** (also called **summer** or **compound**) **coating**. It will not perform in recipes the same way as white chocolate.

COUVERTURE denotes a coating chocolate with a high cocoa butter content, usually 32 to 39 percent, useful for making chocolate candies, decorations, and ultra-smooth glazes. The higher percentage of cocoa butter promotes the flow of melted, tempered chocolate, enabling the pastry chef to create thin chocolate coatings or decorations that have a good snap when set. Couverture is available for any type of chocolate, white or dark.

DUTCH-PROCESS COCOA, also known as **alkalized cocoa** or **European-style cocoa**, is processed with an alkali to neutralize the natural acidity of cocoa powder. Dutchman Conrad van Houten invented this process in 1828, hence the name. Until van Houten's machine, which separated cocoa solids from cocoa butter, chocolate beverages had been made from ground cacao beans. Remember, the beans have an inherent cocoa butter content of 54 percent, making previous chocolate beverages oily. By alkalizing the cocoa, increasing its pH from 5.5 to between 7 and 8, he improved cocoa's ability to disperse in a liquid and also mellowed the flavor. Today, Dutch-process cocoa is made nearly the same way; the machinery is just more sophisticated. Dutch-process cocoa is darker in color than regular cocoa powder, and its flavor is smoother. **Regular cocoa powder** is reddish brown, with a more intense, even fruity, robust flavor than alkalized cocoa. These two types of cocoa powder are not always interchangeable, as they are often paired with specific leaveners that complement their acidity or alkalinity. Most of the cocoa butter has been separated from cocoa powders. **Breakfast-grade cocoas** denote a cocoa butter content of 22 percent, which is higher than typical cocoas. Therefore, substituting breakfast grade for regular cocoa changes the fat content of the recipe. All of these cocoas are unsweetened and should not be confused with hot cocoa mixes.

CHOCOLATE CHIPS are included in this section to differentiate them from basic chocolate. They contain different vegetable fats and special stabilizers that help them retain their shape during baking. They are not interchangeable with regular chocolate, whose cocoa butter behaves (and tastes) differently from other fats. The additional stabilizers mean that sauces, puddings, and mousses will set firmer than ones made with regular chocolate.

QUALITY CONSIDERATIONS

Factors affecting quality include the initial quality of the beans and proper fermentation, roasting, and conching. Some deficiencies are easily detected. Chocolate that has undergone minimal conching is noticeably less smooth. Waxy chocolate may indicate the presence of vegetable fats other than cocoa butter. Certainly, quality chocolates will not contain artificial ingredients, such as vanillin. Beyond that, choosing chocolate becomes a matter of taste. Indeed, wine-tasting terminology is sometimes applied to chocolate these days. Today's consumers are also more status conscious regarding high-end chocolates, and restaurant menus often identify the brand of chocolate used in a dessert as a selling point.

Pastry chefs usually have strong brand preferences. While taste comparisons are key, keeping the end product in mind is just as important. Two high-end chocolates can have equally pleasing tastes, but one may have better flow for making hard shells and decorations. The most wonderful-tasting chocolate may not make the best cake. At the very least, the nuances of flavor may be lost because combining chocolate with other ingredients can change or mask its flavor. Sauces and mousses often convey the purest chocolate flavor. Therefore, pastry chefs may utilize several different brands of chocolate for different purposes.

STORAGE

Cocoa butter, a vegetable fat, will eventually become rancid, like all natural fats. Beyond shelf life, trying to maintain chocolate in perfect form is also a consideration. Newly purchased chocolate should be in temper (see discussion, below), meaning that the most stable form of cocoa butter crystals have been encouraged to form, and the chocolate is smooth and shiny with a pleasant snap to it. In order to *keep* the chocolate in temper and maximize shelf life, it should be stored near 65°F in a room that is not overly humid and is free from temperature fluctuations. Those of you working in a professional kitchen at this moment can start laughing. In these ideal conditions, bitter and dark chocolates will last for a couple years. The key here is to assess how much chocolate you need on hand, since ideal long-term storage is not possible in hot kitchens. White chocolate and milk chocolate should be given priority safe-storage status, since the milk solids they contain are much more sensitive to rancidity. They should also be stored in a dark place. As a last resort, chocolate for baking may be stored briefly in the refrigerator of freezer, but never chocolate to be used for coatings or candymaking (see below).

Warmer or fluctuating temperatures can cause the cocoa butter to melt, separate, and recrystallize with white filmy streaks called **fat bloom**. Humidity changes may cause water to condense on the chocolate. Sugar is dissolved in the water, and then recrystallizes on the surface when the water evaporates. This is called **sugar bloom**. Neither is harmful for baking, but only fat-bloomed chocolate may be used for candymaking, after being retempered, of course.

All chocolate will readily absorb kitchen odors and should be protected accordingly.

WORKING WITH CHOCOLATE

Cocoa butter has a sharp melting point, which means it does not have a long intermediate stage of being semi-soft, like shortening, but is either solid or melting. This melting point is just below our body temperature, so that chocolate melts as soon as it hits the tongue, accounting for its pleasure factor. Cocoa butter is what makes eating chocolate a sublime experience, but it is also what makes chocolate difficult to work with.

Cocoa butter is seldom discussed without an explanation of its unique properties of crystallization. That is not to say that other fats do not possess a unique crystal structure. No one thinks twice about how melted butter will return to its solid form, but much nail biting goes on during the wait to see "if the melted chocolate sets up." The cocoa butter in chocolate must be coaxed into becoming a solid, hard, shiny form. As melted cocoa butter cools, it inevitably begins to recrystallize. But there are four different types of crystals that form, and each form multiples rapidly at specific temperatures.

- Alpha crystals melt between 70° and 75°F.

- Beta crystals melt at 95°F.

- Beta prime crystals melt between 81° and 84°F.

- Gamma crystals melt at 63°F.

Only one of the four types of crystals, called the beta, is considered stable, resulting in a shiny, solid piece of chocolate.

Tempering is simply the melting and cooling of chocolate at specific temperatures to ensure proper solidification. Similar to the idea of seeding in candymaking, where the size of the sugar crystals is controlled to create specific textures, tempering creates the ideal environment for the beta crystals to dominate the crystal formation of the melted chocolate. The theory of tempering chocolate is straightforward. In practice, however, tempering chocolate requires dedication and repetition to be mastered.

MELTING

The chocolate can be melted over a hot water bath, in a double boiler, or even in the microwave. Gentle heat to prevent scorching is the prime consideration, as cocoa butter will separate from cocoa solids at temperatures just beyond 120°F. Care should be taken to prevent water droplets from touching the chocolate. Chocolate will tolerate added water, but only a drop or two causes it to seize. The minimum liquid to add to prevent seizing is $1^1/_2$ teaspoons per ounce of chocolate, but thinning the chocolate to smooth it out also means the chocolate can no longer be used for hard shells and decorations (see Corriher, p. 461).

BASIC TEMPERING

An accurate thermometer is essential for tempering. There are specialized thermometers available for chocolate work, which have a range between 80° and 130°F. Those who become proficient at tempering eventually use their wrist or upper lip to determine temperature. (Fingertips are not adequate, as seasoned pastry chefs have usually lost heat sensitivity from repeated burns.)

1. Melt the chocolate to a temperature of 115° to 120°F. The chocolate must reach this range to ensure that all the cocoa butter crystals have been thoroughly dissolved. There should be no remaining lumps of chocolate in the

mixture. The temperature should not exceed 120°F, or the cocoa butter may separate from the cocoa solids.

2. Let the chocolate sit at room temperature, stirring occasionally, until the temperature of the chocolate falls to just over 80°F. Carefully bring the chocolate back to 86°–91°F, using the lower end of the range for white and milk chocolates and the higher temperatures for dark chocolates. Now the chocolate is ready to use. The tempered melted chocolate may be kept at its ideal range (which ensures good control of flow for making thin coatings) by any gentle means at hand: a warm spot on the stove near the pilot light, a hot water bath, a heating pad, or a even a hair dryer aimed at the bottom of the bowl. If the temperature reaches 92°F, or falls below 77°F, the chocolate is no longer in temper. It must be melted to 115°–120°F and cooled all over again.

OTHER METHODS

In the classic method of tempering chocolate, the melted chocolate is cooled to about 100°F. Between a quarter and a third of the chocolate is poured onto a clean dry surface, preferably marble, steel, or Formica (as opposed to wood or plastic). The chocolate is repeatedly scraped and spread over the surface using a long offset metal spatula or bench scraper. The motion must be continuous to prevent lumps from forming. Gradually the chocolate will thicken and lose its shine. When it reaches 84°F (82°F for milk and white chocolates), the paste is ready to be returned to the bowl of melted chocolate. The term for this paste is "mush." The temperature of the chocolate, after the paste has been stirred in and melted, should be between 86° and 91°F.

If you have a small amount of chocolate on hand that is still in temper, it can be used to "seed" melted untempered chocolate. Once again, let the melted chocolate cool slightly, then stir in the chopped tempered chocolate. For this method, the ratio of melted chocolate to chopped tempered chocolate is about 4 to 1. Some chefs use larger chunks of tempered chocolate as seeds, and simply remove the lumps that have not melted when the ideal temperature is reached.

Blocks of chocolate that are still in temper do not require all these steps. If they are carefully melted so that the temperature never exceeds 91°F, the chocolate will remain in temper.

PATIENCE AND TEMPER

Correct tempering is checked by spreading a small amount of chocolate on a sheet pan or piece of waxed paper and then waiting to see if the chocolate sets with an even surface color and shine. It is better not to hasten the process by placing the chocolate in the refrigerator, as crystal formation is sensitive to air temperature. For example, many hurried chefs have placed chocolate-dipped strawberries in the refrigerator to force the chocolate to solidify. However, when the strawberries are placed on a platter at room temperature, the chocolate quickly softens and begins to sweat. If improperly tempered chocolate does not set up, it can be forced to harden in the refrigerator, but this means that it will revert to being soft and dull at room temperature.

GANACHE

In its purest form, ganache is a mixture of heavy cream and chocolate. But that is just the beginning. Butter, coffee, tea, and even fruit purées make their way into ganache. Despite its simplicity, ganache is one of the most versatile components in the pastry kitchen.

Ganache can be thick or thin by adjusting the ratio of cream to chocolate. Thick ganache has more chocolate than cream. The large proportion of chocolate allows the ganache to set up upon cooling, becoming semisolid. Thick ganache can be used as a filling for cakes and truffles, or spread over a cake as a frosting. Even amounts (by weight) of cream to chocolate make a ganache perfect for glazing tortes. Ganache made from two parts cream to one part chocolate may be chilled and whipped, creating a silky mousse or a frosting.

BASIC GANACHE MAKING

For recipes that call for equal or greater amounts of heavy cream to chocolate, place the chopped chocolate in a bowl. Once the cream has been brought to a boil, pour it over the chocolate. Let the mixture stand for a minute or two, then gently whisk until smooth. If the recipe calls for more chocolate than cream, there will not be enough residual heat to melt the chocolate using the above method. Instead, use a larger pot to bring the cream to a boil. Remove the pot from the heat and stir in the chocolate. The heat held in the pan should melt the chocolate easily.

BROKEN GANACHE

Despite its simple appearance, ganache is actually a fat-in-water emulsion, much like mayonnaise. The milk solids and cholesterol present in the heavy cream stabilize the mixture; indeed, cholesterol itself is an emulsifier. But occasionally the ganache will break, and the fat will separate, giving the ganache a curdled appearance.

When the chocolate and cream are combined, the chocolate solids and the sugar are suspended in the water phase (the heavy cream contains a substantial amount of water) and the cocoa butter joins the butterfat from the cream. So even though ganache consists of two primary ingredients, there are several variables affecting the stability of the emulsion. Too little water and too much fat spells trouble. For example, a thick ganache made with very bittersweet chocolate may break, but semisweet chocolate may work fine. Unsweetened chocolate and (usually) bittersweet chocolates have more cocoa butter and less sugar than semisweet chocolate, a difference that can affect a ganache made with little cream. The semisweet chocolate provides more sugar (to the water phase) and contributes less fat, which brings the recipe into a happy equilibrium.

Every brand of chocolate differs in its ratio of cocoa solids to fat, not to mention other ingredients like sugar. Thus, ganache formulas will have to be adjusted for each specific chocolate used in order to get consistent results. Ganache clearly requires more care and thought than its simple formula would suggest. Butter, for example, provides both fat and water. If alcohol is added, it joins the water phase. Every ingredient affects the emulsion differently.

Even a stable ganache may slowly break during storage. To bring it back, the same principle is employed as bringing back broken mayonnaise. This can be done two ways: The first and foolproof method is to gradually beat the broken sauce into a tiny amount of heavy cream. According to professional chocolatiers, as little as $1/4$ cup cream will bring back a bathtub of broken ganache. The broken ganache and heavy cream should be at the same temperature, preferably just barely warm. The second method also depends on slowly incorporating the broken ganache into the cream but takes a daring shortcut. A small amount of warm cream is directly poured onto the top of the broken ganache. Whisking begins just on the surface of the ganache with the cream at the center and gradually moves outward to incorporate the entire mixture.

If ganache breaks while on the stove top, more cream or sugar can be added immediately. However, the method above is best for preserving the consistency of the original formula. After all, adding large amounts of cream is not helpful if a thick ganache is the goal.

WHIPPED GANACHE

Whipped ganache can be tricky to make because beating the mixture causes the cocoa butter to crystallize and solidify. When this happens, the mixture turns from silky and spreadable to stiff and grainy. The best way to make whipped ganache is not to hurry. Use a ratio of two parts cream to one part chocolate. Let the ganache cool overnight in a cool spot (55°–65°F is ideal) or in the refrigerator. Waiting at least eight hours makes the ganache easier to whip without seizing. Some chefs insist that rapid cooling over an ice water bath will work, but that has not been my experience. Exposing cocoa butter to extreme cold does initiate crystallization, even if it isn't visible to the naked eye.

Ganache should be cool when whipped, but it doesn't have to be truly cold. Some chefs prefer the ease of whipping cold ganache, which, like plain heavy cream, incorporates air quickly when chilled. Other chefs feel 55° to 65°F is safer, since it lessens the probability of sudden hardening. Ganache should be whipped only to soft peaks, since greater agitation only encourages the cocoa butter to crystallize. Beating ganache in a cool room provides better volume (as for whipped cream) but causes the ganache to seize more easily. Some chefs, trying to get the best of both worlds, beat the ganache in a cold room while aiming a heat gun at the bowl of the mixer.

CHOCOLATE PASTE OR MOLDING CHOCOLATE

Chocolate paste can be sculpted, rolled, and cut to form decorations for cakes and tortes. It is a simple mixture of chocolate and corn syrup, usually a ratio of 3 to 1. The chocolate is melted and cooled slightly before the corn syrup is stirred in. The mixture is wrapped and left out at room temperature overnight to ripen. The next day, the chocolate paste is kneaded until smooth and pliable, usually with a small amount of cornstarch or confectioners' sugar. Chocolate paste will harden as it cools, but it easily warms under a lamp or in your hands for reshaping. Different types (white or dark) and brands of chocolate will require slightly different amounts of corn syrup.

CHAPTER 9

WATER

N atural water, whether surface or ground in source, is extremely complex. The composition of water not only varies from town to town but also can fluctuate day to day in a given locale. *Composition* in this case does not refer to the molecular structure—two atoms of hydrogen joined to an atom of oxygen. It refers instead to the varying amounts of trace minerals, dissolved gasses, silicates, metals such as iron or magnesium, clay, silt, salts, organic and industrial contaminants, and purifying agents that may be present. Though we think of water as being tasteless, the presence of certain compounds determines whether or not we think the water tastes "good" or "refreshing." Distilled water, which lacks the minerals and salts found in hard water, is regarded as tasting flat.

Bakers are primarily concerned with three basic aspects*: water hardness, alkalinity, and chlorination. All these factors can impact dough performance, though not as drastically as some would have us believe—the old adage that New York bagels can't be duplicated because of water differences is unfounded.

---

*Even more important than its effect on dough chemistry, water composition can have a huge impact on the life span of kitchen equipment. Hard water is notorious for leaving scale deposits, a buildup that can debilitate hot water lines, heat exchangers, and boilers. Just as the holes on a steam iron become plugged when hard tap water is used—or even worse, release discolored water onto clothes—steam-injected ovens will be affected by water composition. Professional services should be consulted.

HARD VS. SOFT WATER

Water hardness is determined by the amount of calcium and magnesium salts present. Hard water is notorious for reducing the ability of soap to lather, and indeed, determining water hardness involves measuring how much soap solution is necessary to produce a good lather. Though several salts are present in water, such as calcium bicarbonate, calcium sulfate, calcium chloride, calcium nitrate, magnesium bicarbonate, magnesium sulfate, magnesium chloride, and magnesium nitrate, water hardness is denoted by the parts per million of calcium carbonate, which represents the total of all the salts.

Across the nation, very soft water occurs in the Pacific Northwest, the New England states, and in the Southeast from Virginia to Mississippi (excluding Florida). The hardest water occurs in Arizona, New Mexico, and parts of the central Midwest.

Hard water strengthens the gluten in dough and can also increase yeast activity, as some of the mineral salts serve as yeast food. Medium water is considered best for fermentation and gluten development. Very hard water can increase dough fermentation time because the gluten structure is overly strong and resistant to expansion. To compensate, the amount of yeast may be increased and diastatic malt can be added. Also, a small amount of an acidic ingredient, such as vinegar, can be added to the dough, since acids reduce gluten strength.

Very soft water creates slack, sticky doughs because the gluten-enhancing minerals are absent. The amount of water can be reduced to produce a more workable dough. A weaker gluten structure is less able to retain gases produced during fermentation, even though soft water does not inhibit yeast activity. Added salt will improve the dough's texture and gluten structure.

DEGREES OF WATER HARDNESS (parts per million of calcium carbonate)
SOFT WATER = 0-50 PPM
MEDIUM WATER = 50-100 PPM
HARD WATER = 100-200 PPM
VERY HARD WATER = 200+ PPM

Acidity vs. Alkalinity

Acidity and alkalinity are measured on the pH scale, translated from French, *p(ouvoir) H(ydrogene)*, which means "hydrogen power" or potential hydrogen. The scale measures the concentration of hydrogen or hydroxyl ions in a solution. The presence of hydrogen ions denotes acidity (an acid), and hydroxyl ions denote alkalinity (a base). In 1908, the scientist Sören Sörenson suggested pH be scaled from 0 to 14, with 0 denoting an extremely strong acid and 14 an extremely strong base. Each numerical increment represents a tenfold change in ion concentration. The scale is shaped like the letter "V" (see Figure 9.1) with the number 7 at the bottom, representing a solution that is neutral: pure water.

Pure water is neutral, but natural water varies in its acidity or alkalinity. Even treated municipal water can vary in its pH from day to day or week to week. Acidic water is corrosive to pipes, and is usually monitored carefully at treatment plants. Soft water is associated with acidity, and hard water with alkalinity, but since so many variables affect water these correlations are far from absolute.

Doughs made with slightly acidic water will ferment readily, since yeast prefers a slightly acidic environment. The acidity has a negative effect on crust color and texture, though, as it inhibits browning.

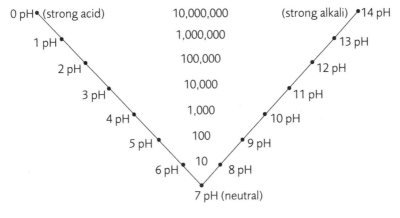

FIGURE 9.1 The pH scale.

Alkaline doughs produce breads with good crust color but poor volume, as the alkaline environment has negative effects on yeast fermentation. Fermentation time will need to be lengthened. High alkalinity means high buffering capacity, so much of the acid added to the dough to compensate will be neutralized. Still, minimizing alkalinity is necessary for yeast. Despite the association of hard water (with its calcium salts) and alkaline water, alkaline water may contain very little calcium sulfate, which bolsters yeast activity. Calcium sulfate is an ingredient in commercial "yeast foods" and can be supplemented.

CHLORINATION

Water is chlorinated to kill unwanted microorganisms. Generally, chlorinated tap water has only a mild effect on commercial yeast. Sourdough starters are a different matter. Not only do they rely on wild yeast for flavor, acidity, and leavening but almost equally need "friendly" bacteria that work in conjunction with the yeast. If you are developing a wild yeast starter, chlorinated water may inhibit the microorganisms you are trying to encourage. This is particularly true if running the hot tap water gives off a swimming pool smell. Bottled water is an alternative, as is simply waiting for the chlorine to dissipate—chlorine gas is highly unstable and will evaporate. Stirring or whisking the water will accelerate this process.

CHAPTER 10

SALT

From a strictly scientific standpoint, salts represent a class of chemical compounds. They are produced from the chemical reaction of an acid with an alkali. While chemists are familiar with hundreds of different salts, for bakers *salt* means only one of these—sodium chloride.

Once upon a time salt was precious, but today it is readily available. Though sodium chloride is essential for human health, salt is currently so ubiquitous that overindulgence, not deficiency, is common. Salt makes food taste better, and though it prevents spoilage and has definite physiological functions, this is why we add it to baked goods.

SOURCES

Salt is derived from the world's oceans and large salt lakes, but the vast majority of salt is mined from deposits in the earth. These deposits are the remains of salted bodies of water.

Rock salt is mined, broken into chunks, and minimally purified depending on its end use. Minerals and harmless impurities give it a grayish cast. Rock salt has a large and irregular crystal structure. It is not used in pastry kitchens, but is known to home cooks as the salt used for old-fashioned hand-crank ice cream makers.

Much of the earth's salt deposits are not pure enough to be mined directly. In this case, water is pumped into the deposit. Salt dissolves in the water and the brine is pumped out. The brine is quite free of impurities, since it contains only the most soluble salts. The brine will undergo any of several evaporation methods, which determine the final shape and size of the crystals.

Sea and salt lake water is a more complex brine containing different mineral salts. When the water evaporates, via sunlight or artificial means, the salt solution becomes overly concentrated (supersaturated) and the grains of salt are forced to precipitate out of the solution. The rule of thumb is that the least soluble salts precipitate first and the desirable, easily soluble salts precipitate last. Sea salt forms irregular crystals and may vary in color from white to pale gray depending on the other minerals present.

Since the other minerals give the salt a distinctive flavor and the process for evaporation (especially sunlight and wind) may be time-consuming, sea salt can be very expensive. Double-check the source of any expensive sea salt, since it is all too easy for another salt to be sold in its place. Most sea salt is no more expensive than kosher salt and has little distinctive flavor. Distinctively flavored sea salt should not be used to salt batters and doughs, but should be reserved for toppings, where its delicate flavor can be savored.

Types of Salt

How a brine is processed determines the final shape and size of the salt crystals. Some are hard and compact, others are hollow or flaked. The shape of the crystals contributes to solubility. More important, the different shapes and sizes of the crystals mean that a teaspoon of one salt will not equal a teaspoon of another. To substitute kosher salt in a recipe that calls for granular salt requires the use of a sensitive scale to be accurate. A teaspoon of granular table salt may equal $1^1/_2$ to 2 times that amount of kosher salt.

The use of vacuum evaporators to process brines is energy efficient, and therefore is the most widely used method. The salt produced this way is hard, cube-shaped, and has medium-fast solubility. **Granular table salt** is the prime example. Table salt also contains anticaking agents, and sometimes **iodine**, which the human body needs in trace amounts.

As a variation, granular salt can be compacted during processing into a grainy but flaked form that is used as a crunchy salt topping on crackers and breads.

A third variation of this process adds minuscule amounts of sodium ferrocyanide (prussiate of soda) to the brine to alter the shape of the crystals. This salt forms irregular, highly porous cubic grains. Increased surface area and porous structure make this salt, called **dendritic**, more soluble in water like flake salt.

Sea salt or mined salt can be processed by the **Alberger process**, which creates **flake salt**. Flake salt is more flat than cubic, with irregular edges. Flake salt made by the Alberger process is often hollow. Greater surface area makes the flakes dissolve easily. Flake salt crystallizes in different sizes, and is sifted and sorted for sale accordingly. Sea salt that undergoes evaporation from sun and wind does not form hollow, flaked crystals.

Kosher salt has been produced in concordance with rabbinical supervision and is not associated with a single type of processing. Though kosher salt is always coarse grained, it may have been produced by crushing granular salt or using the Alberger process. Thus, different brands may have different solubility and density.

EFFECT OF SALT ON BAKED GOODS

YEAST FERMENTATION

Salt inhibits yeast fermentation. In fact, if salt grains come into direct contact with yeast cells—when scaling ingredients, for example—the yeast will be damaged. Either hydrate active dry yeast in warm water and add this mixture to flour and salt, or add fresh or instant active yeast to the flour, and dissolve the salt in the water.

Fermentation time is longer if salt is added to the flour during the initial stage of dough mixing. If it is kneaded into the dough toward the end of the kneading process (or mixing process, depending on whether the dough is mixed in a machine or kneaded by hand), or even after the autolyse or resting period, its inhibitory effect on yeast fermentation will be lessened. Porous, flaked, or fine-grained salts readily dissolve when kneaded into dough. Kosher and table salt work fine.

Some chefs add more salt to bread doughs in warm weather, when high temperatures make fermentation fast and less predictable, to keep the rapid fermentation in check. Naturally, only so much salt can be added without altering the flavor profile of the bread.

GLUTEN STRUCTURE

Adding salt to a dough strengthens the gluten, making the dough feel tighter. Salt makes the gluten more extensible, or more resistant to breaking when pulled and stretched. In slack doughs, caused by soft water or inadequately aged flour, the addition of salt will make a difficult dough workable.

Tightening the gluten in a firmer dough, of course, means that kneading will be more work. Gluten development is only one aspect of kneading; kneading also helps shape the gluten and hydrates the flour evenly. When mixers are doing the work of kneading, the salt is usually not added until the end of the mixing process in order to minimize stress to the machine. Salt can make a firm dough even tighter, which will lengthen fermentation time since the dough is resistant to expanding.

Cakes and cookies are minimally affected by salt.

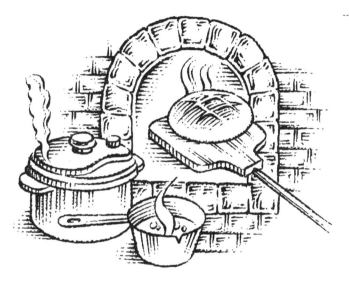

CHAPTER 11

THE PHYSICS
OF HEAT

F or baking and cooking to occur, heat must be transferred from a heat source to the batter or dough. When two touching objects, or different parts of the same object, are at different temperatures, energy is transferred from the region of higher temperature to that of lower temperature. This transfer of temperature is called **heat flow**, and the transfer of energy is called **heat energy**. The flow of heat continues until the two objects attain the same temperature. Placing cold eggs in a bowl of hot water to temper them is an example of this principle. The eggs gradually become warmer and the water cooler, until finally they are both the same temperature.

METHODS OF HEAT TRANSFER

There are three basic methods of heat transfer: **conduction**, **convection**, and **radiation**. The eggs in the warm water above are heated by conduction, since the warm water is the medium that transfers the heat. Actual cooking is usually a complicated affair, and may involve all three methods of heat transfer.

To understand better what takes place when conduction, convection, and radiation heating are used in baking, consider the analogy of a person sitting in a room in front of a fireplace. Fire, the source of radiant heat, warms people sitting close to the fireplace, even if the rest of the room feels cold. **Radiation** is electromagnetic energy that is transmitted by very short waves, and it only reaches those close to the fire. The

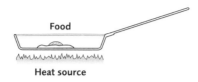

FIGURE 11.1 Cooking by conduction.

bricks in the fireplace become hot through **conduction**—they touch the fire, which warms them, and they transmit warmth to neighboring bricks. The room itself is heated mostly by means of **convection**. Heated air, near the fire, expands and rises while the cooler air falls. The air is continuously in motion, and eventually the entire room becomes warm.

Baking would seem to be a simple example of radiation, since heat radiates out from a heating element or gas flame. However, the dough is not baked owing to its proximity to the heat source. Rather, it is radiation from the walls of the hot oven, as well as the hot air in the oven, that transfers the heat. Air near the heating element gets hot, rises, and is replaced by cold air, which is heavier. As a result, convection currents move around the dough or batter, cooking it. A convection oven takes advantage of this principle, adding a fan to better circulate the hot air. As a result, **convection ovens** cook foods more efficiently (faster), and eliminate hot and cold spots in the oven. Often, baking temperatures must be reduced by 25°F when baked in a convection rather than conventional oven.

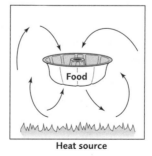

FIGURE 11.2 Convection currents carry the heated air to the surface of the food.

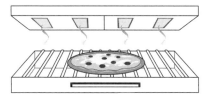

FIGURE 11.3 Broiling. Close proximity to intense, radiant heat cooks the food.

Broiling and **grilling** are better examples of radiation, since close proximity to the direct flame or coals cooks the food. Clearly, cooking by radiation is efficient only when the food is close to the heat source.

Cooking food in boiling water begins by heat radiating from the heating element or flame to the bottom of the pot. The pot conducts heat to the water inside, which cooks the food by convection currents moving through the liquid medium. Deep frying shares the same concept.

Microwave ovens use electromagnetic radiation to cook food; however, microwaves are a different band of electromagnetic energy than the radiant heat discussed above, which registers in the infrared section of electromagnetic waves (see Figure 11.6). Microwaves are considered lower in energy than infrared waves because they do not affect all molecules, only the polar ones. Polar molecules have slightly different electrical charges at their opposite ends, making them more responsive to microwave radiation than nonpolar molecules. Infrared heat, on the other hand, increases the vibration of nearly all molecules. Water is polar, but a heatproof glass (Pyrex) measuring cup is not. The microwaves heat the water, but the glass stays comparatively cool (until the heat of

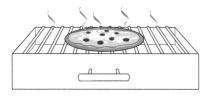

FIGURE 11.4 Grilling.

Heat source

FIGURE 11.5 Boiling. Convection action in the liquid conducts heat to the food.

the water warms it). Microwave ovens cook quickly since they activate all the polar molecules at once; there is no long wait for the heat to penetrate the center of the food, as with baking. Microwave ovens cannot brown foods, which requires that the outside of the food be exposed to more heat (to initiate caramelization and browning reactions) than the interior.

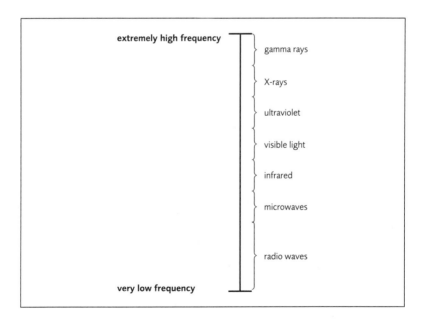

FIGURE 11.6 The electromagnetic wave spectrum.

Induction cooktops use electromagnetic energy to transfer heat. Magnets within the range are electrified, and the energy is transferred directly to the pot, which must be stainless steel or iron (hold a magnet) to conduct. Induction cooktops do not get hot themselves, making them both energy efficient and very safe to use.

Halogen light is used in some ovens as another method of electromagnetic radiation. The heat it gives off is more intense than that of conventional ovens, reducing the cooking time significantly. Usually, halogen is paired with another cooking method, such as microwave, to make the cook time even shorter. Halogen light will brown foods.

How Heat Is Measured

Heat is measured in BTUs, or British thermal units. One BTU is the quantity of heat required to raise the temperature of 1 pound of water 1°F. This energy is about equal to that given off by a wooden match when completely burned. If the burner on a commercial gas range is rated at 15,000 BTUs, then the energy it produces in one hour is about the equivalent of burning 15,000 matches. BTUs are associated only with the Fahrenheit scale.

In the metric system, energy is measured in calories. The heat of one calorie is the equivalent of the heat required to raise the temperature of 1 gram of water by 1°C. Calories are associated with the centigrade (Celsius) scale.

> On the Fahrenheit scale, water freezes at 32°F and boils at 212°F.
>
> On the centigrade scale, water freezes at 0°C and boils at 100°C.
>
> To convert from Fahrenheit to centigrade, subtract 32 and multiply by .55 (5/9).
>
> To convert from centigrade to Fahrenheit, multiply by 1.8 (9/5) and add 32.

The Phases of Matter

There are four phases of matter: solid, liquid, gas, and plasma. Generally, a substance is most dense in its solid state. Water is an exception to this: It expands slightly when frozen, making it technically more dense as a liquid than as a solid, since the same number of molecules take up less space as a liquid. This is why water that freezes in pipes will cause them to burst. In the liquid phase, molecules are *generally* less dense but still have a fixed volume. Liquids assume the shape of their container. A gas is even less dense and has no fixed volume. Unless enclosed, gases will continue to expand. A substance reaches the plasma phase only at extremely high temperatures. In this phase, some or all of the electrons have separated from the individual molecules. Thankfully, pastry chefs have no need to understand the plasma phase unless something dreadful occurs.

It is helpful for bakers and chefs to understand the phase changes of water, from ice to a liquid to steam. It is easy to remember that water freezes at 32°F and turns to steam above 212°F. However, it is harder to comprehend that it takes a substantial amount of energy to accomplish a phase change.

STEAM

At sea level, water boils at 212°F. To change water at this temperature to steam, it is necessary to add 970 BTUs to each pound of water. This amount of heat energy is known as the **latent heat** of steam—it is latent within the steam, ready to be released. When the steam condenses

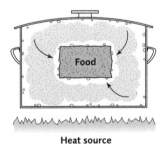

Heat source

FIGURE 11.7 Steaming. Steam surrounds the food and as it condenses gives off latent heat.

on food or in a cooking vessel, changing back into water, the same amount of heat—970 BTUs—is given off and may be transferred to the food present.

Steam becomes hotter under pressure, which accounts for its fast cooking action. Another way of stating this is: Pressure on any gas increases the temperature of the gas. When a pot of boiling water is covered, a small amount of pressure builds and is vented when the lid is lifted. In a tightly sealed pressure cooker, more pressure can build and the temperature rises. Pressure is measured in pounds per square inch (psi). Steam under 5 pounds of pressure has a temperature of 228°F, not 212°F, and contains six times more heat than boiling water.

EVAPORATIVE COOLING

An earthenware jar containing water and sitting in a warm, dry place can keep the water inside cool. The water seeps through the porous walls of the jar and then evaporates, and this process absorbs heat from the water. Because of evaporative cooling, a nonporous container of water placed in a 400°F oven will never boil; in fact, it will evaporate completely, and the water's temperature will not exceed 180°F. If the water was covered with a lid, it would boil because evaporative cooling cannot take place.

Steam created from within a baking dough may cause evaporative cooling. As the steam forms, it absorbs 970 BTUs of heat for every pound of steam formed, which is drawn from the cooking food and thus slows the cooking process. This is called the **heat of vaporization**.

HEAT OF FUSION

Exactly 145 BTUs are required per pound of ice to change it from ice to water. Thus, substantial heat is absorbed by the ice, even though the temperature remains 32°F. This is known as **heat of fusion**. In cooking food from the frozen state, considerable energy is needed to change the ice to water. Conversely, when freezing foods, 145 BTUs of energy must be drawn off a pound of water merely to change it to ice.

THE EFFECT OF SALT

Water with considerable added salt no longer boils or freezes at normal temperatures. The prime example of this phenomenon is using salt to melt the ice on roads and sidewalks in winter. The ice changes to water, but is still at 32°F. In cooking, salt is used in such small increments that there is no good example to demonstrate how the addition of a lot of salt (like a cup) changes the boiling temperature of water.

Hand-crank ice cream makers depend on salt's effect on ice water. Water and rock salt surround the inner canister that holds the ice cream base. The mixture of water, salt, and ice creates an iced brine solution that is well below freezing (around 10° to 20°F) and still liquid. Ice and water would never fall below 32°F, and the temperature needs to be below that to freeze the ice cream base. The ice cream base is not pure water, and freezes below 32°F. As the brine absorbs heat from the ice cream base, more ice melts, but the temperature stays low.

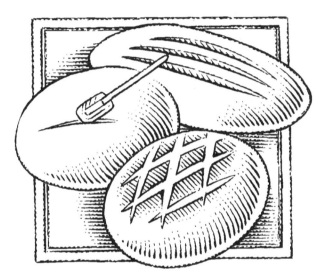

CHAPTER 12

BREAD AND OTHER
YEAST-RISEN PRODUCTS

Only a few simple ingredients are needed to make great bread—flour, water, yeast, and salt. Yet what could be more satisfying than a golden, crackling baguette? This mysterious transformation is baking's first great achievement. But new techniques and machinery, and a desire for richer, more exotic ingredients, mean the bread baker's repertoire may now include everything from the most rustic loaf to the lightest, richest brioche.

Making consistently good bread requires knowledge of which ingredients will function best in a particular recipe. However, bread is more than the sum of its ingredients. Because yeast is a living organism, the baker must understand what happens during the processes of fermentation and baking. Beyond this, a good bread baker must develop excellent hand skills and a feeling for how to correct for day-to-day variations of temperature, humidity, and ingredients.

FLOUR

Flour is the most important ingredient in bread, and the importance of choosing the right flour for the right job cannot be stressed too much. Almost all bread is made with "bread flour," but that is not quite so self-evident as it sounds. American hard wheat flours, with their high protein content and ability to absorb large amounts of water, may make it difficult to produce a European hearth bread with a crisp, brittle

TYPES OF FLOUR AND THEIR COMMON USES

All-purpose flour	Protein content between 9 and 11%, used for yeasted coffee cakes, doughnuts, enriched sandwich bread.
Bread flour	Protein content between 11.5 and 13%, used to make hearth breads.
High gluten flour	Protein content 14%, used in combination with bread or all-purpose flours, good for highly machined doughs, combination with grain flours lacking gluten, highly acidic breads.
Whole wheat flour	Protein content around 13%, used for health breads or to give flavor to hearth breads.
Patent durum flour	Protein content around 12%, particularly good in hearth breads.
Pastry flour	Protein content around 9%, used in enriched breads for tenderness.
Artisanal bread flour	Protein content around 11.5%, performs in hearth breads much like lower protein European flours, equivalent to United States flours with higher extraction rate.
Vital wheat gluten	What is left over when starch has been removed from wheat flour in a washing process; protein content about 40%, used in breads prepared with other grains that lack gluten-forming proteins, such as rye and health breads.
Organic flour	Up to twice the cost of regular flour, especially good for artisan breads.
Wheat bran	Used extensively in health breads and in muffins.
Wheat germ	Provides nutty, pleasant taste in bread.

crust and open crumb. Each type of flour was developed with a specific purpose in mind—how well they live up to that promise determines how "good" they are. Quality flours perform well over a broad range of protein contents. A list of basic flours and how they may be used in yeast bread products appears on page 154.

YEAST CHOICES

There are several different types of yeast (fresh, dry, wild yeast starters) and each has its own advantages and disadvantages. Fresh yeast requires no hydration time and tolerates cold water. Dry yeast must be hydrated in warm water before being added to a water-poor, sugar-rich dough. Wild yeast starters have a tangy, complex flavor. More detail is listed below, with the entries on bread types, but Chapter 2 covers yeast in detail.

SALT

Salt tightens the gluten network, which may be a hindrance to machine-mixed doughs and a blessing to doughs made with soft water. Salt slows or inhibits yeast fermentation. A fast-dissolving salt is preferred for bread doughs. See Chapter 10 for more details.

READ BEFORE YOU KNEAD

EQUIPMENT

There are several different methods for assembling bread doughs. Some involve only a few steps, others are more complicated. Even small bakeries use mixers for assembling and partially kneading the dough. Though any commercial mixer with planetary rotation action is acceptable, dedicated dough mixers are a must for bread made on a moderate scale. Special bread dough mixers have a corkscrew hook that doesn't overwork the dough. Many of those mixers also have a mechanism that will tilt the bowl for gentle dough removal.

MEASURING AND THE BAKER'S PERCENTAGE SYSTEM

All ingredients for breadmaking should be scaled, especially flour. Weighing the water also ensures accuracy from batch to batch, as small inaccuracies can make a big difference in both the dough and the finished bread's texture.

BAKER'S PERCENTAGES When making bread, bakers refer to formulas rather than recipes. Most breads are simple ratios of flour, water, yeast, and salt. From day to day, bakers may vary batch sizes, increasing or decreasing the formula to produce the required number of loaves. The baker's percentage is the easiest way for them to scale formulas up or down, determining exactly how much of each ingredient is needed. It's also a great way to fix mistakes—say, if you accidentally add too much flour to a batch of dough. The system is weight-based and either the metric (kilograms and grams) or avoirdupois (pounds and ounces) system may be used as long as the units are the same for all ingredients. Although metric may be easier in the long run, most home bakers and many bakeries still rely on pounds and ounces, so the following examples use avoirdupois weights.

In the baker's percentage system, each ingredient is expressed as a percentage of the total flour weight: Thus, the flour weight is always 100 percent. If more than one flour is used, their combined weight comprises that 100 percent. In the following formula (not an actual recipe, just an example), the combined weight of the two flours is 50 pounds. Therefore 50 is the number by which we divide each ingredient weight to determine its percentage (in relationship to the 100 percent of total flour).

40 POUNDS BREAD FLOUR = 80%

10 POUNDS WHOLE WHEAT FLOUR = 20%

33 POUNDS WATER = 66%

1 POUND SALT = 2%

0.6 POUND YEAST = 1.2%

Now, this example yields only 84.6 pounds of dough. What if we wanted to make 200 loaves, each scaled at 1 pound 8 ounces? First, determine the total amount of dough needed by multiplying 200 by 1.5 (the weight of each loaf), to get 300 pounds. Then, to calculate the weight of each ingredient in the larger recipe, you add up all the percentages in the above formula. This total percentage value is 169.2. Divide the desired dough weight, 300 pounds, by this number to get 1.77. Then multiply the percentage amount for each ingredient in the above recipe by 1.77 to obtain the larger weight required by the larger recipe.

80% BREAD FLOUR X 1.77 = 141.6 POUNDS

20% WHOLE WHEAT FLOUR X 1.77 = 35.4 POUNDS

66% WATER X 1.77 = 116.82 POUNDS

2% SALT X 1.77 = 3.54 POUNDS

1.2% YEAST X 1.77 = 2.124 POUNDS

For formulas using pre-ferments (see page 159), the weight of all the flour used in the sponge must be added to the weight of the flour used in the final dough to obtain the number to use to determine percentages. For example, in the following formula, the flour weights in the pre-ferment and final dough add up to a total of 60 pounds; so 60 pounds is the 100 percent used in the baker's percentage system. Therefore the percentages for the other ingredients below were obtained by dividing each ingredient's weight by 60.

PRE-FERMENT INGREDIENTS

15 POUNDS BREAD FLOUR = 25%

15 POUNDS WATER = 25%

0.5 POUND YEAST = 0.83%

INGREDIENTS FOR FINAL DOUGH

33 POUNDS BREAD FLOUR = 55%

12 POUNDS WHOLE WHEAT FLOUR = 20%

24.6 POUNDS WATER = 41%

1.2 POUNDS SALT = 2%

This system is also very helpful, as mentioned above, when you make a mistake. Let's say instead of the 33 pounds of bread flour called for in the final dough above, you mistakenly added 43 pounds. This accidental increase means your divisor number would be 70 instead of 60 in determining the corrected new weights of the other ingredients in order to keep the recipe at the correct proportions. This trick thus saves you ingredients cost and labor. Making a few extra loaves is better than having to throw out everything.

To determine the percentage of pre-ferment you need in the final dough, add all the percentage figures together, to get 168.83. Divide the percentage totals for the pre-ferment, 50.83, by this number to obtain 30 percent. Divide the percentage total for the final dough by the same number to get 70 percent.

TEMPERATURE

Controlling water temperature is important for regulating the dough's development. The ideal dough temperature is 75°F. Cold water (usually somewhere between 55° and 63°F) is used in pre-ferment stages (see below). In straight doughs that are mixed at high speed for a relatively long period of time, a percentage of the formula's total water content can be added as ice or ice water.

Prolonged high-speed mixing generates a lot of heat that is transferred to the dough; a dough's temperature increases one degree for each minute it is mixed at medium speed. A reduction in dough temperature (optimum temperature for straight dough is between 75° and 78°F) prevents fermentation from happening too rapidly and avoids off flavors. Compressed yeast works fine with cold water, as do wild yeast–filled starters. Active dry yeast and instant yeast can be rehydrated in a small amount of warm water before being added to the cool dough.

Adequately hydrated doughs have a more appealing open crumb, a chewy texture, and a longer shelf life. The hydration rate of dough can be calculated by adding the weight of all the liquids, then adding all the flours and grains. Divide the weight of the liquid by the weight of the dry ingredients. Ideal hydration begins around 62 percent and extends to 80 percent for really wet doughs, such as for Italian ciabatta. If using a sponge or wild yeast starter, their liquid and dry weights must be factored in as well.

MIXING THE DOUGH

AUTOLYSE

Some bakers begin by mixing all the dough's ingredients together. Today, however, it is common to begin with an **autolyse**. Autolyse is a technique in which the primary portions of flour and water are combined (on low speed in a mixer or by hand) and left to stand for 20 to 30 minutes. This headstart, so to speak, improves the dough-handling qualities of the breadmaking process. The flour hydrates to its fullest potential and the gluten begins developing. Proteolytic enzymes within the flour begin to rearrange the unruly gluten structure into a stronger, more organized form. Any starter, intermediate sponge, commercial yeast, or salt is not added at this point—only the flour(s) and water—because leaveners would begin to acidify the dough and the proteolytic enzymes work best in a neutral environment. Salt is omitted because of its ability to tighten up a dough, preventing the flour from fully hydrating. Though the autolyse adds a step to breadmaking, the final dough comes together in less time with less mechanical kneading. In commercial bakeries, where large batches of bread are mixed in big floor mixers, reductions in mixing time and speed minimize the risk of beating too much oxygen into the dough. Oxygen oxidizes the unsaturated fat in the flour and bleaches its carotene pigments, imparting an off taste to the finished bread.

PRE-FERMENTS

After the autolyse, the yeast and remaining flour and water are added. Pre-ferments are also added at this time. A **pre-ferment** is a long, preferably cool fermentation of the yeast (or wild yeast starter) with a portion of the flour and water called for in a recipe. Pre-ferments are created at least a day before the dough is mixed. Pre-ferments provide complex flavors akin to mild sourdough or wild yeast starters, but are not nearly as acidic; wheat flavor comes through more than anything else. Sometimes pre-ferments are called **sponges**.

Using a pre-ferment allows the fullest range of flavor in the wheat flour to develop and gives time for acetic and lactic acids to form.

TYPES OF PRE-FERMENTS

The following terms usually either indicate the country of origin or differentiate between stiff and liquid mixes.

POOLISH is the French word for "Polish," who the French believed originated the technique. **Sponge** is another word that is frequently used to describe this type of pre-ferment. Flour and water are combined in equal proportions in a soupy starter that begins to develop with the addition of more or less yeast depending on the desired length of fermentation. Different doughs can have different ratios of flour to water as part of the poolish; the general rule is the more liquid (thin or batterlike) a pre-ferment is, the faster the yeast will multiply. Long, cool fermentations from three to fifteen hours with small amounts of yeast produce poolishes whose peak performance is several hours long. When fully fermented, the poolish will have risen completely, then fallen back just a bit; the top will appear slightly wrinkled.

PÂTE FERMENTÉE consists of pieces of scrap dough from the previous day's batch added to a newly mixed dough. The scrap dough contains the same ingredients as the final dough, including salt and a fair amount of yeast. When the final dough is mixed, more commercial yeast is added. Despite salt's inhibitory effect on yeast activity, the dough should be kept cool to prevent overfermentation. If overfermented, the old dough will become too acidic and produce alcohol. Occasionally, cautious bakers will actually make a small batch of "old dough" so that fermentation can be very closely regulated.

CHEFS AND **LEVAIN DE PÂTE** are similar to *pâte fermentée* except that the newly mixed dough gets no additional yeast—the old dough inoculates the new dough with its yeast supply. The yeast in this type of pre-ferment could be either commercial or wild yeast. This term specifies that the leavening agent is a small piece of old dough, and not a starter or storage leaven. The proportion of pre-ferment is greater than that in *pâte fermentée* (5 to 30 percent of the flour's weight) and the dough is fermented at room temperature. Breads made with this method closely mimic the flavors of a mild sourdough and the French *levain*.

BIGA is the Italian version of a pre-ferment. Bigas are usually very firm doughs with only around 50 percent hydration and about 1 percent compressed yeast. Like the others, bigas are best fermented over a long period of time in a cool environment. This gives them time to develop acetic acid, an important flavor component and dough conditioner (reinforcing gluten, especially important with low-protein Italian flours) in the final dough. Bigas tend to be more stable and keep longer at their peak than the more liquid pre-ferments.

TABLE 12.1 ORDINARY BREAD FAULTS AND THEIR CAUSES

Faults \ Causes	Improper mixing	Insufficient salt	Too much salt	Dough wt. too much for pan	Dough wt. too light for pan	Insufficient yeast	Too much yeast	Dough proofed too much	Dough underproofed	Dough temp. too high	Dough temp. too low	Dough too stiff	Dough too slack	Proof box too hot	Green flour	Dough chilled	Too much sugar	Insufficient sugar	Dough too young	Dough too old	Improper molding	Insufficient shortening	Oven temp. too high	Oven temp. too low	Overbaked
Lack of volume	X		X		X	X			X							X			X	X			X		
Too much volume		X		X				X												X				X	
Crust color too pale											X							X		X					
Crust color too dark																	X						X		
Crust blisters											X			X	X				X						
Shelling of top crust		X							X		X	X			X				X	X	X				
Poor keeping qualities								X		X		X						X		X		X		X	
Poor texture, crumbly								X						X				X	X	X				X	
Crust too thick					X													X		X				X	X
Streaky crumb																					X				
Gray crumb								X	X	X	X			X											
Lack of shred								X	X										X	X					
Coarse grain	X	X																	X	X	X				
Poor taste and flavor	X									X															

Reprinted with permission of the publisher from J. Amendola's *The Baker's Manual for Quantity Baking and Pastry Making, 2nd Edition.* Copyright 1956 and 1960 by Ahrens Publishing Company, Inc.

Acetic acid, in addition to its role in flavor, acts as a natural dough conditioner, greatly improving extensibility. The dough is kneaded for a shorter period of time, preventing off flavors that can occur as the dough oxidizes. A minimal amount of yeast is needed for this process, as the little critters continue to multiply during the long wait. Prefermented doughs make breads with complex flavors and great moisture retention. The nomenclature of different types of pre-ferments can be quite confusing, but see Types of Pre-Ferments on page 160.

KNEADING

When wheat flour is mixed with water and stirred or kneaded, the glutenin and gliadin proteins not only bond with the water but also link with one another to form sheets of a flexible, resilient film called gluten. Gluten traps air and gases formed by the yeast, causing the bread to rise. Beyond developing the gluten, kneading serves to distribute the yeast cells evenly through the dough. As the yeast feeds on the sugars, it produces a liquid containing both alcohol and carbon dioxide. The carbon dioxide is released upon contact into the air bubbles, enlarging them. Protein content determines how much water a flour can absorb—the greater the amount of protein, the greater hydration possible.

Kneading the dough by machine is the only practical way to make bread on a large scale. (Small batches for the home baker can be kneaded by hand, of course.) Keeping the initial mix time down as much as possible with an autolyse and pre-ferments means that commercially made bread on a large scale can still be authentically hand-crafted. Bread recipes that use very high-protein flours and have an extremely high water content can be kneaded longer at a higher speed, resulting in a reduced fermentation time. Just keep in mind that more oxygen is being incorporated into the dough in the process; oxidation means the bread will stale faster. Timing the kneading period is a good idea, as is monitoring the temperature with an instant-read thermometer to make sure it is near 75°F. Doughs can be overmixed, and once they are, there is no bringing them back. If the gluten bonds are destroyed from too much stress, the dough disintegrates into a slack, watery mess.

Home mixers and those in most small to medium bakeries use planetary action to knead dough. A dough hook revolves around the bowl, turning the dough and developing the gluten as it tosses the dough repeatedly against the side of the bowl. Several types of mixers are made especially for bread. They knead more quickly without heating the dough or overworking it. Their action seems to mimic hand kneading more closely and doesn't tear the gluten as much.

How can you tell when you are finished kneading? At first the dough will appear shaggy and rough. As kneading continues, the dough smooths out and begins to pick up flour off the sides and bottom of the bowl, combining it into a single mass. The dough ball develops a bit of shine. Gently work a piece of the dough between your fingers, attempting to stretch it as thin as possible—until it is almost translucent. This is called **windowpaning** because well-developed gluten allows the dough to be stretched into a thin, translucent membrane. If the dough rips into ropy strands, it has not been kneaded sufficiently. If it forms a lumpy sheet that tears easily, it's still not there. Keep going, but watch the dough very carefully.

To avoid overmixing, turn the dough once or twice during its initial fermentation. Turning isn't exactly kneading, but it does continue to develop the gluten and redistribute the food supply for the yeast. When the dough has risen a while (the amount of time is variable depending on the dough), gently lift and fold the sides of the dough over onto itself. Then flip the whole thing over. Turning is similar to punching down the dough but avoids excessive deflation. After working so hard to develop precious carbon dioxide bubbles, there is no reason to lose them by being overly rough!

FERMENTATION

Fermentation is equivalent to the home baker's term "first rise." The dough rises as a single piece, before being divided and shaped. This is when the yeast begins to feed and multiply. Organic acids develop that condition the gluten and impart flavor. This first fermentation is usually complete when the dough has doubled in volume.

At lower temperatures, fermentation will be slow and the dough will develop more complex flavors (by products of yeast fermentation), including an acidic or slightly sour flavor. At high temperatures, the dough ferments quickly and unpleasant flavors may be produced. Ideal fermentation temperatures range between 72° and 85°F. When the dough has roughly doubled in size, it's ready to be either gently punched (turned) and given a future rise or scaled and shaped.

Bacteria produce two significant acids during the fermentation period—lactic acid and acetic acid. These acids are what give sourdough breads their characteristic tang, but they also give any slowly fermented bread a deeper, complex flavor. Wild yeast starters will contribute more bacterial activity to a dough, since the bacteria in it have been fermenting for a long time. Straight-rise doughs are not given a long enough fermentation for significant acid to be produced. Lactic acid is milder in flavor than the more sour acetic acid. Temperatures under 72°F or just over 85°F will favor bacterial growth over yeast growth, meaning that the yeast are multiplying more slowly and the bacteria faster—the dough becomes acidic faster than it rises. Keeping the dough at a very cool temperature will retard the action of the yeast, allowing time for acid development.

DIVIDING AND SHAPING

Professional bakers scale the dough to ensure standard loaves, usually dividing it with a bench knife and using a balance scale. The dough should not be stretched or torn, and minimal dividing cuts are made to better to retain air bubbles. Shaping is a whole discipline unto itself, requiring dexterity and skill. Usually after dividing, the pieces of dough are gently shaped, covered, and rested for a short period of time, during which the gluten accommodates itself to these new demands. This procedure makes final shaping much easier. Free-form breads must be shaped so that an outer skin develops to hold the dough within. There are baguettes, batards, hard rolls, boules, intricately braided challah, decorative shapes—the array is staggering.

PROOFING

Professional bakers call letting the shaped bread rise the "proof." Home bakers usually term this the "second rise." This rising period takes less time than the first, since the yeast has already multiplied. During this rise, the texture and crumb of the bread are created. Ideal fermentation temperatures again range between 72° and 80°F, with the lower range producing better flavor. When the dough has roughly doubled in size, springs back when pressed, and feels full of carbon dioxide gas, it's ready to be baked.

Hearth breads may be raised in floured linen-lined bowls (bannetons) or a heavy folded cloth (couche) in order to guide their developing shape. They can also rise free-form on cornmeal-dusted parchment-lined sheet pans. Softer breads like sandwich loaves, brioche, or yeasted coffee cakes are baked in greased pans.

SCORING

Scoring or slashing the risen bread dough has a functional purpose as well as an artistic one. It is usually done just before the bread goes into the oven. The slash allows some of the carbon dioxide a place to vent; otherwise, the bread will explode randomly through its skin, creating strange, uneven shapes. A razor blade or lame is the tool of choice. Slashes are made rapidly and smoothly at about a 45-degree angle, penetrating just under the surface of the loaf. This produces a lovely open, blooming cut or *grigne*. Some breads are not scored—usually those with fat or other tenderizing ingredients that impart a finer, denser crumb.

BAKING

THE INTERIOR

If the process of baking a dough were to be told as a story, the main character would be water. Water's movement during baking weaves the entire narrative together. All bread doughs contain varying amounts of moisture. When the dough goes into the oven, the moisture is tied up with the flour proteins—water and flour proteins together form the gluten network. Ovenspring—the rapid expansion of gas cells—must happen early, before the crust sets for optimum volume. For this reason, hearth-style breads are baked at a very high temperature (450–500°F) since their dough lacks the external support of a pan and must rise and set quickly. Irregular, elongated cells in the finished bread bear witness to good ovenspring in these breads.

As the dough heats up (130°–140°F), the protein structure begins to soften and the yeast is killed. During this phase the dough is fragile and could collapse, but it is also the most flexible to allow the gas cells to expand. As the dough gets warmer (160°F), many of the gas cells coalesce, and the proteins approach the temperature at which they are denatured or cooked (165°F). During this time, the starch in the dough has been absorbing water from the gluten network. By the time the gluten proteins are denatured, they can no longer hold any water, so all of it has migrated to the starch. The starch cooks, or gelatinizes, forming a gel structure with the water. Thus both starch and gluten contribute to the structure of the finished loaf. When bread is done, the internal temperature registers between 185° and 200°F, for enriched breads and hearth-style breads, respectively. The telltale sign is a hollow sound when the bottom of the loaf is tapped, indicating that the water and starch have become a solid gel.

Some of the water in the bread dough is turned to steam, but less than 10 percent is lost. For water to be converted to steam, it must absorb heat from the dough. This is called evaporative cooling since its effect cools the dough.

THE CRUST

Great hearth breads have a thick, chewy but crisp crust, and baguettes have a thin, crisp, and even crackled crust. Several aspects of baking contribute to these crusts. For one, the exterior of the dough gets much hotter than the interior during baking. This is true of all baked goods, but becomes more of an issue as the oven temperature gets hotter. Masonry ovens and good commercial bread ovens not only get hot but their temperature fluctuates less when the door is opened than do conventional ovens. Unless the oven is hot enough, Maillard reactions (browning reactions between carbohydrates and proteins) and caramelization (browning of sugar) will not occur on the surface of the bread to the extent necessary for a good hearth crust. It is these reactions that give bread crust its pleasing, toasty flavor.

STEAM

If steam is sprayed into the oven during the first 10 to 15 minutes of baking, the bread benefits in a number of ways. Ovenspring is maximized, since the skin on the bread is moist and flexible enough to accommodate a rapid expansion. A crackly crust develops from volatile elements precipitated out of the bread into the steam that make the surface of the bread crisp and brown. Wet towels in massive masonry ovens are one way to create humidity. Steam-injected ovens achieve a similar result. Pressurized garden sprayers can duplicate this in the more common deck ovens or even in a home oven. By their nature, convection ovens are dry; the hot, windy aspect of convection ovens makes creating humidity a challenge.

The remainder of the baking should be dry in order to develop a crisp and crunchy crust. Initial moisture wets the surface of the bread dough, causing some of the starch to swell and gelatinize. Later, when the oven air is dry, this thin layer of gelled starch becomes dehydrated, making a chewy but crisp crust.

COOLING

Hot bread should immediately be transferred to wire racks to cool. Otherwise, steam condenses under the loaf and makes it soggy. Once cooled, hearth breads should be stored at room temperature in the open, or in paper bags. Enriched breads should be stored in plastic bags.

Once a bread loaf is fully cooled, it reaches its optimum crumb texture and flavor. After this point, things go downhill. Though moist breads, such as sourdoughs and breads with minimally processed whole-grain flour, keep their moist crumb longer, most breads steadily become hard and dry. This is a result of one of the starches present, amylopectin, which begins to revert back to its granular state. This process is called **retrogradation**, and it is the prime cause of staling.

Bread Varieties

STRAIGHT-DOUGH BREADS

In straight-dough or straight-rise breads, all the ingredients for the finished bread dough are combined in the initial mixing stage: flour, water, yeast, and almost always salt, along with any other ingredients. This is perhaps the simplest and is certainly the fastest way to make bread. Because the fermentation time is short for these breads, their flavor is not complex. Long fermentation also influences shelf life, so that straight-rise breads tend to become stale faster. In richer bread doughs, such as for cinnamon rolls, the added flavor from a longer fermentation is not necessary. French baguettes, on the other hand, consist only of flour, water, yeast, and salt. They are made using the straight-dough method, and they often taste dull and bland by the end of the day unless a small piece of old dough has been included or their fermentation time extended by retarding the dough.

WILD YEAST STARTERS

A wild yeast starter is cultivated from ambient yeast, rather than commercial yeast (see Chapter 2). Various names for wild yeast starters include barm, leaven, sourdough, starter, desem, and levain. Each wild yeast leaven is a little world with distinct populations of wild yeasts and acid-producing bacteria. The bacteria provide two acids that give wild yeast–leavened breads their distinct flavors: mild lactic acid and the more sour acetic acid. These bacteria are lumped under the genus heading of *Lactobacilli*. A wild yeast–leavened dough is quite acidic with a low pH (3 to 4.5). The ratio between the acetic and lactic acids present, plus the overall pH of the dough, gives each starter its characteristic flavor. Within this simple framework, however, a wide range of style and flavor variations exist.

Variables such as fast or slow fermentation, hot or cold temperatures, and the viscosity of the starter determine the flavor profile of the bread, since each variable affects yeast and bacterial fermentation differently. The type of flour also affects overall pH values. Flours with a high mineral or ash content act as buffers, reducing the overall pH value of an acidic dough. But acid-producing bacteria thrive especially well in these same flours, so the dough may have a high free acid content without an extremely low pH. These variables apply not only to the storage starter, but also to intermediate and the final doughs (see Wing and Scott, p. 67). The interaction of all these factors can be controlled to produce the desired result. Two styles of storage starter are widely used: a firm, almost doughlike starter and a thin, more batterlike starter. The firm starters need less frequent feedings and are slightly more storage stable. Firm starters also produce more acetic acid. Batterlike starters, which favor yeast activity and lactic acid production, must be kept on a tight feeding schedule and monitored for excessive acidity.

Pre-ferments made with wild yeast starters are called **leaven sponges** to differentiate them from sponges made with commercial yeast. (This extremely helpful clarification of terminology was developed by Daniel Wing and Allen Scott in *The Bread Builders*.) The same rules apply to sponges made with starters as to other pre-ferments: The amount of water in the starter and how long it ferments before being made into the final dough relates directly to finished flavor. A thin starter may be used to make a firm sponge, or a firm starter may used in a thinner pre-ferment.

The French wild yeast leaven that produces **pain au levain** is only slightly sour and possesses a deep, complex balance of flavors. The presence of both acetic and lactic acids is necessary to achieve good flavor. Lactic acid has no special taste of its own, but it is needed for flavor balance. Acetic acid is primarily responsible for tangy sharpness or sourness, but on its own it will taste too vinegary and harsh. *Pain au levain* undergoes several stages to build its dough, and has a short dough fermentation and a long proof.

Barms are a relatively liquid type of wild yeast starter that produce a pronounced sourness in the bread. Barms are usually built into a firmer pre-ferment to develop a bit more lactic acid to round out the flavor. *Barm* is an English word, descriptive of the alcohol this starter can produce. Sourdough starters for San Francisco sourdough bread are usually a type of barm; liquid starters tend to produce a lot of acetic acid. Acetic acid is well tolerated by the yeast associated with San Francisco sourdough. It has a tangy, even sharp flavor and very high acid level. It receives middle-of-the-road time in fermentation of the intermediate build(s) and a short dough fermentation. It generally has a long proof since the yeast is slowed considerably by the acidic environment. It is usually made with high-gluten flour to retain as much precious gas as possible.

Desem is a stiff type of wild yeast starter maintained in a cool environment. It originated in the Netherlands. Desem is started and always sustained with fresh organic wheat flour. The sponge is made with this same whole wheat flour, as is the finished dough. Desem dough is fermented slowly at a low temperature in order to get the most gluten development from the reduced gluten capability of fresh whole wheat flour. It is then proofed more quickly at a higher temperature. This produces a bread with only mild acidity created by a good balance of lactic and acetic acids. It is a relatively dense bread, given the nature of the flour.

RYE BREADS

Rye flour does not have enough gluten-forming proteins to make light bread by itself. Often at least a portion of the flour in rye bread comes from wheat. Rye bread doughs containing more than 20 percent rye flour rely on the viscosity of starches and pentosans (see page 25) to trap carbon dioxide gas and provide structure. Rye gluten alone is too weak to hold trapped air as it expands. As the loaf of rye bread enters the oven, the gelatinized starch on the outside of the loaf forms a skin that aids in gas retention. Wheat flour is added in varying amounts to strengthen rye breads; the more wheat flour added, the lighter in texture the rye bread.

Rye breads rely on starch for structure, but rye flour itself contains an enzyme, amylase, that destroys the structural capability of starch. Wheat amylase is denatured, or made inactive, before starch gelatinization takes place. Rye amylase is not denatured until much later in the baking process. During baking, the starch granules in both wheat and rye swell as they absorb water, creating a kind of gel. When the temperature gets hot enough, the starch gelatinizes, or sets, providing structure to the baked bread. In rye bread, the amylase is not denatured before gelatinization, and is free to attack not just the initially available damaged starch but also the starch made available by gelatinization. The result is that way too much starch is converted to sugar, and the loaf flattens, sags, and becomes heavy.

Sour rye breads, made from a wild yeast starter or long acid-producing fermentation, do not have this problem. The action of rye amylase is inhibited by an acidic environment, especially in conjunction with salt. Traditional rye breads are made with sour starters—the low pH slows down enzyme action and protects the starch until rye amylase is finally denatured during baking. Long fermentation also makes rye grain more digestible.

Rye flour is hygroscopic, meaning that it will absorb moisture from the environment. This quality gives rye breads an extended shelf life.

WHOLE-GRAIN AND HEALTH BREADS

Breads that contain a significant percentage of whole wheat flour, rye flour, or any other type of grain flour will have fewer gluten-forming proteins available to create structure and height. Depending on personal taste regarding texture and nutritive qualities, a percentage of wheat bread flour is added to the formula. Oats, millet, cornmeal, wheat bran, wheat germ, sunflower seeds, nuts—all are tasty and healthy additions. Whole grains and seeds are usually presoaked overnight to soften them. Slashing of heavy whole-grain breads should be done immediately after the shaping phase, as they have a more fragile structure and are susceptible to collapsing.

BAGELS

Bagels get their unique texture from poaching the shaped dough in simmering water before baking at a relatively high temperature (425° to 475°F). Many believe it takes some sort of magic alchemy to make a good bagel, or insist that New York City water is what makes that area's bagels so great. True, hard water does help, but most likely it is an Old World dedication to technique that makes New York's bagels better (and not all NYC bagels are so great!).

Bagels are made with bread or high-protein flour and very little moisture, which makes them denser than other breads. They can be made with the straight-rise method, or they can be made with pre-ferments or starters. Usually the straight-rise method is used, since it is fast and easy. Artisanal bakers often employ the pre-ferment method for bagels, which gives them complex flavor and more chewiness and increases their shelf life. Artisan bakers are also known to use steam when baking their bagels, which makes the crust both crisp and chewy.

ENRICHED BREADS

Enriched breads contain tenderizing, rich ingredients like butter, sugar, and eggs. They are additionally embellished with chocolate, nuts, dried fruits, and liquor. The flour may be a mixture of bread and cake, or of pastry and bread flour depending on how much weight the dough must support. Added fat changes the texture of these breads, making them more tender and even cakelike. The richer the dough, the more difficult it is to handle. Brioche, for example, may have anywhere from a 1:2 ratio of butter to flour up to equal weights of each, making it delicious and tender when baked but horribly sticky as a dough.

Since the gluten in rich doughs is interrupted by fat and sugar, these breads are often baked in pans for support. Doughs that have lots of sugar and fat, but little water, will ferment sluggishly. The more enriched a dough is, the more yeast is used. The type of yeast has an effect on fermentation as well. Osmotolerant instant dry yeast is formulated for water-poor doughs, such as these. Though instant yeast can be mixed directly with the flour, many chefs take the added precaution of rehydrating the yeast separately for water-poor doughs. Enriched doughs range from the simple, white sandwich loaf to luxurious brioche. Yeasted coffee cakes are popular, as are sweet rolls of all descriptions and holiday favorites from stollen to panettone to babka and hot cross buns.

DOUGHNUTS

The dough for yeast-risen doughnuts, as opposed to cake doughnuts, which are chemically leavened, is closely related to the basic sweet dough used for cinnamon rolls and sticky buns. Usually the dough for doughnuts has more fat and moisture than sweet dough, making it richer but lighter in texture. The dough rises once before it is shaped, and then proofs once more. Instead of being baked, doughnuts are deep fried in oil.

LAMINATES

L aminate doughs include those for puff pastry, croissants, and Danish. **Lamination** is the process of rolling and folding a piece of dough to encase a block of butter, creating hundreds of layers of pastry. For centuries, accomplished pastry chefs have been measured, in part, by how well they have mastered this process. Despite their time-consuming nature and need for precise execution, laminate doughs are rewarding and relatively straightforward to make. The ability of humble ingredients like the flour, butter, and water in classic puff pastry to rise over eight times their initial height during baking is gratifying and truly spectacular.

The method for making all laminate doughs is virtually the same. A dough, the *détrempe*, whose primary ingredients are flour, water, and salt, is wrapped around a block of cool but malleable butter, the *beurrage*. Puff pastry and Danish pastry consist of roughly equal amounts by weight of butter to flour. The puff pastry *détrempe* consists of flour, water, a small amount of butter, and salt. Danish *détrempe* is a rich, soft yeasted dough prepared with flour, milk, eggs, sugar, a very small amount of butter, and salt. The croissant *détrempe* is yeasted, like the Danish *détrempe*, but is much less rich—it contains water and/or milk, flour, a bit of sugar, and salt. Over the years the amount of butter rolled into the croissant *détrempe* has been steadily increasing, from a third of the weight of the flour to half that or even more.

Once assembled into a neat package, the resulting dough blocks, the *patons*, are then rolled and folded in a series of turns, or *tourage*. This process of lamination is the sole leavening agent of puff pastry and what makes yeast-risen croissants and Danish flaky instead of merely breadlike. The repeated rolling and folding of the dough creates pockets of trapped air between the many layers. When the pastry is baked, expanding air and steam (from moisture in both the dough and the butter) force the layers to separate and rise.

The major exception to the general laminate method outlined above is **inside-out puff pastry**. Here, the *détrempe* is encased in the butter, the very opposite of the traditional method. Though it sounds ludicrous to attempt rolling a sticky fat around a dough, only the first turn is any more difficult to execute than regular pastry. Some chefs claim this method creates a more tender product, since the *détrempe* is stressed less during the turns (see gluten development, below). I have not found this to be true. Though it is a fun experiment, the inside-out method is less than practical for hot kitchens.

Ingredients for Laminate Doughs

FLOUR

Choosing the right flour combination is key to achieving the best possible pastry. Hard wheat flours, used in breadmaking, contain more protein than soft wheat and cake flours. When combined with water, two of these proteins, glutenin and gliadin, combine to create long molecules of gluten. When the dough is kneaded or rolled, the strands of gluten coil and join to form an elastic, expansive structure strong enough to contain the expanding gases as the pastry bakes. Without enough gluten a dough will break under pressure rather than stretch. However, the elastic nature of the gluten structure causes the dough to become resistant to rolling as it is handled and stressed.

When making pastry doughs, chefs have traditionally worked around this problem by combining a high-protein flour with a soft flour, such as cake flour. The ratio of high-protein flour to soft changes according to the amount of time a dough is allowed to rest between turns. Rapid or quick puff pastry, for example, is given all its turns at once without resting, and therefore requires a higher amount of soft flour to accommodate the constant stretching and rolling. Balance is essential in creating the best structure for laminate doughs.

FATS

Laminates may have almost equal weights of flour and fat, so naturally the type of fat used has a marked effect on the texture and flavor of the final product. Which fat you choose also affects technique, since the melting point and plasticity of each fat determines how easily it is folded and rolled into the *détrempe*. In the heat of the oven, most of the fat melts into the dough, leaving air pockets behind. As steam builds from the moisture in the dough, the air pockets expand and lift the layers. The layers of dough separate from one another, producing consistent, spectacular lift.

Although butter is certainly the first choice for great-tasting pastry, it doesn't necessarily make the highest or flakiest pastry. Lard, along with hydrogenated vegetable shortenings and hard margarines designed to be rolled into laminate doughs, possess large fat crystals that contribute to the flaking effect. Lard and shortening have a lower water content than butter, meaning that an equal amount by weight will provide more fat, and therefore create a more tender, flaky product. When cooled, pastry made with shortenings may leave a waxy aftertaste, owing to the higher melting point of the fat. Butter, with its mouth-friendly low melting point, will not.

Specialized laminate shortenings, whether lard or vegetable-based, remain plastic over a large temperature range, forming a thin, continuous film that separates the rolled dough layers and prevents them from merging. They will neither melt into the dough before baking nor become so hard when chilled that they rupture the layers when the dough is rolled. Plastic shortenings or margarines can actually be spread over two-thirds of the *détrempe* that has been rolled into a rectangle. The bare bit of dough is folded over the shortening-covered portion and then the remaining dough end is folded over it, just like folding a business letter, achieving the same effect as a turn without actually rolling. This *paton* can then immediately be given a real turn if the working conditions are not too hot. The seal between layers of dough is not perfect, but the resulting volume loss is not appreciable in shortening or margarine laminates.

Working with butter, which has a narrow temperature range for ideal handling, requires more precision, to be sure, but produces superior flavor. The commitment to using all butter requires excellent technique and careful handling of the dough. Be mindful of the ambient temperature, as well as that of the components, and be as diligent as possible in sealing edges and applying even pressure during rolling. Ideally, the *détrempe* and *beurrage* will be close to the same temperature, about 60°F, to ensure even fat distribution, minimize any leakage, and prevent cold butter from tearing through dough layers. Do not use butter softened by sitting at room temperature for laminates, as it will readily melt when handled. It is better to beat large chunks of cold butter into a malleable state by force, with either a rolling pin or a mixer fitted with the paddle. This ensures consistent temperature throughout the block.

Usually the *détrempe* is chilled to bring it to the same temperature as the butter, but using ice water and/or very cold milk to make the *détrempe* is a faster way to achieve a cool dough. To use this shortcut with yeasted doughs, fresh yeast must be used—rather than dry yeast, which requires rehydration in a warm liquid.

DOUGH SHEETERS AND RETARDERS

Dough sheeters are invaluable appliances for making laminate products, and any pastry kitchen that produces laminates and pies on a daily basis should look into investing in one. The rollers of a sheeter are adjustable, able to perfectly roll a dough to the desired thickness. For laminate doughs, which start out as a thick block of dough, the rollers can be set progressively closer together after each pass of the *paton*. In addition to the obvious savings in time and labor, the even pressure applied to the dough by the rollers is hard to duplicate by hand. If the expense of a sheeter is out of the question, organize your daily routine and workstation so that the turns for all laminate products are performed in rapid succession in one area. This will keep production time down and minimize the time any one dough is exposed to the warm kitchen air.

For large batches, working in two-person teams during the rolling process is also beneficial. Do not attempt to skip the resting periods to keep on schedule—it is absolutely necessary for the dough to fully relax between turns. See Laminate Dough tips, page 184, for further hints.

The yeasted laminates—croissants and Danish—really benefit from specialized dough retarders. Retarders are pieces of bakery equipment that hold yeasted doughs slightly above normal refrigerator temperatures, allowing very slow fermentation to occur either in the *paton* or in the formed product. Retarder-proofer combination models can be programmed to steadily, slowly increase the temperature for a controlled rise (ideally overnight). Proof boxes create a warm, humid environment, letting the dough rise uncovered and expand to maximum height. Even if you can't afford a fancy electronic model, a simple proof box can be rigged with a hotel pan filled with water set over a Sterno. Ideal proofing temperatures are between 78° and 82°F at 80 percent humidity.

METHODS FOR LAMINATE DOUGHS

CLASSIC AND RAPID PUFF PASTRY

Classic puff pastry requires the most turns of any laminate dough, usually 6 threefold (or letter turns) or 4 fourfold (or book turns). The goal is the maximum number of turns the dough can withstand without collapsing the layers (see How Many Turns, page 183). In the recipe for puff pastry in *The Baker's Manual*, two blocks of butter are encased in the *détrempe*, folded business-letter style, instead of one block. A turn can be eliminated without losing layers, since folding the butter into the *détrempe* in two blocks accomplishes the same thing. This method works only with puff pasty: Richer croissant and Danish doughs perform best if the butter is encased the traditional way, as a single block.

Classic puff pastry produces the highest rise of any of the laminates. It is best used in any recipe where the pastry itself must shine. Bouchées and vol-au-vents, or pastry shells designed to hold fillings, require the height that can be provided only by classic puff pastry. Elaborate designs can be incised onto pastry, creating a stunning decorative effect. Pithiviers, a French dessert that consists of a rich almond cream baked between two circles of puff pastry, is decorated in this way. More humble, but no less delicious, is the fruit-filled turnover, another product best made with classic puff pastry.

Rapid puff pastry, also called **quick** or **rough puff pastry,** has the same mixing method as pie dough. Very cold pieces of butter, flour, salt, and ice water are briefly mixed, leaving large visible chunks of butter. This dough is given three turns (fourfold or book turns to maximize layers) immediately. During the turns, the pieces of butter are flattened and dispersed throughout the dough, approximating the precise distribution of fat in classic puff pastry. Rapid puff pastry requires only one resting and chilling period, between the final turn and rolling the dough for cutting and shaping. Rapid dough will not rise as high, but the texture is still flaky and buttery. Rapid puff is an excellent all-purpose pastry. Slightly more dense and compact than classic puff pastry, it stands up well to savory fillings that tend to be heavy. Napoleons are much easier to cut from rapid puff pastry; the layers tend to shatter and crumble less than with classic puff pastry when sliced. Classic puff pastry scraps also work well for napoleons. Since the dough for napoleons is docked and weighted to prevent a high rise, scraps are fine.

For both classic and rapid puff pastry, bake small cookies (palmiers, sacristans) at 425°F, sheet-pan-sized puff pastry for napoleons at 400°F, and large filled tortas at 375°F. (These temperatures are for conventional ovens; decrease temperature 25°F for convection ovens.)

DANISH AND CROISSANT PASTRIES

For yeasted **croissant** and **Danish doughs,** the *détrempe* is minimally kneaded to prevent excessive gluten formation before the butter is rolled in. Plenty of gluten development will occur in subsequent rolling and folding of the dough. Some bakers like to retard the yeasted *détrempe* overnight, which improves the extensibility of the gluten network and allows more turns to be done at once. This method is rumored to create flakier layers. Another method used to ensure a flaky product is enclosing a single block of *beurrage* rather than two. Soft yeasted doughs, which have a second leavening source, receive fewer turns than puff pastry in order to preserve distinct visible layers. The *détrempe* is rolled into a square, and the *beurrage* is placed in the center of the square, catty-cornered. The triangular flaps of dough are folded over the *beurrage* and pressed together to seal. The *paton* is given 2 threefold turns and 1 fourfold turn, with appropriate rests between.

Retarding or refrigerating the *paton* overnight improves extensibility when rolling out the dough and reduces shrinkage. Fresh yeast is the best choice for yeasted laminates; it works well with cold liquids, with no need for special rehydration in warm water. The dough should be proofed in a warm (80°F), humid environment until it doubles in volume or barely holds a dent when poked. If the dough springs back to the touch, it is underproofed; if it holds a deep dent that does not offer any resistance, it is overproofed. Overproofing results in a product that collapses after baking and has an unpleasantly strong yeasty flavor. Underproofing yields a doughy, unattractive product with fused layers. Croissants are usually baked at around 425°F.

Classic plain crescent-shaped croissants have their own specific shaping techniques discussed in *The Baker's Manual*. Filled croissants, such as pain au chocolat, are often squares of dough simply rolled around a filling. Croissant dough can also be rolled into logs, sliced, and then proofed and baked in muffin pans like cinnamon rolls. Depending on the client and perhaps location, the texture of croissants can be adjusted. Some patrons like their croissants bready, sweet, and pale gold in color, but most prefer a deep gold, delicate pastry whose distinct layers disintegrate into flakes with each bite.

Danish dough is popular and versatile. Individual-sized Danish, with a wide array of shapes and fillings, are the mainstay of bakeries. Larger products made from Danish dough, such as kringle strips, Swedish tea rings, and coffee cakes, can be sold whole or by the slice. Danish are usually baked between 350 and 400°F, depending on size and filling type.

HOW MANY TURNS?

Puff pastry may be known as *millefeuille*, meaning "thousand leaves," but there is no fixed number of layers or turns for sublime pastry. Two common folding methods exist: the threefold, called a single turn or

LAMINATE DOUGH

Croissant and Danish dough can be frozen in *paton* form, though they fare better when frozen after being cut and shaped, either unfilled or filled and ready to bake. To freeze these doughs for more than two days, increase the amount of yeast by 10 to 25 percent to ensure proper performance. Some yeast cells may be damaged during long-term storage in the freezer, usually owing to temperature fluctuations. Thaw the dough completely in the refrigerator, and allow it to warm slightly at room temperature before rolling and shaping. Keeping the dough well covered during the thawing process prevents condensation, which makes the dough soggy. Allow the dough to come to room temperature before proofing also to prevent condensation.

Rolling pastry cutters are available that cut entire rows of croissant triangles in a single pass. Adjustable pastry cutters with multiple wheels make cutting strips or squares quick and accurate.

Except for rapid puff pastry, laminate doughs require at least a four-hour time commitment. Two-thirds of the turns must be completed in succession (about an hour apart) before the dough can be refrigerated and finished at your convenience. Large areas of extremely cold butter can tear the dough when rolled. Chilling the dough for one hour allows the gluten to relax while keeping the butter cool but pliable (ideally, both the dough and butter should be the same temperature in order to move together as one). Once the majority of turns are completed, the butter will be thin enough to pose no threat to the dough.

Refrigerate, never freeze, the dough between turns. Freezing the dough halts the relaxing process; the gluten strands are simply frozen in place. A one-hour rest in the refrigerator gives the dough time to relax while keeping the butter cool. If the dough seems to be rubbery and resistant to rolling, it needs to rest longer.

If the *beurrage* mixture becomes too soft, mound it on plastic wrap, form it into the desired shape, and chill until workable.

If the butter comes through the dough at any point, flour heavily and chill before finishing the turn.

To ensure even, stable gluten structure, roll the dough in all directions. Do not roll over the ends of the dough, as the pressure will push the butter out the end.

LAMINATE DOUGH (Continued)

After rolling out puff pastry, lift and flap the dough gently to allow it to contract before cutting into shapes. This will prevent shrinkage. When cutting pastry for multiple-part structures, such as vol-au-vents, chill pieces fifteen to twenty minutes before assembling.

Cut straight down with a sharp knife to avoid compressing the layers. If the pastry is glazed on top with either egg or milk, do not glaze over the edges. The glaze can glue layers of pastry together, preventing an even rise.

Puff pastry can be refrigerated three to four days without losing quality. Freeze assembled products, such as apple turnovers, rather than the *paton* when possible for best results. Thaw filled products in the refrigerator overnight before baking. Unfilled or minimally filled products (e.g., cheesestraws or palmiers) can be baked frozen. Doughs with vinegar will break down and lose volume if stored for a long time.

Bake pastries on parchment paper for even browning and easy transfer.

To get the most height when using scraps of dough, stack and chill them before rolling.

letter fold, and the fourfold, the double turn or book fold. If you consider the initial butter-dough package as three layers, then the traditional four double turns yield 768 layers, and the traditional six single turns yield 2,187 layers. Compulsive counters who do not consider dough upon dough in the folding process as two distinct layers, as we do (since no butter separates them), can use Bo Friberg's table for counting in *The Professional Pastry Chef* (see Bibliography). Friberg provides a detailed chart for puritanically precise pastry chefs, correcting the number of layers to 513 and 1,459, respectively.

Recipes often combine double and single turns to achieve the maximum number of layers for each type pastry, while other recipes have noticeably fewer turns. To test whether the dough can take another turn, cut off 2 inches of the dough. If you can still see distinct layers (for rapid puff pastry, make sure there are visible areas of butter in the dough), try giving this portion one more turn. Then bake the test dough and a small piece from the remaining *paton* and compare.

CHAPTER 14

CAKE BAKING

Cake baking requires precision and care to achieve optimum texture and height. Having the ingredients, and thus the batter, in the appropriate temperature range is the single most important factor in determining the final texture and height of the cake. Eggs must be 70° to 90°F to provide maximum volume for the finished cake. Butter should be at least 60°F to incorporate air when it is creamed with the sugar, but not so warm that it melts from the friction of mixing. In general, the optimum batter temperature for sponge-type cakes is 90°F, while for butter-type cakes it is 70°F (see Pyler, p. 997).

The second most important factor is oven temperature. When it comes to temperature accuracy, ovens are assumed guilty until proven innocent. A mercury thermometer is preferable for testing oven accuracy, not the more inexpensive spring type. If you do not have access to a good thermometer, prepare a simple recipe you are familiar with and check the results. You can learn much from that experiment, as even generally well-behaved ovens may have hot spots that cause foods to bake unevenly.

The center of the oven is the best place to bake cakes. If the oven has multiple racks, the pans near the top and bottom of the oven should be switched at the baking midpoint to ensure even volume and browning. Greasing and flouring pans not only assists in releasing the finished cake but also ensures good volume. The floured sides of the pan give the batter something to cling to as it rises. For certain types of sponge cakes, the bottoms of the cake pans may be greased and/or lined with paper to allow easy release; the sides of the pans may be left ungreased to allow the egg foam batter to climb and cling most tenaciously—preserving the best volume and texture.

Beyond these factors, choosing or developing a correctly balanced formula appropriate for each specific type of cake is supremely important. Chemists in large industrial-sized bakeries have actually conducted studies that determined the optimum specific gravity and pH levels for each type of cake. Knowing this, of course, makes it all the more worrisome to be at the mercy of a plain old recipe in a book, with no such equipment on hand to provide guidance or reassurance. Fortunately, some room for variation exists in cake baking. Once you understand how each ingredient affects the outcome of the baked cake, you can adjust any less-than-perfect recipe yourself.

INGREDIENTS

Ingredients in cake making can be divided into several categories by what they do to the final product. In order to help the chef to pinpoint problems, make ingredient substitutions, and improve the texture of the cake, it is helpful to group the ingredients into two major dichotomous categories: the tougheners (structure builders)/tenderizers and the moisteners/drying agents. Some ingredients, of course, may fall into both categories depending on what role they are called upon to play in the cake.

STRUCTURE-ENHANCING INGREDIENTS

Wheat flour, with its gluten-forming proteins, supplies the primary structural foundation of most cakes, excepting egg-based sponge cakes. High-protein flours, also known as high-gluten, make chewy breads but tough cakes. Bread baking is all about maximizing gluten formation and cake baking is about minimizing it. Too much gluten makes a tight, unyielding batter that turns into a tough, rubbery cake. Gluten begins to form when the flour is moistened and stirred; it is easy to create a tough cake just by overmixing. One of the telltale signs is tunnels in the cake. Low-protein flours are preferable for minimizing gluten development, particularly cake flour.

Cake flour is more finely ground than other flours, giving the crumb a fine texture. It is specially bleached with chlorine gas, which makes it easier for fat to stick to the starch. Bleaching disperses the fat more evenly, and since the creamed fat contains air bubbles, it disperses air throughout the batter more effectively, too. The result is that cakes made with cake flour are more finely grained. Chlorine bleaching allows the wheat starch to absorb more liquid, typically a hallmark of high-protein flours. Cake flour is more acidic than normal flour. Since acids promote faster setting, this means the starch will gelatinize sooner in the oven, reducing baking time and keeping the cake moister.

Some cake recipes have little flour in proportion to other ingredients, so gluten formation is of little structural consequence. However, **starch gelatinization**, from the starch present in the flour and any other added starch, is important to the structure of all cakes. In the heat of the oven, the starch granules begin to swell and absorb liquid (see Chapter 7). The starch gelatinizes at a higher temperature than the gluten proteins become cooked (denatured). Once denatured, the gluten is unable to hold all the liquid it has absorbed, and that liquid is then transferred to the starch. Unlike sauces, cake batters do not provide enough liquid for all the starch to absorb enough moisture to burst, so only partial gelatinization takes place. The gluten structure interacts with the flexible starch granules, which allows the gluten film to stretch and become thinner around expanding gas bubbles. When the gluten network finally denatures or bursts owing to expansion (losing its liquid to the starch and becoming semi-rigid), the starch takes on the released liquid and keeps it dispersed evenly throughout the rapidly setting cake. As the starch itself finally begins to gelatinize, it provides even more structural support.

Egg proteins stabilize cake batters. When the eggs are heated, their proteins coagulate and become rigid, helping to set the crumb of the cake. **Dry milk powder**, added to a batter in small amounts, creates a stronger structure, owing to its protein content. The milk solids also increase browning in the crust. Dry milk helps the baked cake retain moisture and also improves the crumb. Additional water must be added to batters made with dry milk for adequate rehydration.

TENDERIZING INGREDIENTS

The presence of **sugar** dilutes gluten proteins, making it a tenderizer. The **starch** in wheat flour contributes to cake structure (see above). Replacing a small portion of flour specified in a recipe with a pure starch, such as cornstarch or potato starch, makes for an even more tender cake. Starch competes with gluten for water, as well as dilutes its strength. **Fat** tenderizes by coating individual flour particles, making gluten formation difficult. Fat helps cakes retain their tenderness since it prevents loss of moisture.

Beyond **cocoa powder's** small amount of fat, its primary function as a tenderizer is a result of its lack of gluten-forming proteins. Thus, if present in a recipe in any significant amount, cocoa powder will reduce the overall percentage of gluten in the cake. Dutch-processed cocoa is alkaline and should be paired with baking powders, whereas baking soda is used to leaven and neutralize the acidity of natural cocoa (see Chapter 2).

Egg yolks do contain protein, a structure-building component, but their high fat and emulsifier content also put them squarely in the tenderizer camp. Cholesterol and lecithin, both found in egg yolks, are emulsifiers that help to evenly disperse the fat in a batter. Even dispersion of fat in a batter causes a cake to be more tender.

Chemical **leaveners** belong in this category of tenderizing ingredients because they make the finished crumb tender and light through their action.

INGREDIENTS THAT ADD OR DEPLETE MOISTURE

Fat, egg whites, yolks and whole eggs, liquid dairy products, and sugar syrups all provide moisture to a cake. Flour, granular sugar, starches, cocoa powder, and dry milk powder compete for moisture in a cake batter.

SPONGE CAKES

Sponge cakes are characterized by a higher proportion of eggs to lower amounts of flour. They are leavened primarily by beating air into eggs, though chemical leaveners are sometimes added as a preventive measure. Eggs, either whole, yolks, or whites, will trap air as they are beaten, creating a foam made from millions of bubbles. In the oven, these bubbles expand and lift the cake until the temperature of the batter is hot enough to set it. Sponge cakes are usually baked at higher temperatures to help set the cake as quickly as possible, preventing the bubbles from rising, escaping, and then collapsing the batter. As the egg proteins cook, they coagulate and help set the cake's structure. The gluten created by the small amount of flour is too widely dispersed to be the sole structural foundation. High egg protein and very little flour cause sponge cakes to be flexible and springy.

Even cakes made with unbeaten eggs and added chemical leaveners, such as American-style layer cakes, get a lift from eggs. First, lecithin and cholesterol—the emulsifiers in eggs—help disperse fat and air evenly in a better, creating better volume. When the eggs are mixed into the batter, their proteins form a film that helps capture the air bubbles released by the chemical leavener. As the egg proteins cook and coagulate, they prevent these bubbles from escaping and coalescing.

Successful sponge cakes begin with good egg foams. It is essential to use room-temperature eggs for maximum volume. If sugar is beaten into the eggs, warm eggs are better for dissolving the grains of sugar. Whole eggs are beaten to the ribbon stage, when they become pale and thick, and a ribbon of egg foam dropped from the whip remains on the surface of the foam below. The sugar should not be added until this late stage, and even then it should be added very slowly, with the mixer running to prevent volume loss and to give the sugar time to dissolve.

For egg white foams, grease-free utensils are required to achieve the greatest volume. Cream of tartar, an acid, is often added to prevent overwhipping and give stability. Sugar, too, will add stability. It should be added in the last stage of beating, as described above. Beating the egg whites at medium to medium-high speed results in better cake volume. Though it is faster to whip the whites at high speed, a slightly lower speed creates a greater number of air bubbles, which are smaller and more consistent in size. Care must be taken not to overbeat egg whites. Once they have reached the soft peak stage, the whites must be watched closely. Though most recipes call for folding stiffly beaten egg whites into the batter, it is better to err on the side of caution. Once the whites have been beaten to the stiff peak stage, they quickly become overbeaten. Overbeaten whites look grainy and dry, rather than shiny, and have lost much of their leavening ability.

BISCUIT

Biscuit (pronounced *bis-kwee*, rather than *bis-kit*, the Southern breakfast food), the classic European sponge cake, contains eggs, sugar, and flour, but no added fat. There are three basic types of biscuit, based on the amount of flour present in the recipe. **Jelly rolls**, or **roulades**, are cakes baked in thin sheets that will be rolled around a filling. These sponge cakes have the least amount of flour, which makes the cake flexible enough to roll without breaking. Since the cakes are thin rather than tall, they don't need much flour for structural support. Roulades are baked in greased parchment-lined pans for easy removal. They are loosely rolled while still warm, and allowed to cool in this position before the parchment is removed and the cake is filled and frosted.

Regular **biscuit**, also called **sponge cake**, can be baked in layers, as it has more flour. Plain sponge cake, which has no butter or oil, is usually brushed with a flavorful sugar syrup to make it moist. Sponge cakes are tender and are perfect for rich fillings like mousse or buttercream.

Last are **ladyfingers**, the sponge cake formula with the most flour. Also called **biscuit à cuillière**, which indicates the batter was dropped and shaped by a spoon, ladyfingers are finger-shaped cakes used to line charlottes and in tiramisù. The added flour makes the batter thick enough to be piped, but it is more difficult to prepare than the other batters since more flour must be folded into the separated egg foams without deflating them.

Sponge cake batters are usually made by beating the yolks and whites separately, each with a portion of the sugar. The two foams are folded together with the sifted cake flour, or a combination of all-purpose flour and corn or potato starch. Egg yolk foams are notoriously thick, easily deflating the egg whites when the two are combined. To make yolks less viscous, beat a whole egg with the yolks (more if the batch is large), effectively transferring one white to the yolks. Even though this reduces the volume of beaten egg whites in the recipe, less total batter volume is lost.

ANGEL FOOD CAKE

Egg white–based **angel food cake** is the lightest and most tender of the sponge cakes, a remarkable feat for a cake that has virtually no fat. Leavened with the air contained in the beaten egg white foam, angel food cakes get their moisture and tenderness from the egg whites and a proportionally large amount of sugar.

Naturally, careful beating of the egg white foam is essential to the success of the cake. Clean, nongreasy utensils should be used to maximize volume, and generally cream of tartar is added for stability. Usually some of the sugar is beaten with the whites for a more stable foam. The batter is very delicate and tolerates minimal flavor additions.

Angel food cakes are generally baked in ungreased tube pans, since fat collapses the egg white foam. The cakes are cooled upside down because egg proteins, which form the primary structure of the cake, firm and set as they cool. If cooled upright, gravity may collapse some of the air cells before the cake is set. Angel food cakes are tender at either room temperature or cold.

CHIFFON CAKE

Chiffon cake, developed by a California baker in the 1920s, is a decidedly American form of the sponge cake. Unlike other sponge cakes, chiffon cakes are made rich with the addition of oil and include baking powder as a leavener. They are still exceptionally light from their high egg content, but unlike European sponge cakes they don't need to be brushed with sugar syrup to stay moist. Chiffon cakes have an unusual mixing method: The dry ingredients are whisked together with the oil and yolks, and beaten egg whites are folded into this mixture.

Chiffon cakes, like angel food cakes, were traditionally baked in ungreased tube pans and inverted to cool to prevent the loss of volume that occurs before egg proteins firm. But because chiffon cake works well with a variety of fillings and remains tender even when cold, it makes wonderful layer cakes. In this case, the bottom of the cake pans should be greased, lined with parchment, then greased and floured. Do not grease the sides; the cake needs something to stick to when inverted. If the pans are filled just under halfway, the cooked cake will fall to just under the level of the rim within moments of leaving the oven, and the pan can be safely inverted to cool the cakes. The layers can be cooled right side up, but inverting them does maximize the finished height.

GENOISE

Genoise contains butter and so is sometimes categorized as a butter cake rather than a sponge cake. However, the technique for making genoise is a specialized version of the sponge method. Butter is primarily a flavoring agent in this classic French cake that retains the airy, light texture of other sponge cakes. Genoise layers are the base for elegant French *gateaux*, filled with mousse, ganache, or buttercream. Like biscuit, it is customary to brush the layers with a flavored simple syrup before filling to keep the cake moist.

Successful genoise begins with melted butter that is cooled until it is barely warm. The butter is often browned for flavor, called *beurre noisette*, or clarified (skimmed of milk solids). Meanwhile, whole eggs are placed in the mixing bowl with the sugar. The eggs and sugar are whisked together over simmering water until the sugar dissolves and the eggs feel warm. The egg and sugar mixture is beaten to the ribbon stage, and the sifted flour is then gently folded in. Last, the melted butter is folded in quickly to prevent the batter from being deflated by the fat. The baking pans are greased, lined with parchment, greased over the paper, and lightly dusted with flour.

Genoise and chiffon layer cakes lose a little height as they cool. When they have settled, the cakes should still be double the height of the batter. The cake should not sink in the middle, or lose over 20 percent its greatest volume. These cakes have as much, if not more, egg than flour. The large amount of egg makes them light and airy, and keeps them relatively flexible. When the cakes come out of the oven, the egg proteins are fully cooked, but are not firmly set. They will set as the cake cools.

BUTTER- AND SHORTENING-BASED CAKES

There are three main mixing methods used for butter- and shortening-based cakes. The most familiar is the **creaming method,** where the fat and sugar are beaten together until they form a light, fluffy mass. The sharp edges of the sugar crystals create small pockets of air in the fat as they are beaten together. Butter must be soft enough to beat, but cool enough not to melt—around 65°F is ideal. If the butter begins to melt, it will not be effective at trapping air. Shortening already has small air bubbles in it, about 12 percent by weight, and they are very finely dispersed. This gives shortening an edge over butter at aerating. Shortening is all fat, unlike butter, which is 4 to 8 percent water. Shortening has a greater temperature range for creaming than butter; it has a higher melting point and is softer when cold. As a fat, it performs better than butter, but the flavor of butter is associated with fine baking. Margarines have varying amounts of water—more so than butter—and do not possess its sweet flavor. Some margarines are available that have a very low water content and behave more like shortening in baked goods.

Though many batters contain additional leaveners, the creaming of the butter and sugar establishes the foundation for raising the batter. The one-bowl method for mixing relies on chemical leaveners rather than creaming for aeration, and produces cakes with a slightly lower volume. Chemical leaveners may react when mixed into the batter and create carbon dioxide bubbles, but their primary role is to expand the bubbles created by creaming.

The eggs are beaten into the creamed butter next, usually at small increments to ensure even absorption. If the eggs are not the same temperature as the creamed butter, the batter may look curdled. The last step in the creaming method is to add the sifted dry ingredients and any additional liquids, usually starting and ending with the dry ingredients. A portion of flour is added first so that it may be coated with fat particles. This helps minimize gluten formation when the liquid is added to the mixer (water allows the proteins in wheat flour—glutenin and gliadin—to combine and form gluten). Adding the liquid ingredients too fast can result in a curdled-looking batter, as the fat-in-water emulsion inverts to a water-in-fat one. When the remaining flour is added, the batter will smooth out. The creaming method aerates better than the other methods, but the volume difference between creamed batters and those mixed with the high-ratio method is relatively small.

The **high-ratio method**, also known as **two-stage**, came about with the advent of chlorinated cake flour and modern shortenings in the 1930s. Soft, low-gluten flour cannot absorb as much moisture as high-protein flours, but bleaching with chlorine gas created cake flours that tolerated higher levels of liquid. Improved shortenings dispersed the fat and air pockets better in batters, creating tender cakes. Cakes made with these two ingredients came to be known as high-ratio cakes because they absorbed a higher amount of moisture.

Today, the high-ratio mixing method is used for batters whose sugar exceeds the weight of the flour. Pound cakes and yellow or white layer cakes are candidates for this method, but very thin batters such as for devil's food cake are not. Though either butter or shortening can be used, cake flour is essential for success. An adequate amount of liquid, such as milk, is also needed in high-sugar cakes; the sugar competes with any starch present for liquid. An insufficient amount of liquid can cause dryness.

The liquid ingredients, such as milk, eggs, and vanilla extract, are combined separately. For large batches, where it is inconvenient to combine them, only the eggs have to be lightly beaten until homogenous. All the dry ingredients are combined at low speed in a mixer, which replaces the repeated sifting used in other methods. The shortening or softened butter is added next and is cut into the flour by the action of the beaters. After the flour begins to be coated with the fat, just enough liquid is added to the running mixer (low speed) to disperse the fat. The eggs are added first if they have not been mixed with the other liquids. This step also aerates the batter. The rest is added slowly, creating a homogenous batter. The batter is beaten at a higher speed until fluffy. The high-ratio method yields a more velvety and tender crumbed cake than other methods.

For cake recipes using a liquid fat such as melted butter or oil, there is another mixing method, called the **one-stage** or **dump method**. All the dry ingredients are mixed in a bowl, and all the liquid ingredients, including the oil or melted butter, are combined separately. The liquid ingredients are "dumped" into the dry ingredients and mixed only until they are evenly dispersed to minimize gluten formation. Some recipes call for all the ingredients to be added to the mixer at once and combined, but this creates a tougher cake since it requires more mixing to combine all the ingredients evenly. Clearly, the one-stage method is faster than the others, but it does pose the threat of developing too much gluten. The best way to minimize gluten formation is to add the oil or melted fat to the flour first. By coating the flour with the fat, the liquid is prevented from being immediately absorbed by the flour to create gluten. This method can be used for muffins, quickbreads, and for oil-based devil's food cakes. Still, muffins made by creaming are taller and more tender than ones made by the one-stage method; some volume and texture are sacrificed for the sake of speed.

Many other hybrid mixing methods exist. Some carrot cake recipes, for example, start by beating the oil, sugar, and eggs together. Many older recipes for cakes use the creaming method, but beat the egg whites separately and fold them in for even more volume.

One last word about mixing method and cake volume. Though this book stresses the importance of incorporating air in a plastic fat, such as butter or shortening, or using an egg to create volume, it is possible to make a light cake without using either process. In the 1970s, food scientists made a landmark discovery about emulsifiers: Though it had been known that emulsifiers improved solid shortening's performance in cake batter, chemists discovered that liquid shortenings with added emulsifiers made cakes with equal volume. Suddenly solid fats were not necessary for aeration. Today, many food companies use these high-emulsifier liquid fats instead of the time-consuming practice of creaming the fat with sugar. Emulsifiers, like lecithin and cholesterol, disperse fat and air evenly in a batter, ensuring tenderness and high volume. Commercial emulsifiers are even more sophisticated.

Home bakers have known that there is more than one way to aerate a cake. Recipes abound for mayonnaise cake, where the mayonnaise provides the fat, air, and eggs, and cakes made with whipped cream as the aerated fat. Both whipped cream and mayonnaise contain natural emulsifiers.

POUND CAKE

Modern **pound cakes** are derived from an old formula for which the cakes are named: a pound each of butter, sugar, eggs, and flour. Traditionally, the only leavening came from creaming the butter with the sugar. Today, pound cake recipes reflect the current preference for tender cakes with a more delicate crumb. Pound cakes are still more dense than layer cakes, but they are more moist, sweet, and open-crumbed than their ancestors. Baked in loaves or decorative Bundt-shaped tube pans, pound cakes are commonly sliced and eaten unadorned, or lightly glazed.

Added sugar, milk, or sour cream and a small amount of leavening are the hallmarks of modern pound cakes. Reducing the amount of eggs or flour (the structure-building components) slightly will also make a more tender, moist cake. Pound cakes usually rise by one third of their initial batter volume during baking.

AMERICAN-STYLE LAYER CAKES

The great **American layer cake** was once considered a dowdy cousin to European *gateaux*, probably because the use of chemical leaveners was first greeted with skepticism. European cakes depend on good technique for their leavening, rather than a powder, and they tend to contain less fat. But the rich, fluffy, tender mile-high layer cake is now beloved. Early versions were topped with light, fluffy frostings, such as meringuelike seven-minute frosting (also called boiled icing) and whipped cream. Today's layer cakes are more often covered with rich buttercreams. White, yellow, devil's food, lemon, and carrot are the most common cake flavors sold in bakeries, though coconut, mocha, and nut cakes are also popular.

Cake formulas have changed over the past century, owing to both changes in consumer taste and the development of new ingredients, such as shortening and chlorinated cake flour. Older recipes share a basic formulation:

- The weight of the sugar is less than or equal to that of the flour.

- The weight of the total liquid (eggs included) is equal or less than the weight of the flour.

- The weight of the eggs is greater than or equal to that of the fat.

Sturdy cakes are the hallmark of these old ratios. Though certainly rich, the high amount of egg and flour makes them seem less moist than modern cakes. Modern high-ratio formulas have created tender, fluffy, and sweet cakes by increasing the sugar, liquid, and eggs. Though the formula and mixing method were developed for use with high-ratio shortenings and cake flour, it can also be used with butter and/or mixed with the creaming method. Cake flour is needed, however, since it can support more moisture than other low-protein flours. High-ratio cakes have the following characteristics:

- The weight of the sugar equals or exceeds that of the flour.

- The weight of the total liquid (eggs included) exceeds the weight of the sugar.

- The weight of the eggs is greater than the weight of the fat.

There is always some room for variation, and perfectly good cakes are made that stretch these parameters. Layer-cake batters double their height as they bake, so pans should not be filled more than halfway.

BISCUITS AND SCONES

To make both biscuits and scones, cold chunks of fat are cut into the dry ingredients, as for pie dough. **Biscuits** usually have no sugar and are generally a mixture of fat, flour, and milk with a leavening agent. Though the pieces of fat left in the dough make plain biscuits quite tender, many bakers give the dough a turn or two to create flaky layers.

Scones are slightly sweet and richer than biscuits, with the addition of eggs and even cream. Some recipes for scones have no cold butter or fat cut into the flour, but rather are a simple combination of flour, leavening, and heavy cream. These are cream scones, and they are exceptionally tender and moist.

MUFFINS AND QUICKBREADS

Muffins and **quickbreads** are more closely related to cakes than breads, since they are chemically leavened and share the same mixing methods as cakes. The only difference is that they are less "cakey" than cakes, although these days bakeries often sell little cakes with the name of muffins. If it is too rich to tolerate a pat of butter, it's not a muffin. Muffins are less rich than cakes, a bit less tender, less sweet, and have a more open crumb texture. A good muffin is ephemeral; the combination of their small size and large surface area with a modest amount of fat means they do not keep well. Quickbreads, on the other hand, retain moisture better. Fruit-based breads, like banana, pumpkin, zucchini, and apple, are very moist and actually improve in flavor after the first day. Most formulas for quickbreads and muffins are interchangeable. Like other American-style cakes, the mixing methods for muffins and quickbreads vary.

TROUBLESHOOTING

Pound cakes should form a nice peak, muffins should stand tall, but in general, cakes shouldn't be overly rounded on top. Or sunken. Or have their sides caved in. Below is a list of cake problems along with possible culprits.

TROUBLESHOOTING GUIDE

Poor volume	Batter not well aerated; batter overmixed; egg foam not whipped or folded in properly.
Domed top	Batter has too much flour or oven is too hot.
Sunken top	Stale or wrong kind of leavening; batter has too much fat.
Sides caved in	Too much liquid in recipe.
Dense layer at bottom of cake	Too much liquid or fat, or cake flour should be used.
Cake is dry	Too much egg; too much flour; not enough fat or liquid.
Air tunnels in cake	Too much gluten developed in mixing, wrong mixing method, too much egg or flour protein in cake.
Cake is gummy	Too much buttermilk, banana, applesauce, zucchini, or any acidic purée.
Cake is tough	Too much egg; too much flour; wrong mixing method; not enough sugar.

CAKE PANS

BROWNING

Pan color affects browning. Dark pans absorb more heat than light-colored ones, and batters baked in a dark pan will be darker. Ingredients also affect browning. Sugar, especially corn syrup, honey, and molasses with their invert sugar content, helps foods brown. Milk products also aid in browning. Acidic ingredients, including cake flour, lessen browning. Baking soda can be used to reduce the acidity of batters to aid in browning.

PAN SIZES

Cake recipes usually specify a pan size, but substitutions can be made if the recipe is adjusted. Generally, to bake cupcakes instead of cake layers, the only change is a small increase in oven temperature. Rich, thick cake batters, like pound cake, are baked in loaves or tube pans in a moderate oven (325° to 350°F) and have enough fat to keep the cake moist during the long baking time. But baking a devil's food cake batter in a tube pan may not work: The batter contains more liquid, and in a pan with limited surface area the baking time will increase, drying out the sides. The cake may even collapse. To convert this recipe, less liquid and more fat and egg are needed.

Baking cake layers in sheet pans rather than several round pans may require a decrease in leavening (since the cake batter will rise more easily when it has more surface area) and a decrease in baking time.

SELECTING CAKE LAYERS, FILLINGS, AND FROSTINGS

The fun part of being a pastry chef is creating new combinations of flavors and textures. There are several considerations when pairing cake layers with fillings and frostings. One is serving temperature. Buttercream and butter-rich layer cakes are hard when chilled because butter is hard when cold, so neither is good straight from the refrigerator. Even a fresh, moist, and tender butter cake at room temperature seems hard and dry when cold. Butter's sharp melting point also means that buttercream frostings cannot sit out at room temperature too long in hot weather.

Mousse fillings are a staple of European cakes, or *gateaux*, where they are paired with a sponge-type cake that remains soft when cold. Even genoise, which contains a small amount of butter, is still soft when cold owing to its high egg content. American-style layer cakes do not do well with mousse, which is served directly from the refrigerator—either you have a hard, dry cake and perfect mousse, or a room-temperature tender cake and melting mousse.

Flourless chocolate tortes, or any cake containing a high amount of chocolate (not cocoa powder, but chocolate that contains cocoa butter), will also be hard when cold. These cakes do not taste or feel fudgy unless they are allowed to come to room temperature.

For catering chefs, the hot summer months may mean bolstering Bavarians with additional gelatin, or making ganache fillings thicker than normal.

Temperature can be an important parameter when designing a dessert menu. American layer cakes are perfect for buffets, but European-style sponge cakes filled with mousse can be served straight from cold storage in a busy restaurant. If you sell cakes wholesale, educate your clients about how to store and present the dessert. Otherwise, it is your own reputation that will suffer.

CHAPTER 15

EGG COOKERY:
CUSTARDS, SOUFFLÉS,
MERINGUES, BUTTERCREAM,
AND PÂTE À CHOUX

T he methods used to make custards, meringues, and pâte à choux have little in common, yet each of these owes its unique texture to the humble egg. Flour is the pastry chef's central ingredient, and chocolate is certainly the most glamorous, but no ingredient is so versatile as the egg, as the range of dishes in this chapter demonstrates.

CUSTARDS

All custards rely on eggs for their richness and texture. Custards fall into two major categories, stirred and baked, which reflect the method by which they are produced.

STIRRED CUSTARDS

Stirred custards range from sturdy pastry cream, a custard also thickened with starch that will not curdle when brought to a boil, to delicate crème Anglaise, which will curdle if you look away for a second too long. Egg whites cooked alone will begin to set at 145°F, and yolks at about 155°F. Sugar and starch, among other ingredients, raise the temperature at which the eggs are cooked. Thus, the cooking temperature for stirred custards is variable. Most chefs strain all their stirred custards after cooking to ensure a perfectly smooth texture and to hide what few egg particles may have scrambled. After cooking, plastic wrap should be placed directly on the surface of stirred custards to prevent a skin from forming.

Pastry cream is a starch-thickened custard, usually made with milk, sugar, eggs/yolks, and a starch. The starch raises the temperature at which the sauce thickens and buffers the eggs to prevent scrambling. Thus, pastry cream can be brought to a boil without curdling, assuming that the sauce is stirred constantly. In fact, starch-thickened custards must be brought to a boil to kill alpha amylase. This enzyme, present in egg yolks, breaks down the amylose present in starch and causes the pastry cream to thin. Pastry cream is used for filling napoleons, eclairs, cakes, and tarts. Its consistency is usually quite thick, but chefs routinely adjust the formula to suit the product at hand. Cream pies require a pastry cream filling thick enough to slice, for example, but have a better texture if cream replaces some of the milk. Pastry cream can be combined with whipped cream for a light filling or used as the base for making buttercream.

Crème Anglaise is a classic rich dessert sauce, consisting of milk or cream, egg yolks and/or eggs, and sugar. It is a thin sauce, having the consistency of barely thickened cream. Because it contains no starch, it must be heated gently and never brought to a boil to prevent curdling. Crème Anglaise is fully cooked at 175°F. The visual test for doneness involves lifting the sauce-coated wooden spoon and running a horizontal streak through it with your fingertip. If the path remains clear, the sauce is done. Though commonly served as a dessert sauce with fruit desserts, soufflés, and warm unadorned cakes, crème Anglaise is extremely versatile. It can be used as an ice cream base, combined with chocolate to make an incredibly rich ganache, and beaten with butter to make a super creamy filling.

Lemon curd is a thick, intensely flavored custard made only with lemon juice, zest, sugar, butter, and eggs or yolks. Rich lemon curd, made with all yolks, is usually cooked gently in a double boiler. Other recipes may be made in a saucepan. Lemon curd is thick enough to be spread on a scone, and it is used as a filling for cakes and tarts. It can be lightened with whipped cream or used to flavor buttercream. Rich, creamy lemon tarts can be made by baking lemon curd in a precooked shell until smooth and set, and then glazing the surface. Lemon curd differs from the lemon filling used for lemon meringue pie. Lemon curd is too rich and intense to eat in any quantity, and lemon pie filling has added water and starch. Because acid prevents starch from swelling and thickening, lemon pie filling is thickened before the lemon juice is added.

BAKED CUSTARDS

Baked custards are rich with cream and eggs, especially egg yolks, which gives them their ultra-silky texture. With the exception of flan, baked custards have no defining flavor and leave much room for creativity. These custards generally contain little starch, if any, so they must be cooked carefully and slowly to prevent curdling. They are usually baked in a moderate to slow oven (350° to 300°F) in a protective water bath. A water bath, or bain-marie, is made by placing the custard dish in a larger pan that is filled with enough hot water to come halfway up the side of the custard dish. For ease of transport and to prevent sloshing the custard with water, the large pan containing the custard dish is placed directly on the extended oven rack *before* the water is poured in. A water bath insulates the custard and makes for slow, gentle, and even cooking. The custard warms as a whole, preventing the edges from cooking too fast. For crème brûlée, pot de crème, and flan, the milk or cream is usually scalded before being combined with the rest of the ingredients, so the mixture is almost as warm as the water bath. A towel may be placed under the custard dishes to insulate them from the hot bottom of the pan.

Custards are considered done when their top surface no longer wiggles, except in the very center when the pan is gently shaken. Each type of recipe, however, may have its own test for doneness. Custards will set upon cooling, and if they are overcooked they may crack or curdle. Prompt removal from the water bath is essential, since its residual heat will continue the cooking process. They are chilled before serving.

Crème brûlée translates as "burnt cream," referring to the crisp caramel (burnt sugar) topping of this custard. The ingredients for the custard are combined and poured into very shallow ceramic crème brûlée dishes. Like pot de crème, crème brûlée is served in its baking dish. The dishes are shallow and wide to provide the maximum surface area for creating the brittle caramel crust, the most beloved part of the dessert. After the crème brûlée has been chilled, a layer of sugar (white, brown, Brownulated, or confectioners') is evenly spread across the top of the custard and caramelized with a torch, salamander, or even under the broiler. Beginners will have better control with a torch, and should place the crème brûlée dishes on ice to prevent the custard from getting hot while the top is browned. When served, the custard should be cool underneath the warm, brittle crust.

Pot de crème is a custard baked in a pot-shaped cup, or any small decorative tea cup. It is like a silkier version of stovetop pudding. Pot de crème is baked in a water bath, covered, and chilled before serving.

Flan or **crème caramel** is a custard baked in a caramel-lined mold or ramekin. The caramel is prepared first, poured into the molds, and swirled to coat the sides. The ingredients for the custard are combined and poured into the prepared molds. Crème caramel is baked in a water bath until just set or a knife inserted in the center comes out clean. It should be promptly removed from the water bath and refrigerated until cold. Invert the crème caramel to unmold.

Many forget that the ubiquitous **cheesecake** is actually a custard baked in a crumb or cookie crust. The creamiest cheesecakes contain little if any flour and a high amount of added cream or sour cream, and are baked in a water bath for a smooth, even texture. Removing the cheesecake from the oven when it is just set and using a water bath will prevent the top from cracking. Dense New York–style cheesecakes are different. Their formula includes flour and more eggs and cream cheese than usual, but less liquid. These cakes start out in a very hot oven for 10 minutes, which causes them to rise and develop a golden top. They cook in a moderate oven, without a water bath, and rest in the turned-off oven for an hour after baking. When cool, New York–style cheesecakes fall a little, leaving a characteristic rim around the edge. Home cooks constantly fight soggy crusts resulting from ineffective springform pans, but professional bakers simply use round cake pans with 2- to 3-inch sides. If the pan has been greased, the cooled cheesecake is easily released after a pass or two over a warm burner.

Savory **quiches** are custards baked in a pastry crust, usually pâte brisée or pie dough. No water bath is used. The easiest way to make quiche is to blind-bake the pastry shells; fill them first with grated cheese and next with sautéed vegetables, bacon, or ham; and pour a custard mixture on top. Six whole eggs with enough half-and-half poured in to equal 3 cups makes a custard that sets to perfect consistency. Quiches are baked until set, or a knife comes out clean two-thirds of the way toward the center. They can be seasoned and flavored infinite ways, and they will always turn out well so long as the vegetables in the filling have been sautéed long enough to give up their water content. If they haven't, the custard will have a curdled appearance.

SOUFFLÉS

There are two types of soufflés: baked and chilled. Though sweet or savory would seem to divide soufflés into two categories, the method for both is virtually the same. Chilled or frozen soufflés, on the other hand, have nothing in common with baked soufflés—they are actually frozen mousses or Bavarians served in a soufflé dish.

Inexperienced cooks shudder at the word *soufflé*, which has been maligned as a difficult dish to master. Soufflés are leavened with beaten egg whites that have been folded in to an egg yolk–rich base. The base is flavored with fruit purée, chocolate, or even cheese, herbs, and other savory flavors. When a soufflé falls, usually technique is blamed: Overly beaten egg whites, which are dry, grainy, and incapable of expansion in the oven, and deflating the whites when folding them into the base are the first suspects. But structures that depend on eggs are ephemeral and prone to collapsing, since the structure of eggs (egg foam that surrounds the trapped air) is still soft when removed from the oven.

Flour-strengthened bases, however, prevent collapse by providing additional support. The base for a dessert soufflé is a flour-thickened custard made with egg yolks, much like pastry cream. For a savory soufflé, the base is like an egg yolk–enriched white sauce. Though less flour makes a more tender soufflé, restaurant chefs have relied on the presence of flour to ensure that the hot soufflé makes it to the table before it begins to shrink.

Soufflés are baked in straight-sided ceramic dishes made specifically for this purpose. The dishes can be large or individual size. It is

SOUFFLÉS

As with other egg white foams, always lighten the thick base with a quarter or third of the egg whites before folding in the rest. Fold gently and quickly with a balloon whisk that has few wires, or a large rubber spatula or flexible bench scraper.

Make sure the base is flavorful enough to taste good after it has been diluted with the egg whites. The base should taste too intense to be eaten on its own.

Create the most stable egg white foam possible by using fresh eggs (they make more stable foams) and room-temperature eggs (for best baking volume), and if possible, beat the whites in a copper bowl (stability). Of course, grease-free utensils are essential for good foam volume.

Strong convection ovens may blow the tops right off of delicate soufflés.

very important to butter the dishes well, and to coat them with something for the egg mixture to cling to as it rises. For dessert soufflés, sugar is used, and for savory ones, grated cheese or bread crumbs. The prepared dish is chilled before filling, which prevents the outside of the soufflé from setting before the inside cooks. If parchment collars are wrapped around the dish, extending their height, the dish may be filled to $1/2$ inch of the top of dish. Some soufflé formulas are strong enough to rise evenly without the help of a collar. The collar is removed before serving. With no collar, the dish should be filled from two-thirds to three-fourths full. Bake soufflés near the bottom of the oven for best lift.

One final note to pastry chefs: Chocolate soufflés fare better than other dessert soufflés. They are so stable that they can be assembled ahead, poured into prepared dishes, and baked as needed.

MERINGUES

As soon as an egg white foam is combined with sugar, it becomes a meringue. There are many types of meringues, such as French, Swiss, and Italian, and they are differentiated mainly by how the sugar is incorporated into the egg foam.

Meringues may be folded into cake batters for aeration, folded into a mousse for lightness, used as the base for buttercream, baked on a pie as a soft topping, or piped and baked alone to form crisp meringue cookies and cake layers. Soft meringue toppings usually have equal weights of sugar and egg white, but meringues that are baked in the oven to become hard have twice as much sugar as egg white.

The amount of sugar present is important to the stability of the meringue. An egg white is mostly water, but it also contains several proteins. The action of whipping the whites reconfigures the proteins, so that they become loosely linked to one another and to the water molecules, enabling pockets of air to remain trapped in a protein network. Overbeating the egg whites causes the proteins to tighten so much that they can no longer hold moisture, and water separates from the foam as it breaks down. At this point the egg proteins are no longer elastic and can not stretch to hold the expanding air bubbles in the oven. In meringue, the added sugar melts into the water of the egg white, making the solution more slippery, which lubricates the air cells. If the air cells are lubricated, they are less likely to hit one another and coalesce into larger air cells. This keeps the air cells small, which makes for a smoother, consistent foam. The sugar also interferes with protein linkages, just as it interferes with gluten formation, so that the meringue can be beaten longer without causing the proteins to tighten and squeeze water out. This means more air can be beaten into the foam and the foam stays moist. In the oven, the water evaporates while the egg proteins cook and set, leaving the sugar to dry and harden on the network of proteins. If less than an ounce of sugar per egg white is used, the meringue will not be stable.

MERINGUE-MAKING BASICS

Basic meringue, also called French meringue, is simply egg whites beaten with sugar. Eggs are easiest to separate when cold, but warm whites whip faster and provide better finished volume when used as a

USES FOR BAKED BASIC MERINGUE

Meringue with toasted, finely chopped nuts folded into it is piped into rounds and baked crisp for dacquoise, a dessert layered with buttercream. If the dessert is rectangular, it is a Marjolaine.

Meringue mushrooms are a standard accessory for bûche de Noël.

Vacherin is a baked meringue shell filled with practically anything, from ice cream to whipped cream, lemon curd, or fruit.

Meringue may also be flavored with cocoa or grated chocolate, citrus zests, or flavor extracts.

Pavlova is an Australian dessert of a decorative crisp meringue shell filled with whipped cream and fruit.

leavener in cakes and soufflés (for more about egg whites, see Chapter 4). Egg whites should be beaten with grease-free utensils. A copper bowl is useful for creating a more stable meringue that resists overwhipping, thanks to a reaction between the copper and conalbumin protein in the egg. For a foam with lots of small bubbles, beat the egg white at medium-high rather than high speed. Cream of tartar, an acid that prevents overcoagulation, is added near the beginning of mixing. The sugar, preferably superfine since it dissolves faster, is not added until the eggs are near the soft peak stage. If the sugar is added too soon or too quickly, the volume of the foam is reduced and the beating time must be increased to compensate. In small mixers, the sugar should be added to the running mixer a tablespoon at a time. In large mixers, the amount is increased to around a quarter of a cup. Beating in the sugar takes several minutes, after which the mixer speed is increased for a minute to finish the meringue. The meringue should be shiny and fluffy, with no grittiness from undissolved sugar.

Hard meringues are baked on parchment in a very low oven, between 200° and 225°F. The goal is to completely dry out the meringue without letting it color. Since meringue absorbs moisture from the air, many chefs bake meringue at the end of the day, turn off the oven, and leave the meringue overnight. The next day the meringue is cool but dry, and can immediately be wrapped in airtight containers for storage.

OTHER TYPES OF MERINGUE

Swiss meringue is valued for its stability (compared to basic or French meringue). It is heavier than either basic meringue or Italian meringue. Swiss meringue begins with the egg whites and sugar in the mixing bowl together. The bowl is placed on a low burner or in hot water, and the eggs are stirred and warmed until the sugar dissolves. When no grains of sugar can be detected, the whites are beaten at medium-high speed until stiff but not dry peaks form.

Italian meringue, the sweetest of the meringues, is a whipped egg white foam that is cooked with a hot sugar syrup. The meringue is safer than unpasteurized meringues used to top pies and baked Alaska. The egg whites are beaten until they barely hold firm peaks, then the syrup is poured down the inside of the bowl with the mixer running. The sugar syrup is cooked to the soft ball stage, 234° to 240°F. To ensure that the egg whites reach a high enough temperature to be cooked (160°F), a warm mixing bowl and room-temperature whites are essential. The cooked meringue is then beaten until it has cooled to room temperature. An alternative method for making Italian meringue is to combine sugar and egg whites in a mixing bowl and whip them over simmering water until they reach 160°F. This second method works with a hand-held mixer. Technically, Italian meringue is the most stable since it is cooked.

MERINGUE FOR PIES

Pies are usually topped with basic meringue and baked until golden. This is tricky business, however, since the interior and exterior cook at vastly different rates. An overcooked meringue will form beads of moisture on its surface from the proteins coagulating so much that they squeeze out moisture. A meringue that did not cook through in the center weeps as it slowly dissolves and releases its liquid. With pies, it is possible to do both things at once. Two factors lead to success. First, the filling needs to be hot when the meringue is applied in order to assure that it cooks through. Second, a hot oven temperature (425°F) for a shorter period of time will prevent overcooking (see lemon meringue pie, pages 233–234).

Since shrinkage can be a problem with meringue-topped pies, as well as weeping and long-term stability, many chefs and cookbook authors have taken to adding a thickened cornstarch-water solution to basic whipped meringue. The addition of starch eliminates all these problems and makes the pie easier to slice neatly. It takes only a teaspoon or two of cornstarch to stabilize meringue for a pie. The cornstarch must be brought to a boil in just enough water so that it can be beaten into the meringue without clumping. This is more efficient for large-scale use than for one pie: About 2 teaspoons of cornstarch should be cooked with ¹/₃ cup water. A couple of teaspoons of this mixture will stabilize the meringue for one pie.

For pies that have cold fillings, Italian meringue is a good option. It is stable since it is precooked, and quick browning under a broiler or with a blowtorch will finish it nicely. One last option is to whisk the whites and sugar over simmering water until their temperature reaches 160°F and then beat them. This makes a fully cooked meringue; however, like Swiss meringue, it is heavier than normal.

Pasteurized egg whites or powdered pasteurized egg whites should be used for any meringue that may not reach temperatures high enough to be fully cooked.

BUTTERCREAM

Buttercream is the single most important type of frosting and filling for cakes and desserts. It comes in a variety of textures and flavors— chocolate, vanilla, praline, coffee, banana rum, lemon, orange, and caramel are just a few of the possibilities. Buttercream is simply softened butter that has been gradually beaten into an egg foam until smooth, creamy, and light. The butter is softened, but not melting, and should be added in small increments to the running mixer. The egg foam should be close to the same temperature as the butter. Usually during the beating stage, the buttercream may briefly appear grainy and ruined, but by the time all the butter has been added it will be silky smooth.

There are many styles of buttercream, and as a component they encourage much creativity. Flavored components, such as chocolate, pastry cream, or fruit purée, can be added to Italian, French, and Swiss buttercream so long as the weight of the flavoring is between 25 and 50 percent of the weight of the butter in the frosting. Adding pure liquids, like liquors, may cause the buttercream to have a curdled appearance if more than a few tablespoons are added.

Buttercreams should be stored in the refrigerator, where they will last a week. Any buttercream with pastry cream or crème Anglaise will have a shorter shelf life. Buttercreams may also be frozen. Before using any chilled buttercream, it must stand at room temperature until softened. Once soft, it may be stirred or beaten until fluffy. If it has a slightly broken appearance, very gently warm the sides of the bowl while stirring constantly. If the buttercream still refuses to behave, beating in a small amount of melted butter should do the trick. Usually the curdled appearance is a result of temperature variations within the mixture.

TYPES OF BUTTERCREAM

Swiss buttercream is valued for its stability. It begins with Swiss meringue, into which the softened butter is beaten. It is heavier than Italian buttercream but faster to make. It should not be overworked during spreading and piping, as it quickly melts.

Italian buttercream is made by beating softened butter into Italian meringue. It is the lightest and sweetest of the buttercreams, and it is the safest way to make egg white–based buttercream if pasteurized eggs are unavailable. Italian buttercream is prettier to spread and swirl on cakes, and holds a piped edge well.

Classic **French buttercream** is based on yolks, not whites, which makes it richer than Swiss or Italian buttercreams. The initial preparation, beating hot sugar syrup into fluffy egg yolks, is called a pâte à bombe, and is a component of other desserts such as frozen mousses. French buttercream can be lightened with Italian meringue for the best of both worlds—rich and light.

Pastry cream can be used as a base for buttercream, making a soft, creamy filling that seems lighter and less rich than regular buttercream. This type of buttercream is called **crème mousseline**, and though it may have less butter than standard buttercream, the weight of the pastry cream prevents it from being lighter. Crème Anglaise can also be used as a base for buttercream, but more butter must be beaten into it to prevent curdling. Both of these mixtures are more perishable than Italian or Swiss buttercream. Naturally, to beat butter into pastry cream or crème Anglaise, both components need to be the same temperature or the mixture may appear curdled.

MOCK BUTTERCREAMS

Decorator's buttercream is made by beating shortening and confectioners' sugar together with a small amount of milk, water, and possibly powdered egg whites. Novices use this buttercream to practice piping and decorative techniques, since it does not melt easily when held in a piping bag, as real buttercream will. Many supermarkets use similar frostings, since they are fluffy, hold piped edges and shapes, have a longer shelf life, and are more resistant to warm temperatures. They lack the richness and depth of flavor of other frostings, and they are often cloyingly sweet.

Homemade American layer cakes are often frosted by what is known as **confectioners' sugar buttercream**, an overly sweet and rather grainy topping made by beating butter or shortening and confectioners' sugar together, perhaps with added milk, cream, or vanilla. Some customers prefer it to buttercream. The addition of a small amount of milk, cream, or sour cream and powdered egg whites will make it much smoother, creamier, and lighter. There is no easy way to compensate for the sweetness.

PÂTE À CHOUX

Pâte à choux, the dough used to make cream puffs, eclairs, profiteroles, and croquembuches, does not fit well into other egg categories. Made by beating eggs into boiled water, butter, and flour, pâte à choux does not resemble any other type of pastry. But since the high proportion of eggs makes it rise, puff, and gives the product its distinctive character, pâte à choux belongs with egg cookery as well as anywhere else.

Choux paste, as it is called in English, is more of a gooey paste than a dough. And this pasty consistency signifies a well-balanced formula.

Choux paste begins in a saucepan, where the water, milk, and butter are brought to a boil. The pot is removed from the heat, and all at once the flour is stirred in, creating a very thick paste. This paste is stirred constantly over low heat only until the flour has lost its cooked flavor and the mixture pulls away from the sides of the pan. Just like a roux, which loses its thickening ability (the ability to hold liquid) the longer it is cooked, the flour in pâte à choux will not be able to absorb the maximum amount of egg if it is overcooked.

The flour mixture is next transferred to a mixing bowl and beaten with the paddle attachment until it is warm but not hot. One at a time, the eggs are beaten into the flour mixture. Since no two eggs in a dozen may weigh the same, the recipe for choux paste is not fixed. Rather, the baker is instructed to test the batter by watching how it flows off a wooden spoon. If it drops in large blobs, it is too thick and another egg (or part of an egg) should be added. If it runs in a steady stream, it is too thin. The perfect consistency is in the middle, which yields a dough that can be piped without oozing but has plenty of egg to be as light and high as possible. As soon as the mixture is shiny and falls into a drooped peak when pulled, it has absorbed enough egg and is ready to be piped. Usually a $1/2$-inch plain tip is used to pipe eclairs and cream puffs, though a star tip may be used for eclairs. Choux paste is very sticky and should be cooked on parchment. Using the paste to glue the corners of the paper down prevents the paper from lifting in convection ovens, though strong oven fans may cause the puffs to rise unevenly. Like soufflés, pâte à choux gets the best lift near the heat source toward the bottom of the oven. That said, no restaurant or bakery has the time to bake one pan at a time.

There are two schools of thought about oven temperature. Some chefs start the choux paste at a high (425°F) temperature, reducing it after 15 minutes. Other chefs preheat the oven to a moderate temperature (350°F), increasing the temperature as soon as the sheet pan goes in the oven to give the puffs a burst of heat. Either method works well. After the puffs are cooked, the oven is turned off, its door propped open, and the puffs are left to dry. Another method of preventing the puffs from getting soggy is to pierce them or even slice them to let steam escape. Before they are filled, the eggy interiors are usually hollowed out with a knife. The cooked pastries freeze well.

TIPS

HINTS FOR CHOUX PASTE

Choux paste dough may be glazed with an egg wash to add shine.

A very small amount of sugar may be added to the dough, but too much causes overbrowning.

Milk makes the puffs richly flavored but tender; using all water makes them crisp, and using half milk and half water is a compromise.

Choux paste is usually made with whole eggs, but for crisper puffs a few egg whites may be substituted.

All-purpose flour or bread flour may be used. Bread flour, which is higher in protein, can absorb more moisture (egg in this case) and makes a lighter puff.

CHAPTER 16

PIES AND TARTS

T hough apple pie may be our national symbol, Americans do not differentiate between pies and tarts except on the basis of size. A tart is just a shorter pie, right? Our pies and tarts appear to be different versions of the same thing. In this country, you are just as likely to see a chocolate tart as a chocolate pie, a key lime tart as a key lime pie, a caramel pecan tart as a caramel pecan pie. This is not true, however, in Europe, and it is, in fact, a recent development in this country. This chapter is traditional, keeping classic tarts, like frangipane, in one category and classic pies, such as pumpkin, in another.

PASTRY DOUGHS

Pastry doughs used for pies and tarts are distinguished from other doughs by their mixing method. Generally, a good pie crust is flaky and crisp but tender, and this texture is a result of how the fat is incorporated into the flour.

The best **American pie dough** is made with a combination of butter and shortening, which is a happy compromise between the wonderful flavor of butter and the superior flaky texture provided by shortening. Americans prize texture over flavor when it comes to pie crust, so all-shortening is often the norm. Lard has fallen out of favor. Good-quality lard, with its large crystal fat structure, makes the flakiest pie. **Pâte brisée** is the French version of pie dough. It is made with all butter, which makes it wonderfully flavored but not as flaky as American pie dough.

Pâte sucrée, or sweet dough, is not flaky. Usually it is made as if it were a cookie dough, using the creaming method. Pâte sucrée has egg instead of water, which changes its texture. The egg white makes the baked dough crisp, but the emulsifier and protein-rich yolk binds the dough into a cohesive mass. Pâte sucrée is stronger and easier to roll into large pieces than the other doughs.

DOUGH INGREDIENTS

The type of **fat** used in pie pastry has a profound effect on the texture of the finished crust. Plastic fats, fats that are solid at room temperature, make for flaky crusts because they remain in pea-sized lumps and interrupt the gluten at irregular intervals. Oil, on the other hand, would coat the flour so thoroughly that very little gluten would form and the crust would be overly tender and crumbly rather than crisp and flaky. In the heat of the oven, the pieces of fat melt into the dough, leaving an air space behind. As they melt, steam forms and causes the dough to puff slightly, making the pie crust flaky. Butter contains water, so ounce for ounce it provides less fat than shortening or lard. Shortening and lard melt at a higher temperature and create a flakier crust. At the same time, these fats are pliable and easy to work with over a wide range of temperatures. Butter must be kept very cold to hold its shape in the oven until the dough around it begins to set, and it must be cool when the dough is mixed and rolled so that it doesn't begin to melt into the flour. Though shortening is the easiest and most reliable fat to use, butter has superior flavor and never leaves a waxy aftertaste. The best pie doughs are a compromise between taste and texture.

The **flour** used in pie dough is usually all-purpose, or an even softer pastry flour, in order to minimize gluten formation. Pastry flour is made from soft winter wheat, and if it is not available, it can be approximated by combining three parts all-purpose flour with one part cake flour. A side effect of using cake flour is less browning owing to its acidity. High-protein flours are avoided since they will make a tough crust.

Acidic ingredients, such as vinegar, lemon juice, or sour cream, make pastry tender by breaking down the gluten proteins. Acidic doughs brown less readily.

Sugar promotes browning, and in any quantity it interferes with gluten formation, tenderizing the crust. Dairy products have naturally occurring sugars and will also promote browning.

Protein, from dairy products or high-protein flours, promotes browning.

Using a fatty liquid, like sour cream or an egg yolk, instead of all water to bind the dough will result in a more tender crust.

DOUGH PREPARATION

MIXING To make flaky pie dough or pâte brisée, all the ingredients should be as cold as possible. First, the flour and salt are put in the bowl of the mixer. Using the paddle attachment on low speed, toss small (1-inch) pieces of cold fat into the running mixer a few at a time. If several different fats are used, add the butter first since it is the hardest and shortening last since it is the softest. The fat is flattened and cut into the flour until it forms pea-sized lumps; it should not be overmixed. Lumps of fat should be clearly visible. With the mixer still running, slowly drizzle ice cold water into the mixer bowl, just until a shaggy dough forms. Since water contributes to gluten formation, which toughens the crust, the minimum amount should be added. Getting the dough too wet also makes it difficult to handle. The dough can be lightly kneaded to gather up the dry flour particles. Then it is scaled and formed into discs. If all the dough will be used soon, place the discs on a sheet pan, cover with plastic, and chill. Otherwise wrap the discs individually and freeze for later use.

RESTING THE DOUGH After mixing and scaling, refrigerate the dough for several hours or overnight. During this time the flour becomes more evenly hydrated, which makes the dough easier to roll and gives the finished crust a superior texture. This rest time also relaxes any gluten that has been developed, which facilitates rolling and prevents the shrinkage that would result if the dough were immediately rolled, shaped, and baked. At this point, some chefs like to do a turn on the dough, but this is optional.

ROLLING AND SHAPING THE DOUGH Dough for pies and tarts is rolled to a $\frac{1}{8}$-inch thickness. A dough sheeter makes fast, consistent work of rolling pie dough. When placing the dough into the pie or tart pan, take care not to push or stretch the dough, as it will spring back in the oven. Trim the overhanging dough to $^1/_2$ inch, fold over, and decoratively crimp. After rolling and shaping, the dough for blind-baked shells should rest in the refrigerator for a half hour to relax the gluten. It is especially important to chill butter-rich doughs, which prevents the butter from melting too rapidly in the oven and collapsing the decorative edge. The unbaked pie shells may be frozen if not needed right away.

PREBAKING PIE AND TART SHELLS Blind baking pie or tart shells is necessary for all cream pies, chiffon pies, fresh fruit tarts, lemon meringue pie, and any filling that does not require additional cooking. Prebaking is also helpful for pies with wet fillings, such as pecan, pumpkin, custard, and quiche, that may make the dough soggy. Blind baking is done at a high temperature, usually 400° to 425°F, to immediately set the crust and promote flakiness. The rolled and crimped dough should be well rested to prevent shrinkage and cold to prevent sliding and collapsing. The pastry dough is docked, or pricked with a fork, if the shell will not be baked again with a liquid filling. Docking prevents large air bubbles from causing the pastry to rise unevenly, but some of the holes may remain after baking. Pouring a thin liquid filling into such a shell may cause leakage and sticking. However, chiffon and mousse fillings do fine.

Well-stocked bakeries place empty pie pans on top of the dough. This is called double panning, and it is done to prevent the dough from puffing as it bakes. The pans can be filled with dry rice or beans, or inverted onto sheet pans and weighted with a sheet pan on top. If extra pans are not available, line the chilled pie shells with parchment and pour dry beans or rice into the shell. After 15 minutes, when the dough is set, the pie weights or pan is removed from the shell to let the crust brown.

Chefs will go to great lengths to keep pie and tart shells crisp. Some pour leftover cake crumbs onto the bottom before adding the filling. Others brush the baked bottom crust with egg or fruit preserves, and then briefly bake the crust again until it is dry and sealed. Tart and cream pie shells may be brushed with melted chocolate. Obviously, this takes additional time. If the desserts are promptly sold or served, the crust will be in good condition.

PAN CHOICE The goal of pie making is to cook the crust as quickly as possible, getting it brown and crisp. Often this is much more difficult than properly thickening the fruit. Upon standing, all pie crusts soften as they absorb moisture from the filling. The key to a crisp crust is cooking the dough so quickly that it sets before absorbing too much liquid from the filling. With fruit pies this isn't a problem, but custard fillings like pumpkin should be placed in a shell that is at least partially prebaked.

The best pans for baking pies are inexpensive thin metal pie plates, either dark or light. Though dark pans absorb heat better than shiny metal pans, which reflect heat, dark pie plates are usually heavy. Heavyweight pans, perhaps because they take longer to initially heat up in the oven, do not make as crisp a crust as a thin pan. Ceramic and glass do not fare as well as metal. Bakeries, as opposed to restaurants, use disposable aluminum pie pans made for carryout service. Once filled, these pans should be transported on sheet pans for support.

Baking near the bottom of the oven is best for creating a crisp bottom crust. However, an almost equally good alternative is to place sheet pans on oven racks and preheat them before placing the pies in the oven. The hot sheet pans will help the bottom crust cook faster, and will capture any pie liquid that dribbles over. Pies baked on sheet pans should be turned midway through the cooking time.

GLAZING Double-crust pies are usually brushed with an egg wash before baking (egg whisked with a little water and salt to make it smooth) for color and shine. Butter, milk, or cream are used for mere browning. Cinnamon sugar or coarse-grained sugar can be sprinkled onto the wash for textural appeal.

OTHER TYPES OF CRUSTS

Crumb crusts are not a type of pastry dough; however, they are used to hold many pie and tart fillings, not to mention cheesecakes. Key lime pie, peanut butter pie, and mousse pie are commonly served in crumb crusts. Easy to prepare, crumb crusts are made from crackers or cookies that are crushed or finely ground and combined with enough melted butter to clump firmly when squeezed. The mixture is pressed into pie pans. If sweet cookies are used, such as amaretti or biscotti, no additional sugar is used. Graham crackers, ginger snaps, and chocolate cookie crumbs benefit from a small amount of sugar. Finely chopped toasted nuts can be added for extra richness and depth of flavor. Crumb crusts are baked for 8 to 10 minutes at 350°F, which binds the crust, making it crisp rather than merely crumbly.

FRUIT PIES

Fruit pies of excellent quality can be made from IQF (individual quick frozen) fruit as well as fresh fruit. Freezing makes available year-round seasonal fruits of consistent quality, though fresh, ripe fruit is almost always preferable. Fresh fruit is less reliable than it used to be, since long-distance shipping has necessitated picking and packing the fruit before it is perfectly tender, ripe, and sweet. Since some fruits never get sweeter after picking while others do, creating a pie of consistent quality is challenging. Frozen fruit can be picked later, when the fruit may be too tender to ship, since it is usually processed nearby. Obviously, the variability of fruit requires adjustments in the amount of sugar and thickener. Fresh, ripe fruit at its peak almost always gives off the most juice.

METHODS OF PREPARATION

HOMEMADE METHOD Fruit pies with superior texture are made by placing the uncooked fruit mixture (which includes sugar, spices, starch of some sort, flavorings, and perhaps juice) into pastry dough. The filling is sometimes dotted with butter before it is topped with pastry dough. The dough is trimmed, crimped to seal, and vented. Most starch-thickened pies, such as those that contain flour or cornstarch, must be baked until the filling at the center of the pie is bubbling in order to properly set up.

The telltale sign of a homemade pie is the empty air space between the fruit and the top crust, created when the mounded fruit cooks down after the structure of the pie dough sets. Unbaked pies can be frozen and baked as needed with no noticeable reduction in quality. Fresh or frozen fruit can be used, but pies made with frozen fruit should be baked or frozen immediately (before the fruit thaws) to prevent the crust from becoming soggy.

PRECOOKED FRUIT OR FRUIT JUICE METHOD Another method employed for pie making is to cook and thicken the fruit mixture on the stove top, let it cool, then pour it into unbaked pie shells. This eliminates the air gap between fruit and crust, since the fruit has already been cooked, and it also eliminates the long wait for the center of the filling to reach a boil, since the starch has already been thickened. The major drawback of this method is that the fruit is cooked twice, once by itself and again in the pie shell, yielding a pie with the consistency of baby food. Precooking the fruit works best if the filling goes into blind-baked shells, but that only works for single-crust pies.

COMBINATION METHOD A compromise between the two methods calls for only the liquid juices from the standing fruit mixture to be precooked. Once thickened, the juices are combined with the uncooked fruit in a bowl. When cool, the filling can be arranged in pie shells and baked. Naturally, the uncooked fruit will release more juice as it cooks in the oven, so the juices must be adequately thickened to compensate. This method requires the extra step of separately cooking the fruit juice, but it eliminates the need to wait for the filling to bubble at the center of the pie. In large, well-filled pies, the crust is golden and the fruit is hot long before the juices actually boil in the center of the pie. This often requires careful watching of the crust, whose edges may need to be covered with foil to prevent overbrowning.

THICKENERS Several factors affect the choice of thickener for fruit pies. For a detailed discussion of thickeners, see Chapter 7. Basic considerations are whether or not the pie will be frozen, reheated before serving, should have a clear or opaque appearance, or has an open or lattice top crust.

- Pies that will be frozen will not weep moisture from the gel (syneresis) of the cooked filling if root starches or a waxy cornstarch is used.

- Pies that will be reheated and served warm stay thicker if grain starches, such as cornstarch or flour, are used.

- For shiny, transparent juices that don't dull the bright color of fruit, like berries, use a root starch to thicken.

- Instant tapioca granules should not be used for pies with a lattice top or open-topped pies with decorative cut-outs. The pellets must be submerged in liquid to dissolve or they will remain hard. Double-crust pies hold in moisture and steam, but open pies expose fruit and tapioca granules to the hot, dry oven air.

Custard Pies (Baked Custards)

Custard pie is an umbrella term for any egg-thickened pie, like pumpkin pie, but here it refers to a regional specialty pie that is a creamy custard baked in a pie shell. The pie shell is at least partially baked, since the custard has little, if any, starch and requires gentle heat. Pie dough, of course, does best in a hot oven. Like other baked custards, the pie is removed when the center is just set.

The key to great **sweet potato** and **pumpkin pie** is using a partially baked pie shell. These pies are easy to throw together, since their ingredients need only be whisked together before going into the shell. Canned pumpkin purée is such a good product that there is no reason to roast and purée pumpkin in a pastry kitchen. Sweet potatoes, on the other hand, are best roasted in house. If your pies keep cracking on top and overcooking isn't the culprit, additional whole eggs or yolks may do the trick.

Key lime pie was not originally a baked custard. The recipe came from the Florida Keys, with ingredients convenient to locals: Key limes and canned sweetened condensed milk. Before refrigeration and without land for grazing dairy herds, canned milk was the norm in that hot area. Home cooks whisked egg yolks, the sweetened milk, lime juice, and zest together and poured it into a prepared pie shell. The mixture was not even baked, since the acid in the limes caused the proteins in the milk and egg to set without any heat. The egg whites were used to make a meringue topping (see Anderson, p. 337). Modern pies are baked unless pasteurized yolks are available. Graham cracker crust and a whipped cream topping are modern changes to this old recipe. Tart Persian limes are more available than sweet key limes, and taste perfectly fine.

Pecan pie is a sweet, translucent, corn syrup–based custard into which toasted pecans are stirred. Bourbon, rum, brown sugar, and butter are common additions. As with other custard pies, partially baking the pie shell prevents sogginess. Pecan pie freezes well.

CREAM PIES (STIRRED CUSTARDS)

Cream pies, also called pudding pies, are classic American pies. Basically, they are pastry cream poured into a prebaked pie shell and topped with whipped cream. The filling is usually richer and creamier than pastry cream, though it must be thick enough to slice. Like pastry cream, it is a stirred custard. Chocolate, banana, and coconut are the most common flavors. Banana cream pie and coconut cream pie begin with a vanilla base, and simply have sliced bananas or toasted coconut for flavor. Peanut butter pie is a cream pie also, but it is not a custard. Usually it is made from beating peanut butter, cream cheese, and confectioners' sugar until smooth, and then folding in whipped cream.

The filling for **lemon meringue pie** is a stirred lemon custard, tart but less intense than lemon curd. The water, sugar, and starch are cooked before the eggs and lemon juice are added, since starch's ability to thicken is impaired by the acidity of so much lemon juice. The filling is then carefully brought to a boil, which kills the enzyme in eggs that feeds on starch and thins the gel. The filling should be immediately poured into a prebaked pie shell and topped with meringue. If the filling is not hot, the meringue will not be cooked all the way through by the time it is browned. The meringue must touch the crust all the way around the pie, or it will shrink and pull away in the oven. The meringue is baked to both cook it and to lightly brown its surface. Eggs are cooked when they reach 160°F. Generally, the pie is baked quickly at a high temperature (425°F) for a topping that contains only a few whites, but longer at a lower temperature (350°F) if a lot of meringue is used. Overcooking causes water to bead on the surface of the meringue and undercooking causes weeping. Humid days wreak havoc on meringues, as their sugar content causes them to attract moisture in the air and become sticky, if not downright weepy. See Chapter 15 for pie meringue methods and alternatives.

CHIFFON PIES

Chiffon pies are gelatin-stabilized fruit purées to which beaten egg whites have been added. The beaten whites are folded into the barely warm gelatin mixture and mounded into a prebaked pie shell. Once chilled, the pie is like a sliceable mousse. Chiffon pies can be any flavor. When pasteurized egg whites are not available, Italian meringue may be used instead, if the sugar in the recipe is reduced.

MOUSSE PIES

Any mousse can be served in a prepared shell or crumb crust, though chocolate mousse piped into tiny tart shells is the most common variety.

TARTS

There are more varieties of tarts than pies, making them difficult to classify coherently. In the United States, where pie reigns supreme, favorite pie flavors and styles are adapted to tart form. Beyond that, tarts often showcase nuts, dried fruit, caramel, or chocolate ganache. And that's aside from the classic fresh fruit tart, French apple tart, linzer tart, and frangipane-fruit tart.

The only givens in this category are that tarts are short and shallow compared to pies, and that they are baked in fluted pans with removable bottoms. The classic doughs used for tarts are pâte brisée, essentially a sturdy all-butter pie dough, and pâte sucrée, which is like a cookie dough. Both of these doughs are firm enough to hold the filling when removed from the pan.

In most cases, tart shells are prebaked before filling. All the usual glazing tricks can be employed for keeping the crust separate from the wet filling (see Glazing, page 229). European chefs sometimes line the tart shell with a layer of sponge cake so thin that it is hard to detect.

FRESH FRUIT TARTS are made with sweet dough (pâte sucrée) and topped with pastry cream and fresh berries and fruit. The fruit is glazed with melted and strained apricot or currant preserves to keep it fresh and make it visually appealing.

FRENCH APPLE TART is made with pâte brisée or even regular pie dough, a layer of applesauce, and a top layer of very thinly sliced peeled apples. The slices are arranged in a decorative pattern. The entire assemblage is baked together, and the tart is glazed with strained apricot preserves after it cools.

LINZER TART is made from a soft cookie dough scented with toasted nuts and spices. A layer of dough is pressed into the pan and spread with raspberry preserves. The dough is then piped or rolled into ropes by hand to form a lattice top. After the tart is baked and cooled, it will be crispy at the edges and chewy in the middle. Linzer tart freezes well.

FRANGIPANE is not a dough or a custard, but something in between. Made from almond paste, toasted ground almonds, butter, sugar, eggs, and flour, frangipane is a component used in many desserts. Since frangipane is sweet, it is best paired with a pâte brisée crust. The tart shell is partially baked, spread with frangipane, and usually topped with nuts or fruit such as sour cherries, plums, or wine-poached pears. The assembled tart is baked until the frangipane is puffed and golden.

GALETTES

Galettes are essentially rustic free-form pies. The dough is softer than pie dough, but flaky. To make a galette, a small amount of fruit filling is placed on a piece of dough rolled into a round. The edges of the dough are folded over the fruit, leaving the center open. The dough is brushed with water or an egg wash, and sprinkled with sugar. It is baked at a higher temperature than a fruit pie, around 425°F, to make the dough as flaky as possible. Since a galette holds less filling than a pie, it is possible to cook it quickly at a high temperature. The fruit used for the filling can be fresh or frozen, but it should not be overly juicy. Sugar and cornstarch (or flour) should be tossed with the fruit before it is placed on the dough.

QUICHE

Quiche is a savory custard pie. It is discussed with egg cookery (Chapter 15), since many consider it an egg dish more than a pie.

CHAPTER 17

COOKIES

T he term "cookie" covers an absurdly wide array of baked goods. Only the convenient snack-portion size serves to unify the disparate products, such as gooey brownies, crunchy biscotti, and candylike florentines. Brandy snaps, lace cookies, and florentines are related to candies, and ephemeral little madeleines are certainly small sponge cakes. The Dutch gave us the word *koekje* (*koekie*), literally "little cake," that became the umbrella term for all those small beloved treats.

Cookies are so easy to make that they are seldom given serious consideration. This is unfortunate because elegant, well-decorated, and nicely presented cookies are what turn window-shoppers into customers. Most cookie doughs can be made ahead and frozen, making stockpiling for the busy holiday season a convenience that doesn't compromise quality. As an added bonus, many finished cookies have a longer shelf life than cakes or pies, valuable in keeping the display case filled and appealing.

CONTROLLING SPREAD AND TEXTURE WITH INGREDIENTS

People (chefs included) have specific expectations of cookies. For some, a chewy cookie is best and for others only a crispy cookie will do. The following ingredients and their effects on cookie doughs will help you manipulate any recipe to attain the desired texture.

Fat is key in determining the final texture of a cookie. The small amount of water present in **butter** causes doughs to spread more than shortening. Butter has a sharper melting point than shortening, meaning that it can retain its shape over a narrow temperature range (10 to 20 degrees) before turning to liquid. This factor also affects spread. Butter-based cookies are very crisp. The exception are cookie doughs that contain a significant amount of egg, which gives cookies a soft cakey quality. **Shortening** melts at a higher temperature. Shortening-based doughs spread less and make cookies that are crisp at the edges and chewy in the center. The amount of water in **margarines** varies, but the higher the fat content, the less spread. Combining butter and shortening will create cookies that stand taller without compromising flavor. An all-shortening–based sugar cookie has little flavor, and an all-margarine one will have an artificial taste. Many cookies, like sugar, spritz, and shortbread, get their primary flavor from butter. **Oils** are rarely used in cookie recipes. They provide a crisp, even crumbly texture to cookies if little egg is present, such as with nut sandies, and are used in fruit-based cookies, such as apple or pumpkin, which are soft.

Choosing a dry sugar or a syrup will drastically change the finished texture of the cookie. **Granulated sugar** is the standard. **Moist brown sugar**–based doughs will spread more and stay moist after baking, while **confectioners' sugar**, with its added cornstarch, prevents spread and keeps the texture dry. Syrups increase browning, and when used in any quantity have a softening effect on texture. **Molasses** and **honey** both contain the hygroscopic sugar fructose, which attracts moisture from the air to keep baked goods soft. Small amounts of **glucose syrup (corn syrup)** will brown without softening cookies, but check the label before using corn syrup for this purpose, as some corn syrups contain significant amounts of fructose.

High-protein flours can absorb more moisture (from eggs or the water content of butter) and therefore lessen spread. The higher the protein content, the more the cookies will brown. **Bleached flours** produce paler cookies than unbleached. **Cake flour** is bleached by chlorination and is more acidic than other flours, so it makes cookies that spread little and remain pale (acidity decreases browning but makes the batter set faster). Excess moisture in doughs made with low-protein flour will turn to steam in the oven, creating a cakelike puff, since low-protein flours absorb less liquid than gluten-forming high-protein flours. Because cookies contain a considerable amount of fat and very little moisture, the danger of toughness from too much gluten development is small. Still, low-protein soft wheat flours, like cake flour, produce cookies that are more tender. Obviously **unbleached all-purpose flours** (not southern) are in the middle: They will spread a little more than cake or high-protein flours, and provide moderate browning capabilities.

Whole eggs will soften cookies and provide puff. If a recipe that calls for one whole egg is reduced to an **egg white**, the cookie will be more crisp than chewy. Using a single **yolk** will provide a little moisture from the fat but still help to bind the batter, reducing spread. Tender and crumbly doughs like shortbread and pâte sucrée will be more stable with a yolk or two (even whole eggs can be used for very large batch sizes) without compromising the rich, crisp texture.

Leaveners differ in their effect on cookie doughs. In general, batters and doughs are acidic. **Baking powder** is designed with both acids and alkali that neutralize each other, therefore it does not neutralize the acidity of the batter. This acidity prevents the dough from spreading too much, but it can also inhibit browning. In butter cookie recipes, baking powder leavens more and makes the cookies seem dry compared to baking soda. It is worth experimenting with leavening to adjust texture. **Baking soda** by far is the most common leavener employed. Many cookie recipes call for more baking soda than is needed to neutralize the acidity of the batter. The Toll House recipe on a package of Nestlé's semisweet chocolate chips is a good example: 1 teaspoon of baking soda is used with only $2^{1}/_{4}$ cups of flour. The dough's acidity would be neutralized by less than an eighth of a teaspoon, but here the baking soda helps the cookies to brown. No unpleasant residue is discerned above the flavors of the brown sugar, vanilla, and chocolate. If your cookies are pale, a small amount of baking soda can help promote browning.

Very small amounts of **milk** or **cream** will aid in browning, but liquids in general make for a cakelike texture. This is especially true of **sour cream, buttermilk,** and **yogurt,** which add puff to cookies.

Oven Temperature and Dough Temperature

Oven and dough temperatures contribute to spread and browning. Obviously, higher oven temperatures will promote browning, but they also help the dough to set faster, thus halting spread. Chilling the dough before it goes into the oven also reduces spread: The cold dough melts more slowly, letting the heat of the oven set the crust before the cookie has spread too much.

The following section provides tips for handling a few general types of cookies. It is a brief discussion that in no way attempts to describe the vast array of cookies out there. For madeleines, see the section on sponge cakes in Chapter 14.

DROP COOKIES

American classics such as chocolate chip and oatmeal raisin cookies fall under this category. Because their doughs are so similar, I include ginger snaps and peanut butter cookies here also, though technically they are shaped cookies. Drop cookies are almost always made by the creaming method (see Chapter 14), though creaming the fat with the sugar is not essential. Wonderful chocolate chip cookies can be made with melted butter, for example, but the yield of cookies per batch will drop by 30 percent. The creaming method apparently builds volume by trapping air in the dough.

ROLLED, SHAPED, AND ICEBOX COOKIES

This category includes cut-outs and slice-and-bake cookies whose doughs are chilled before use. Sugar cookies, gingerbread cut-outs, and checkerboard cookies fall into this category. Slice-and-bake icebox cookies are doughs that are shaped into logs and chilled before being sliced and baked. Refrigeration is essential for handling and rolling butter-rich doughs. In the case of slice-and-bake cookies, it makes the dough stiff enough to slice.

The best rolled cookies exhibit minimum spread and retain their cut edges during baking. The trick is to keep the fat content high without destroying the decorative shape. All too often, an excess of flour is added to prevent spread and make the dough easier to handle during the rolling and cutting steps. These cookies are hard and dry rather than crisp and buttery. Keeping the dough cold prevents fat-rich doughs from becoming sticky, and chilling the cut-outs again before baking helps retain their shape in the oven.

Rolling buttery doughs between sheets of waxed paper, by hand or using a sheeter, helps minimize contact with the dough and makes transferring the rolled dough to the freezer easy. Many chefs cut out shapes, but remove only the trimmings. This leaves the cut-outs on the parchment, which can be dragged onto a sheet pan.

BAR COOKIES

Bar cookies encompass a broad range of textures, from moist brownies and blondies, made from batters baked in a pan, to layered bars created from components such as linzer dough, shortbread, jam, lemon curd, fruit, cream cheese filling, and streusel. They are generally easy to assemble and keep well, either assembled and frozen unbaked or portioned and wrapped after baking.

PIPED COOKIES

Of all types, piped cookies require the most care and precision. Butter cookies, like langues de chat (cat's tongues), are buttery crisp and thin, easily ruined by too much spread. Spritz dough must hold its edge to be decorative, and fluted cookies like Viennese fingers lose their charm if they spread. Adding more flour is not an option; it would make the langues de chat less palatable and the spritz dough too stiff to pipe. Proper butter temperature and creaming method are crucial for the success of these doughs, unlike drop cookies, which are more resilient.

The creaming method for these cookies can be applied to any recipe, such as layer cakes, but this is the only place in this book the method is covered. Presumably it is French in origin, taught to me by someone who studied with a French pastry chef. Unlike the basic creaming method, where sugar and fat are creamed together, cool butter is beaten alone first until it is smooth and shiny and holds a peak. It is essential that the butter be cool and not too soft, 60° to 65°F. To start with cold butter, throw all but a fourth of the butter into the mixer bowl. Melt the remaining butter and pour it into the bowl with the cold butter. Cream the two together. Only when the proper consistency is reached can the sugar be added, and the sugar should be added gradually to preserve the texture of the butter as much as possible.

For doughs that are stiff and difficult to pipe, such as French macaroons and spritz, the technique of "breaking the bag" will stave off carpal tunnel surgery for a few years and provide better control. When piping, usually only the top of the bag is twisted, preventing the contents from oozing out. To put a break in the bag means to twist off the bag in the center of the contents, thereby creating two chambers of dough from one. Pipe the first section of the bag first, then push down the remaining contents. It will take less force to pipe.

BISCOTTI

Italian biscotti are crisp, twice-baked cookies (the word *biscotti* translates as "cooked again") that have a tremendous following in American coffee-house culture. Authentic Italian biscotti do not contain butter, and only occasionally call for a small amount of oil. The addition of butter changes their texture from brittle and crisp to dry and crumbly. Nuts dominate the flavor of biscotti, though in the United States additions such as dried fruit and chocolate have created endless variations.

The method for making biscotti is straightforward: All the dry ingredients are combined in a bowl, including toasted ground or chopped nuts, and the eggs (and oil) are added just until a dough can be formed. The dough is shaped into long logs, slightly flattened, and baked in a moderate oven (350°F). When the logs have cooled enough to handle, they are sliced crosswise with a serrated knife. The slices are cooked in a slow oven (300°F) until dry and crisp. The flavor of biscotti gets better with age. If stored in an airtight container they will last for weeks.

SHORTBREAD

Shortbread, hailing from Scotland, is a simple, not too sweet formula of butter, sugar, flour, and perhaps salt. Butter is the dominant flavor, and despite the many flavor variations (chocolate, espresso, nut, brown sugar, lemon, maple, and oat), the flavor of butter is still the reason people buy shortbread. Most recipes derive from a basic ratio of 2 cups of butter to 1 cup of sugar for 4 cups of flour. Beyond that, it is a matter of preference. Some chefs prefer the creaming method, others like to "cut in" the butter to form a more crumbly, tender cookie. Using melted butter is not unheard of either.

Tenderness is not much of a problem with shortbread, whose name indicates that the recipe has enough fat to shorten or interrupt gluten formation. Choice of flour and sugar is used to control texture, creating a range of sandy and crumbly to smooth and crisp. Substituting a small amount of cornstarch or rice flour for all-purpose flour is a common technique for achieving a more tender cookie. Most chefs have strong preferences for a specific sugar. Confectioners' sugar makes a smooth cookie that some find pasty, preferring the granular texture of regular sugar.

Shortbread dough may be pressed into a pan, docked (to prevent puffing), and baked, or it can be chilled and rolled, though rolling rich shortbread dough requires a cool room and patience. Any shortbread recipe that is not overly crumbly is suitable as a base for bar cookies. An egg or yolk(s) will give more structure to shortbread, making it easier to use for crusts and tarts.

TULIPE

Tulipe batter, or paste as it is usually referred to, is a versatile make-ahead component especially helpful for restaurant and catering pastry chefs. The cookies are flat and flexible when still hot from the oven, and can be shaped into bowls or cones. Once cool, the cookies are crisp and can be used to hold other components such as mousse or ice cream. The recipe is called *tulipe* because the fluted bowl shape resembles a flower. Tulip paste can be spread with an offset spatula, but more commonly it is spread over stencils to create decorative shapes. You can make your own stencil if you have a piece of flexible plastic, the sort that forms the cover on spiral notebooks, by tracing the shape you want and cutting it out. Discard the cut-out; spread the batter into the empty shape in the plastic. Melted chocolate can be piped onto the batter in decorative patterns before baking; it will bake into the cookie. The batter can also be tinted.

CHAPTER 18

SUGAR SYRUPS
AND CANDYMAKING

T hough it must seem improbable, the same principle guides the making of peanut brittle and marshmallows. Controlled crystallization of varying concentrations of sugar syrups is the foundation for all candymaking, which for most pastry chefs centers on making syrup for Italian meringue or making golden caramel for croquembuche, rather than taffy or hard candy. Still, if you can make praline, you can make lollipops.

The finished texture of candy is defined by two things: the size of sugar crystals formed and how concentrated the sugar syrup is. The concentration of sugar increases the longer a mixture of sugar and water (the sugar syrup) cooks, since the water evaporates. After the mixture reaches a boil, the temperature continues to rise (only pure water does not rise above 212°F no matter how long it is boiled). Generally, a longer cooking time corresponds to higher sugar concentrations and results in harder candy. The exception to this is the caramel stage. Hard crack syrup, used for pulled and blown sugar sculptures and the pale blond caramel used for making sugar cages, becomes harder and more brittle than deep amber caramel (like praline) when cooled. Caramelization is a complicated chemical reaction, in which the sugars begin to break down and create literally hundreds of flavorful compounds. The darker the caramel, the less unconverted sucrose is present to crystallize into a hard candy (see Corriher, p. 423).

Each type of candy requires a specific concentration of sugar to form properly, and the easiest way to determine sugar concentration is with a candy thermometer. The temperature range between 234°F and 310°F

SUGAR SYRUP STAGES

No two candymaking charts are the same. Each one gives slightly different temperature ranges, and some break down larger categories, such as the crack stage, into three stages instead of two. Despite the lack of uniform charts, most sources agree on the temperatures for specific candies. All recipes for fondant, for example, bring the syrup close to 238°F.

Thread	220–233°F	simple syrup
Soft ball (a soft ball that flattens when pressed)	234°–240°F	fondant, fudge, syrup for Italian meringue
Firm ball (a ball that resists flattening when pressed)	242°–249°F	soft caramel candies, marshmallows
Hard ball	250°–265°F	nougat, divinity
Soft crack (flexible strands that can be shaped)	270°–290°F	taffy
Hard crack (brittle, easily broken strands)	300°–310°F	brittle, toffee, pulled sugar, blown sugar
Caramel	320°–370°F	praline

NOTE These temperature ranges are accurate at sea level. Subtract one degree for every 500 feet increase in altitude. At 2,000 feet, soft ball is 230° to 236°F.

is broken down into smaller intervals. These intervals are named for the shape a spoonful of syrup takes after it is dropped into ice cold water, removed, then pressed or pulled.

METHODS

On rainy and humid days, bring the sugar syrup to the top edge of the range. Moist air makes it difficult to achieve consistent results. Sugar is hygroscopic, meaning that the candy can attract moisture from the air. This is especially true of any invert sugar that has been formed from boiling the syrup in the presence of a crystal-inhibiting acid, such as lemon juice or cream of tartar. At the very least, it may become sticky, and at the worst, it may not set up properly. If you cannot postpone candymaking to a dry day, be sure to cook the syrup as long as possible to reduce the moisture present in the candy. For fondant, this would be 240°F rather than the more conservative temperature of 238°F.

Naturally, checking the shape the sugar syrup forms in ice water is less convenient than checking a thermometer, since the temperature of the remaining syrup cooking in the pan is rising while one is dipping and shaping. Since the syrup remains in each candy stage for only a short time, a good thermometer is the best guide for beginners. With time and practice it no longer becomes necessary to stand guard over the thermometer, as visual clues will let you know when the correct stage is approaching. Just as a breadmaker knows when a machine-kneaded dough has developed enough gluten by the sound it makes as it hits the side of the bowl and how it clings to the dough hook, the seasoned candymaker relies on the popping sound and appearance of the bubbles in the boiling syrup.

Bringing sugar syrup to a specific concentration is one half of candymaking. The other half is controlling the size and number of sugar crystals that form as the syrup cools. Fudge, for example, is composed of millions of crystals so tiny that they don't register on the tongue, giving it a smooth, creamy mouthfeel. Large crystals, on the other hand, give rock sugar its characteristic texture.

Understanding how a solution of sugar and water behaves is fundamental to candymaking. A cup of water at room temperature can dissolve only a fixed amount of sugar. When no more sugar will dissolve, the solution is called **saturated**. Heat, however, allows more sugar to dissolve in the given amount of water because a hot solution keeps the sugar molecules moving faster, lessening their attraction to one another. This is what happens when 2 cups of sugar are combined with only 1 cup of water in a pan over low heat: At first, the sugar will not completely dissolve, but as the solution approaches a boil, the sugar granules slowly disappear. When the pan is removed from the stove and the syrup begins to cool, the solution becomes **supersaturated**, meaning that the water is holding (temporarily) more sugar in solution than it normally can for that given temperature. Because the sugar molecules are essentially packed beyond the point at which they are able to remain dissolved, the slightest movement of the syrup or exposure to any foreign particle will cause the sugar molecules to cling to one another and fall out of solution. This is called **precipitation**, and the second half of candymaking is about controlling this process.

There are two basic laws of sugar crystallization. The hotter the syrup is when crystallization is initiated, the larger the crystals. The cooler the syrup, the smaller the crystals. Many candies, such as brittles, divinity, and chewy caramels and taffy, are not crystalline. Crystalline candies, such as rock candy, fudge, and fondant, must be carefully controlled to get the right crystal size.

Ingredients that inhibit crystal formation in sugar syrups are glucose syrup or corn syrup, often added to concentrated sugar solutions, since their high content of glucose and/or fructose sugars resists crystal formation. The viscosity of these syrups, owing to long chains of sugar molecules that were not broken down into simple sugars during processing, also inhibits crystal formation. For widespread crystal growth to occur, small sugar molecules must have proximity to an existing crystal, which encourages precipitation. The long-chained molecules create a traffic jam of sorts, making it harder for the smaller molecules to meet up. Using too much corn syrup, naturally, may prevent candies like fudge from setting up properly (see McGee, *On Food and Cooking*, pp. 413–414).

Various acids, such as lemon juice, vinegar, and cream of tartar may also be added in minute quantities to inhibit crystallization. The acids, in combination with the high heat, break down the sucrose molecules into its component parts, glucose and fructose, which themselves are more resistant to crystallizing than pure sucrose.

MAKING FOOLPROOF SUGAR SYRUPS

1. Heat the sugar and water gradually, stirring frequently, to give the sugar time to dissolve. When the syrup reaches a boil, cover the pot for a minute or two to let steam and water condensation dissolve any remaining granules clinging to the side of the pot. The lid must be removed for the water to evaporate and for the sugar concentration to increase. Continue to boil the syrup without stirring, which may instigate crystallization.

2. Prewarm your thermometer before inserting it into the hot syrup.

3. Have a pastry brush sitting in a cup of hot water. If necessary, use it to wash down crystals that form on the side of the pan.

4. Always use utensils that do not conduct heat for stirring, such as wooden spoons. A metal spoon will quickly get hot enough to burn during cooking, and a cold metal spoon may cause crystals to prematurely precipitate in a cooling syrup. Use a fresh spoon if the one you start cooking with becomes encrusted with crystals, and never re-dip a spoon (that has not been washed) into the syrup.

BASIC SYRUP/CANDY TYPES

SYRUPS

Simple syrup is a sugar-and-water solution that has been brought to a boil to ensure complete dissolution of the sugar granules. The syrups can vary in viscosity, depending on the amount of water present. Equal weights of sugar and water are used to make **heavy syrup**. Sugar syrups may be flavored with rum, fruit, or coffee and used to brush genoise layers. They are also used to candy fruit peel.

Syrup for Italian meringue has been brought to the soft ball stage. The greater heat and viscosity of this syrup literally cooks the egg whites as it is added to them, making them glossy, stable, and easy to work with.

FONDANT AND FUDGE

Candies can be made from **fondant**, but it is more commonly employed to coat petit fours, napoleons, and smooth-surfaced wedding cakes. Like syrup for Italian meringue, fondant is cooked to 238°F, often with the addition of cream of tartar or corn syrup to prevent crystallization. The syrup is poured onto a marble or Formica surface and left to cool, undisturbed, until it reaches 120°F. With a bench scraper (or two), the fondant is then kneaded until it turns milk white and opaque. The kneading process initiates crystallization, and must be done quickly. It can be strenuous work by hand, since the fondant becomes stiffer as it is worked. Many chefs prefer using a mixer fitted with the paddle attachment, or even the food processor for small batches (the fondant can be warmer for machine processing, about 140°F). Fondant is usually covered with sugar syrup and left to sit for 24 hours in an airtight container to smooth out and ripen. It can be gently heated (to around 100°F) and thinned with sugar syrup to make a pourable glaze, or rolled and cut for draping over cakes. Fondant should be ultra smooth and not the least bit grainy, which is accomplished by creating millions of minuscule crystals that are so small the tongue cannot discern them.

Fudge requires the same tiny crystals as fondant, and is cooked to the same temperature. However, fudge is richer than fondant, with its added milk, butter, chocolate, or nuts. Small batches of fudge can be "shocked" by placing the pot in a bowl of cold water. This immediately stops the cooking, as well as provides a jump start on the cooling process. The longer a candy cools, the greater the danger of accidental crystallization.

CARAMEL AND TAFFY

Soft, **chewy caramels** are cooked just a few degrees beyond fudge and left to cool without agitation, preventing any crystallization. The milk solids in the butter and cream brown at a lower temperature than pure sugar, allowing the candy to caramelize by the time it reaches the firm ball stage. **Taffy** is cooked just a little longer, making it more chewy. Taffy is also pulled, folded, and pulled some more until it loses its shine. The pulling process incorporates tiny air bubbles, which gives the candy a light texture despite its chewiness.

TOFFEE AND BRITTLE

Toffee and **brittle** are cooked to the hard crack stage, well below the temperature that pure caramel praline reaches. Though toffee is crunchy, it has a meltingly smooth texture because of the addition of butter, unlike praline, which is just plain hard. The milk solids in the butter caramelize (brown) at a lower temperature than sugar, so toffee is caramel in color despite the lower cooking temperature. Peanut brittle sometimes contains the addition of baking soda, usually added toward the end of the cooking time. While acidic ingredients prevent premature crystallization, they inhibit browning. Baking soda neutralizes the acidity, allowing the candy to caramelize easily. When baking soda reacts with the acidic sugar syrup, tiny air bubbles are created, which make the candy lighter in texture and even a bit flaky.

DIVINITY, NOUGAT, AND MARSHMALLOWS

Divinity, nougat, and marshmallows are candy cousins. **Divinity** is made from sugar syrup (hard ball) beaten into whipped egg whites. Because the syrup is hotter and therefore more concentrated than syrup made for Italian meringue, and less egg white is used, the resulting candy is stiffer. Divinity is somewhere in the middle between soft and hard meringues in texture, as it is dry on the outside but fluffy, moist, and slightly chewy on the inside. The difficulty in making divinity is getting the syrup to mix into the eggs before hardening. To prevent this from happening, up to half the syrup may be beaten into the egg whites at the soft ball stage to temper them, and the rest returned to the heat and brought to the higher end of the hard ball stage (see Corriher, p. 443).

Nougat is similar to divinity in concept, since it involves sugar syrup beaten into egg whites in two stages. However, the final syrup beaten into nougat is caramelized, creating a chewy rather than creamy or fluffy candy. Nougat commonly has nuts or dried fruit folded into it, and may be coated with chocolate to create individual candies.

Marshmallows were once made from the juice extracted from the marsh mallow plant, combined with hot sugar syrup (firm ball) and egg white to create a fluffy, soft candy. Modern marshmallows use gelatin instead of plant extracts.

CARAMEL

Caramel is the last stage of cooking sugar syrups, the point at which sugar browns or caramelizes. Beyond this, the sugar is simply burned. This stage is completely different from that for making soft caramel candies, which are made at a lower temperature. When sugar cooked to the caramel stage is poured onto a pan, it forms a hard, glasslike candy. Since the flavor of caramel is determined by the depth of its color, a thermometer is not necessary.

By the time sugar reaches the caramel stage, there is almost no moisture left. Thus, the fastest way to make caramel is simply to melt sugar without water in the first place. This is called the dry method for making caramel. Though eliminating the water saves time in waiting for the water to boil off, it is less foolproof for beginners. Dry sugar melts at 320°F and quickly darkens from there. The pan shape best suited for caramel is disputed between chefs. Some prefer a wide, shallow skillet to keep as much sugar in contact with the heated surface as possible. Once the sugars melt and darken, however, a wide pan with its large surface area is harder to stir and control.

The foolproof method for making caramel is called the wet method, which involves adding a small amount of water to the sugar, usually less than half the weight of the sugar. The less water added, the more difficult it will be to dissolve the sugar and prevent crystallization. A small amount of cream of tartar, corn syrup, or lemon juice will help.

TABLE 18.1 FORMULAS FOR CANDIES

	Crystalline		Amorphous or Noncrystalline				Special Textures	
	Fondant	Fudge	Caramels	Taffy	Toffee	Lollipops	Divinity	Marshmallows
	1 cup sugar	1 cup sugar	1 cup sugar	1 cup sugar	1 cup sugar	1 cup sugar	1 cup sugar	1 cup sugar
	1 tbsp corn syrup or 1/16 tsp cream of tartar	1 tbsp corn syrup	1 cup corn syrup	1/4 cup corn syrup	1 tbsp corn syrup	1/2 cup corn syrup	2 tbsp corn syrup	1 tbsp corn syrup
	1 tbsp butter		1/4 cup butter		3/4 cup butter		1 egg white	1 tbsp gelatin
	1/2 cup water	1/2 cup milk	1 cup cream or evaporated milk	1/2 cup water	1/4 cup water	1/2 cup water	1/4 cup water	1/4 cup water
	238°F	238°F	248°F	261°F/275°F	300°–310°F	310°F	252°F	248°F
	Soft ball	Soft ball	Firm ball	Hard ball/ Soft crack	Hard crack	Hard crack	Hard ball	Firm ball

Adapted with permission from Shirley O. Corriher, author of *Cookwise: The Hows and Whys of Successful Cooking*. New York: William Morrow, 1997; based on Helen Charley, *Food Science*, second edition. New York: John Wiley, 1982.

Pale, blondish straw-colored caramel is used for making **caramel cages**, **golden syrup** for drizzling over croquembuche, and **spun sugar** decorations. The syrup usually reaches this color at 310° to 320°F, and to ensure that the syrup does not darken too quickly, the wet method for making the caramel is best.

Praline is caramelized sugar with toasted almonds or hazelnuts. The caramel is cooked until it is light amber for maximum flavor, then the nuts are stirred into the pan (the nuts may be added earlier if they are not toasted to give them time to color). The mixture is poured onto a greased marble slab or sheet pan, and left to cool and harden. Praline is crushed or ground and added to fillings and buttercreams. Large pieces can be used as a garnish.

Caramel sauce is made by adding butter and cream to amber-hued caramel.

COOKWARE

Copper-lined pans, with their superior conductivity, are wonderful for candymaking. Unlined copper is reactive and should not be used, especially if acids such as cream of tartar are added to syrups. The dark color of copper pans makes it difficult to judge the color of caramel.

Good-quality stainless steel pans are perfectly fine. Candymaking, which involves high temperatures, may damage pans that are not well made. Inexpensive pans with hot spots or flaws may cook unevenly, burning one area of a sugar syrup while the rest has not even begun to color.

APPENDIX

HIGH-ALTITUDE BAKING

As altitude increases, atmospheric pressure decreases. With less atmospheric pressure, it takes less energy to convert water to steam—water evaporates more readily. This is exemplified by the change of temperature at which water boils, which becomes steadily lower as the altitude rises. At sea level, water boils at 212°F, but at 10,000 feet it boils at 194°F. Naturally, the temperature chart for candymaking and sugar syrups will be off slightly.

Stove-top adjustments are more straightforward than changes for baked goods, however. The following is a list of possible recipe adjustments for high-altitude pastry work. They are not hard-and-fast rules. Generally, each recipe may need to be tested as written for sea level to assess the extent of changes necessary.

BUTTER- AND SHORTENING-BASED CAKES AND QUICKBREADS

- Reduce leavening slightly because gas bubbles rise more easily and pop with less atmospheric pressure. The danger is that a cake may fall because it will rise faster than it can set.

- Reduce fat and sugar slightly, which lowers the temperature at which the cake will set. (Remember that sugar competes with starch for moisture, and it raises the temperature of starch gelatinization.) Decreasing the baking time prevents the cake from drying out before it is set. *Or* increase the flour (the protein structure from gluten) to set the batter faster.

- Increase the oven temperature by 25°F to promote faster setting of cake structure, which will help trap bubbles and retain moisture.

- Increase the number of eggs to provide more structure. Eggs, especially the yolks, provide additional moisture for longer shelf life. Dryness is associated with high-altitude air, which shortens the shelf life of baked goods.

- Grease the pans well and turn out cooled cakes promptly, as baked goods have a greater tendency to stick at higher altitudes.

SPONGE CAKES

- Decrease the sugar slightly to allow faster coagulation of eggs. This will prevent moisture loss.

- Increase the oven temperature by 25°F. Cooking the cake faster lets the structure set before the cake becomes dry.

YEASTED BREADS

- Decrease the amount of yeast, since less gas is needed to raise the dough.

- Be careful of overproofing. Since gas bubbles will rise and expand more readily, proof time may shorten.

- Flour is likely to be drier at high altitudes, so more liquid may be needed to achieve the same moisture as the same dough at sea level.

- Reduce the sugar in sweet doughs to promote faster gelatinization of starch.

- Choose a flour with a higher protein content to create a stronger gluten network that will set faster and trap the rapidly expanding air bubbles.

- Increase the oven temperature by 25°F to promote faster setting of bread, which will help trap bubbles and retain moisture.

METRIC CONVERSIONS AND OTHER HELPFUL INFORMATION

FRACTIONS AND THEIR DECIMAL EQUIVALENTS

$1/25 = .04$	$1/8 = .125$	$1/2 = .5$	$4/5 = .8$
$1/20 = .05$	$1/6 = .167$	$3/5 = .6$	$5/6 = .833$
$1/16 = .063$	$1/5 = .2$	$5/8 = .625$	$7/8 = .875$
$1/12 = .083$	$1/4 = .25$	$2/3 = .667$	
$1/10 = .1$	$1/3 = .333$	$3/4 = .75$	

DECIMAL EQUIVALENTS FOR OUNCES

1 ounce = .0625	5 ounces = .3125	9 ounces = .5625	13 ounces = .8125
2 ounces = .125	6 ounces = .375	10 ounces = .625	14 ounces = .875
3 ounces = .1875	7 ounces = .4375	11 ounces = .6875	15 ounces = .9375
4 ounces = .25	8 ounces = .5	12 ounces = .75	1 pound = 1.0

FAHRENHEIT TO CELSIUS

32°F = 0°C	110°F = 43°C	210°F = 99°C	290°F = 143°C
40°F = 4°C	120°F = 49°C	212°F = 100°C	300°F = 149°C
50°F = 10°C	130°F = 54°C	220°F = 104°C	325°F = 163°C
60°F = 16°C	140°F = 60°C	230°F = 110°C	350°F = 177°C
70°F = 21°C	150°F = 65°C	235°F = 113°C	375°F = 190°C
80°F = 26°C	160°F = 71°C	240°F = 115°C	400°F = 205°C
85°F = 29°C	170°F = 77°C	250°F = 121°C	425°F = 220°C
90°F = 32°C	180°F = 82°C	260°F = 127°C	450°F = 233°C
95°F = 34°C	190°F = 88°C	270°F = 132°C	475°F = 246°C
100°F = 38°C	200°F = 94°C	280°F = 138°C	500°F = 260°C

METRIC CONVERSIONS

- Ounces to grams: multiply by 28.35

- Pounds to kilograms: multiply by .454

- Fluid ounces to milliliters: multiply by 29.57

- Quarts to liters: multiply by .946

Note: To convert from metric, simply divide by the same number.

WEIGHT-VOLUME EQUIVALENTS FOR COMMON INGREDIENTS	
Food	**Volume Conversion**
Flours/Grains/Crumbs	**Ounces in 1 cup**
All-purpose flour	4.25
Cake flour	4
Bread flour (organic)	4.75 (4.6)
Whole wheat flour	4.5
Rye flour	4
Pumpernickel flour	4
High-gluten flour	4.75
Fine cornmeal	5
Coarse cornmeal	6
Rolled oats	3.5
Bran cereal	2.25
Bran flakes	2
Wheat germ	4
Graham cracker crumbs	4
Chocolate cookie crumbs	4

Note: The dry ingredients were measured by the spoon-and-sweep method, meaning that the flour was lightly spooned into the measuring cup and swept with the edge of a knife to level. Other chefs prefer dipping the measuring cup directly into the bin of flour, which yields a higher weight by compacting the flour into the cup. Liquid measures were used for liquids, dry measuring cups for the dry ingredients.

WEIGHT-VOLUME EQUIVALENTS FOR COMMON INGREDIENTS (Continued)	
Food	Volume Conversion
Starches	**Ounces/Volume**
Cornstarch	1 oz = 3 Tbs
Tapioca	.5 oz (.43) = 1 Tbs
Potato starch	.37 oz = 1 Tbs
Gelatin	.25 oz = $2^{1}/_{4}$ tsp
Sugars/Syrups	**Ounces in 1 cup**
Granulated	7
Confectioners'	4
Dark/light brown	8
Superfine	7.33
Dark corn syrup	12
Light corn syrup	12
Molasses	11
Honey	12
Dark honey	12
Malt syrup	12
Maple syrup	12
Leavenings/Salt	**Ounces/Volume**
Cream of tartar	.33 oz = 1 Tbs
Baking powder	.50 oz (.45) = 1 Tbs
Baking soda	.50 oz (.57) = 1 Tbs
Fresh yeast	.66 oz = 2 Tbs crumbled

WEIGHT-VOLUME EQUIVALENTS FOR COMMON INGREDIENTS (Continued)	
Food	Volume Conversion
Leavenings/Salt	**Ounces/Volume**
Active dry yeast	.13 oz = 1 tsp
Instant active dry yeast	.11 oz = 1 tsp
Gold Saf Yeast, osmotolerant	.11 oz = 1 tsp
Diastatic malt powder	.3 oz = 1 Tbs
Salt (granular/kosher)	.50 oz = 1 Tbs/.33 oz = 1 Tbs
Chocolate	**Ounces in 1 cup**
Chocolate chips (regular)	6
Chocolate chips (mini)	6
Cocoa powder (Dutch processed)	3.75
Nuts	**Ounces in 1 cup**
Natural whole almonds	5
Natural sliced almonds	3
Blanched slivered almonds	4.5
Walnut pieces	4
Pecan pieces	3.75
Pecan halves	4
Hazelnuts, whole, unblanched	4.75
Macadamia nuts	4.75
Peanuts	4.75
Almond paste	9.5
Peanut butter	8

WEIGHT-VOLUME EQUIVALENTS FOR COMMON INGREDIENTS (Continued)	
Food	**Volume Conversion**
Nuts	**Ounces in 1 cup**
Sweetened flake coconut	3
Unsweetened coconut	2.75
Flavorings	**Equivalents**
Vanilla extract	.5 oz = 1 Tbs
Vanilla beans	4 beans = 1 oz
Espresso powder	4 oz = 1 cup/.25 oz = 1 Tbs
Malted milk powder	4 oz = 1 cup
Spices	**Equivalents**
Poppy seeds	.65 oz = 1 Tbs
Ground spices	.25 oz = 1 Tbs
Dried Fruit	**Ounces in 1 cup**
Chopped candied fruit	5.5
Figs and prunes	6
Dried apricots	4.5
Raisins	6
Tart cherries	5
Jams/Glazes	**Ounces in 1 cup**
Apricot jam	12
Gelstar apricot glaze	12
Raspberry preserves	12
Coulis	9

WEIGHT-VOLUME EQUIVALENTS FOR COMMON INGREDIENTS (Continued)	
Food	**Volume Conversion**
Dairy	**Ounces in 1 cup**
Milk	8.5
Half-and-half	8.5
Heavy cream	8.5
Sour cream	8.5
Baker's dry milk powder	4.75
Eggs	**Equivalents**
Fresh-large	1 egg (no shell) = 1.70 oz 5 eggs (1 cup + 2 Tbs) = 8.75 oz
Frozen yolks, sugared	1 yolk = .55 oz
Frozen whites, pasturized	1 white = 1.15 oz
Meringue powder	.25 oz = 1 Tbs
Canned Goods	**Ounces in 1 cup**
Pineapple, crushed	8
Pumpkin	8.57
Cream of coconut	10
Coconut milk	8.5
Evaporated milk	9
Sweetened condensed milk	11
Fats/Oils	**Ounces in 1 cup**
Vegetable shortening	5.75
Vegetable oil	8
Butter	8

BIBLIOGRAPHY

The majority of information in this edition comes, naturally, from the previous edition of *Understanding Baking*. As stated in the preface, both editions rely on E.J. Pyler's two volume *Baking Science & Technology* for food science facts. Though scientists Shirley O. Corriher and Harold McGee have translated the complexity of food chemistry into everyday language, changing the terrain of popular cooking forever, Pyler's volumes remain standard texts for professional programs. Anyone interested in the detailed baking chemistry and the studies behind many of our current assumptions should purchase Pyler's invaluable volumes.

PRIMARY SOURCES

These books provided useful information, usually covering a wide range of topics. Rather than list them under each chapter, I have grouped them together here. These titles are valuable resources for any kitchen.

Corriher, Shirley O. *Cookwise: The Hows and Whys of Successful Cooking.* New York: William Morrow, 1997.

Davidson, Alan. *The Oxford Companion to Food.* New York: Oxford University Press, 1999.

Fortin, Francois, and Les Editions Quebec/Amerique Inc. *The Visual Food Encyclopedia.* New York: Macmillan, 1996.

Gisslen, Wayne. *Professional Baking,* 2nd ed. New York: John Wiley, 1994.

Glezer, Maggie. *Artisan Baking Across America.* New York: Artisan, 2000.

Healy, Bruce, and Paul Bugat. *The Art of the Cake: Modern French Baking and Decorating.* New York: William Morrow, 1994.

Herbst, Sharon Tyler. *The New Food Lover's Companion: Comprehensive Definitions of over 4000 Food, Wine, and Culinary Terms,* 2nd ed. Woodbury, NY: Barron's Educational Series, 1995.

Lang, Jenifer Harvey, ed. *Larousse Gastronomique: The New American Edition of the World's Greatest Culinary Encyclopedia.* New York: Crown, 1988.

Kiple, Kenneth, and Kriemhild Conee Ornelas, eds. *The Cambridge World History of Food.* Cambridge, UK: Cambridge University Press, 2000.

McGee, Harold. *On Food and Cooking: The Science and Lore of the Kitchen.* New York: Charles Scribner's Sons, 1984.

Wing, Daniel, and Alan Scott. *The Bread Builders: Hearth Loaves and Masonry Ovens.* White River Junction, VT: Chelsea Green, 1998.

ADDITIONAL SOURCES

Books listed here by chapter provided additional information specific to each chapter topic.

CHAPTER 1: WHEAT AND GRAIN FLOURS

David, Elizabeth. *English Bread and Yeast Cookery.* Newton, MA: Biscuit Books, 1994.

Field, Carol. *The Italian Baker.* New York: Harper & Row, 1985.

Jacob, H. E. *Six Thousand Years of Bread.* New York: Lyons & Burford, 1997.

Sands, Brinna B. *The King Arthur Flour 200th Anniversary Cookbook.* Woodstock, VT: Countryman Press, 1991.

Scherber, Amy, and Toy Kim Dupree. *Amy's Bread.* New York: William Morrow, 1996.

CHAPTER 2: YEAST AND CHEMICAL LEAVENERS

Healea, Tim. *Bread Baker's Handbook for Pearl Bakery.* Portland, OR: 2000.

CHAPTER 3: SUGARS AND OTHER SWEETENERS

Sizer, Frances, and Eleanor Whitney. *Nutrition: Concepts and Controversies,* 8th ed. Belmont, CA: Wadsworth Thomson Learning, 2000.

CHAPTER 4: EGGS

American Egg Board. *Egg Handling & Care Guide,* 2nd ed. Park Ridge, IL: American Egg Board, 2000.

CHAPTER 5: FATS AND OILS

Clayton, Jr., Bernard. *The Complete Book of Pastry, Sweet and Savory.* New York: Simon & Schuster, 1981.

Sands, Brinna B. *The King Arthur Flour 200th Anniversary Cookbook.* Woodstock, VT: Countryman Press, 1991.

Sizer, Frances, and Eleanor Whitney. *Nutrition: Concepts and Controversies,* 8th ed. Belmont, CA: Wadsworth Thomson Learning, 2000.

CHAPTER 6: MILK AND DAIRY PRODUCTS

Jenkins, Steven. *Cheese Primer.* New York: Workman, 1996.

McGee, Harold. *The Curious Cook: More Kitchen Science and Lore.* New York: Macmillan, 1990.

Sands, Brinna B. *The King Arthur Flour 200th Anniversary Cookbook.* Woodstock, VT: Countryman Press, 1991.

CHAPTER 8: CHOCOLATE

Bau, Frederic. *Au Couer Des Saveurs.* Spain: Montagud Editores, 1998.

Bishop, Jack. "Supermarket Baking Chocolate Takes Top Honors," *Cook's Illustrated* 24 (February 1997):26–27.

Boyle, Tish, and Timothy Moriarty. *Chocolate Passion: Recipes and Inspiration from the Kitchens of Chocolatier Magazine.* New York: John Wiley, 2000.

Gonzalez, Elaine. *The Art of Chocolate.* San Francisco: Chronicle Books, 1998.

Goodbody, Mary, and eds. of *Chocolatier. Glorious Chocolate.* New York: Simon & Schuster, 1989.

McGee, Harold. *The Curious Cook: More Kitchen Science and Lore.* New York: Macmillan, 1990.

Medrich, Alice, and Jack Bishop. "Are Expensive Chocolates Worth the Money?" *Cook's Illustrated* (November 1994):25–26.

———. "Dutched vs. Natural Cocoas," *Cook's Illustrated* (October 1995):26–27.

Montenegro, Lisa. Notes and instruction materials from "Master Class in Baking," a course at the New School (New York); March 1997 session.

Peterson, James. Sauces: *Classical and Contemporary Sauce Making,* 2nd ed. New York: Van Nostrand Reinhold, 1998.

Rees, Nicole. "Secrets of Foolproof Ganache." *Pastry Art & Design* (February 2000):42–46.

Richardson, Terry. "The Well-Tempered Bean," *Cook's Magazine* (April 1992): 64–68.

CHAPTER 9: WATER

Healea, Tim. *Bread Baker's Handbook for Pearl Bakery.* Portland, OR: 2000.

CHAPTER 10: SALT

Healea, Tim. *Bread Baker's Handbook for Pearl Bakery.* Portland, OR: 2000.

CHAPTER 12: BREAD AND OTHER YEAST-RISEN PRODUCTS

David, Elizabeth. *English Bread and Yeast Cookery.* Newton, MA: Biscuit Books, 1994.

Field, Carol. *The Italian Baker.* New York: Harper & Row, 1985.

Greenspan, Dorie. *Baking With Julia: Based on the PBS Series Hosted by Julia Child.* New York: William Morrow, 1996.

Healea, Tim. *Bread Baker's Handbook for Pearl Bakery.* Portland, OR: 2000.

Kamman, Madeleine. *The New Making of a Cook.* New York: William Morrow, 1997.

Reinhart, Peter. *Crust and Crumb: Master Formulas for Serious Bread Bakers.* Berkeley, CA: Ten Speed Press, 1998.

Rosada, Didier. *National Baking Center Reports* (Minneapolis):1999–2000.

Sands, Brinna B. *The King Arthur Flour 200th Anniversary Cookbook.* Woodstock, VT: Countryman Press, 1991.

Steingarten, Jeffrey. *The Man Who Ate Everything and Other Gastronomic Feats, Disputes, and Pleasurable Pursuits.* New York: Knopf, 1997.

CHAPTER 13: LAMINATES

Bilheux, Roland, and Alain Escoffier. *Doughs, Batters, and Meringues,* French Professional Pastry. New York: Van Nostrand Reinhold, 1988.

Clayton, Jr., Bernard. *The Complete Book of Pastry, Sweet and Savory.* New York: Simon & Schuster, 1981.

Friberg, Bo. *The Professional Pastry Chef,* 3rd ed. New York: Van Nostrand Reinhold, 1996.

Greenspan, Dorie. *Baking With Julia: Based on the PBS Series Hosted by Julia Child.* New York: William Morrow, 1996.

———. *Desserts by Pierre Hermé.* New York: Little, Brown, 1998.

Healy, Bruce, and Paul Bugat. *Mastering the Art of French Pastry.* Woodbury, NY: Barron's Educational Series, 1984.

Rees, Nicole, and Lisa Bell. "Puff Pastry Primer." *Pastry Art & Design* (August 1999):58–66.

CHAPTER 14: CAKE BAKING

Anderson, Jean. *The American Century Cookbook: The Most Popular Recipes of the 20th Century.* New York: Clarkson Potter, 1997.

Anderson, Pam, and Karen Tack. "Big, Beautiful Muffins," *Cook's Illustrated* 24 (February 1997):18–19.

Beard, James. *James Beard's American Cookery.* Boston: Little, Brown, 1972.

Beranbaum, Rose Levy. *The Cake Bible.* New York: William Morrow, 1988.

Sands, Brinna B. *The King Arthur Flour 200th Anniversary Cookbook.* Woodstock, VT: Countryman Press, 1991.

Sax, Richard. *Classic Home Desserts: A Treasury of Heirloom and Contemporary Recipes from Around the World.* Shelburne, VT: Chapters, 1994.

Time-Life Books. *Cakes,* The Good Cook/Techniques & Recipes. Alexandria, VA: Time-Life Books, 1981.

Walter, Carol. *Great Cakes.* New York: Clarkson Potter, 1998.

CHAPTER 15: EGG COOKERY: CUSTARDS, SOUFFLES, MERINGUES, BUTTERCREAM, AND PATE A CHOUX

American Egg Board. *Egg Handling & Care Guide,* 2nd ed. Park Ridge, IL: American Egg Board, 2000.

Bilheux, Roland, and Alain Escoffier. *Doughs, Batters, and Meringues,* French Professional Pastry. New York: Van Nostrand Reinhold, 1988.

———. *Creams, Confections, and Finished Desserts,* French Professional Pastry. New York: Van Nostrand Reinhold, 1988.

Friberg, Bo. *The Professional Pastry Chef,* 3rd ed. New York: Van Nostrand Reinhold, 1996.

Lenotre, Gaston. *Lenotre's Desserts and Pastries.* Woodbury, NY: Barron's Educational Series, 1977.

Montenegro, Lisa. Notes and instruction materials from "Master Class in Baking," a course at the New School (New York); March 1997 session.

Peterson, James. *Sauces: Classical and Contemporary Sauce Making,* 2nd ed. New York: Van Nostrand Reinhold, 1998.

Sax, Richard. *Classic Home Desserts: A Treasury of Heirloom and Contemporary Recipes from Around the World.* Shelburne, VT: Chapters, 1994.

CHAPTER 16: PIES AND TARTS

Anderson, Jean. *The American Century Cookbook: The Most Popular Recipes of the 20th Century.* New York: Clarkson Potter, 1997.

Beranbaum, Rose Levy. *The Pie and Pastry Bible.* New York: Scribner, 1998.

Healy, Bruce, and Paul Bugat. *Mastering the Art of French Pastry.* Woodbury, NY: Barron's Educational Series, 1984.

Heatter, Maida. *Maida Heatter's Pies & Tarts.* New York: Cader Books, 1997.

Longbotham, Lori. *Luscious Lemon Desserts.* San Francisco: Chronicle Books, 2001.

Sax, Richard. Classic *Home Desserts: A Treasury of Heirloom and Contemporary Recipes from Around the World.* Shelburne, VT: Chapters, 1994.

Steingarten, Jeffrey. *The Man Who Ate Everything and Other Gastronomic Feats, Disputes, and Pleasurable Pursuits.* New York: Knopf, 1997.

Walter, Carol. *Great Pies and Tarts.* New York: Clarkson Potter, 1998.

CHAPTER 17: COOKIES

Beard, James. *James Beard's American Cookery.* Boston: Little, Brown, 1972.

Field, Carol. *The Italian Baker.* New York: Harper & Row, 1985.

Friberg, Bo. *The Professional Pastry Chef,* 3rd ed. New York: Van Nostrand Reinhold, 1996.

Healy, Bruce, and Paul Bugat. T*he French Cookie Book.* New York: William Morrow, 1994.

CHAPTER 18: SUGAR SYRUPS AND CANDYMAKING

Benning, Lee Edwards. *Oh, Fudge! A Celebration of America's Favorite Candy.* New York: Henry Holt, 1990.

Dodge, Jim, and Elaine Ratner. *The American Baker.* New York: Simon & Schuster, 1987.

INDEX

ABOUT THE AUTHOR

To the surprise and dismay of her family, Nicole was born with a persistent sweet tooth. By the age of nine she was using her mother's copy of *Joy of Cooking* as the foundation for creating strange new dishes, usually cakes and cookies. Driven by the desire to understand the hows and whys behind cooking, and various hunger cravings, she took this hobby to a legitimate profession when she began catering and recipe development. Nicole has served as associate food editor, test kitchen director, and writer/contributor for several magazines, among them *Woman's World, Chocolatier*, and *Pastry Art & Design*. She is a member of IACP and contributes her spare time to anti-hunger efforts such as Share our Strength. Recently, she moved from New Jersey to Portland, Oregon, where she continues to bake every day.